T0330198

PORTUGUESE ECONOMIC DEVELOPMENT AND EXTERNAL FUNDING IN THE MODERN ERA

The
Portuguese-Speaking World

ITS HISTORY, POLITICS AND CULTURE

The Series Editors
António Costa Pinto (University of Lisbon)
Onésimo T. Almeida (Brown University)
Miguel Bandeira Jerónimo (University of Coimbra)

This new series will publish high-quality scholarly books on the entire spectrum of the Portuguese-speaking world, with particular emphasis on the modern history, culture, and politics of Portugal, Brazil, and Africa. The series, which will be open to a variety of approaches, will offer fresh insights into a wide range of topics covering diverse historical and geographical contexts. Particular preferences will be given to books that reflect interdisciplinarity and innovative methodologies. The editors encourage the submission of proposals for single author as well as collective volumes.

The Lusophone World: The Evolution of Portuguese National Narratives   Sarah Ashby

The Politics of Representation: Elections and Parliamentarism in Portugal and Spain, 1875–1926   Edited by Pedro Tavares de Almeida & Javier Moreno Luzón

Inequality in the Portuguese-Speaking World: Global and Historical Perspectives   Edited by Francisco Bethencourt

Marcello Caetano: A Biography (1906–1980)   Francisco Carlos Palomanes Martinho

From Lisbon to the World: Fernando Pessoa's Enduring Literary Presence   George Monteiro

The First Portuguese Republic: Between Liberalism and Democracy (1910–1926)   Miriam Pereira

PORTUGUESE ECONOMIC DEVELOPMENT AND EXTERNAL FUNDING IN THE MODERN ERA

Edited by **Nuno Cunha Rodrigues** and **Alice Cunha**

sussex
ACADEMIC
PRESS
Brighton • Chicago • Toronto

2 4 6 8 10 9 7 5 3 1

First published in 2022 by
SUSSEX ACADEMIC PRESS
PO Box 139
Eastbourne BN24 9BP

Distributed in North America by
SUSSEX ACADEMIC PRESS
Independent Publishers Group
814 N. Franklin Street
Chicago, IL 60610

The European Commission support for the production of this publication does not constitute
an endorsement of the contents which reflects the views only of the authors, and the
Commission cannot be held responsible for any use which may be made of
the information contained therein.

This book is co-funded by Portuguese funds through FCT – Fundação para a Ciência e a
Tecnologia under the project UIDB/04627/2020.

CIDEEFF
Centro de Investigação
de Direito Europeu,
Económico, Financeiro
e Fiscal

Faculdade de Direito da Universidade de Lisboa
Law School of Lisbon
Instituto
Europeu
European
Institute

INSTITUTO
PORTUGUÊS DE
RELAÇÕES
INTERNACIONAIS

IPRI

British Library Cataloguing in Publication Data
A CIP catalogue record for this book is available from the British Library.

Hardcover ISBN 978-1-78976-132-0

MIX
Paper from
responsible sources
FSC® C013056

Typeset and designed by Sussex Academic Press, Brighton & Eastbourne.
Printed by TJ Books Limited, Padstow, Cornwall.

Contents

Chapter 7
*Guilherme Waldemar d'Oliveira Martins and
Joana Graça Moura*

Chapter 8
José Renato Gonçalves

Conclusion
Ricardo Paes Mamede

Series Editors' Preface

Portuguese Economic Development and External Funding in the Modern Era is the first systematic, critical effort to understand the role played by external funding in Portuguese modern and contemporary history and politics. Authored by a group of economists, legal scholars and economic historians, this book provides a thorough analysis of external funding in the Portuguese economy since the Marshall Plan (1949–1952) to the present, exploring its contexts, provenance, uses, purposes and impact, under authoritarianism and democracy. After democratization in 1974–76, Portugal suffered three International Monetary Fund (IMF) interventions (1977, 1983 and 2011) and a strong influx of funds for the European Union. Mobilizing different perspectives from the social sciences, the editors and contributors provide an overview of the legal, economic and financial implications that external funding had on the country in different economic contexts and critical junctures, offering new, original researches and arguments regarding economic development, crisis management, financial assistance and European funds and its role, among other topics. The work is a crucial contribution to the study of recent Portuguese and European economic history, rewarding those interested on the history of the European Union, the IMF and other international organizations connected to external funding and assistance.

The editors of this series are more than pleased to see this impressive collection of texts published in English.

ANTÓNIO COSTA PINTO (University of Lisbon)
ONÉSIMO T. ALMEIDA (Brown University)
MIGUEL BANDEIRA JERÓNIMO (University of Coimbra)

Introduction
Portuguese Economic Development and External Funding in the Modern Era

NUNO CUNHA RODRIGUES AND ALICE CUNHA

The economic History of Portugal is in close connection with external funding. The country entered the twentieth century with the external debt problem to solve. According to Medeiros Ferreira (2010: 44), "the history of Portuguese foreign policy is, to a large extent, the history of capturing capital abroad for the needs of the national economy", including the 1902 agreement with external creditors or the League of Nations` loan in 1927.

Notwithstanding the relevance of external funding to the Portuguese State, literature has yet a lot to contribute to this topic, particularly from an historical and international relations point of view. The volume *Portuguese Economic Development and External Funding in the Modern Era* is our contribution to the deepening of the study on the subject of outmost importance for the past, present and future of Portugal.

After World War II, with the triumph of multilateralism, several international organizations were created, including two which would be of special meaning for the external funding of the Portuguese economy in the second half of the twentieth century and in the early twentieth first century as well. These two organizations are: the European Union (EU, in its current designation) and the International Monetary Fund (IMF). Combined they have been responsible for providing large amounts of funding, both in periods of economic development and of financial crisis. Hence, they are perceived differently by the public opinion and stakeholders: whereas the EU is seen as a source of easy money (the `Brussels` millions`), the IMF has a bad reputation associated to sacrifices.

This collective volume aims at providing a thorough analysis on specific case studies, such as the Marshall Plan (a sort of predecessor of European funding that Portugal benefited from 1949–1952); the three IMF interventions (in the seventies, eighties and the 2011 bailout), including a specific analysis of the impact of the 2011's Troika intervention in Portugal on the national legal framework; the implementation of the first EU funds the country received prior to accession; the relation of EU funds and Taxation (lessons from Portugal in times of Covid) and an analysis of the international monetary and financial system and the right to assistance from the International Monetary Fund.

Together the chapters combine a precise overview of the legal, economic and financial implications that such external funding has had on the country in different moments and economic contexts, while providing new research data and an original contribution to the study of the country`s economic history. Altogether, *Portuguese Economic Development and External Funding in the Modern Era* provides important insights into economic development, crisis management, financial assistance and European funds.

In detail, Maria Fernanda Rollo focus on the participation of Portugal in the Marshall Plan, and argues that it was important in terms of restraining and overcoming the multifaceted crisis that at the time affected the Portuguese economy and society, while it was also of major importance in structuring a controlled process of postwar economic development and modernization; in addition to ensuring the country's presence in the international payments system and in the European economic cooperation movements, and contributing to the intensification of the country's involvement in a process of increasing internationalization and opening up abroad. The chapter addresses Portugal's initial and later response to the launch of the Marshall Plan, the Portuguese Program and the nature and amounts of such aid; and determines that Portugal benefited from financial assistance amounting to approximately US$ 90 million, which affected a significant part of the Country's economic agents, including the State itself.

After the end of the *Estado Novo* regime and before the new democracy was fully consolidated two IMF interventions took place in the country. It was a period of transition, not only in political terms, but also of economic need, during which the Portuguese government received higher amounts of funding through external debt, from different institutional funders, such as the World Bank, the USA government, the European Investment Bank and the Council of Europe.

Luciano Amaral writes about the May 1978 Stand-by Arrangement (SBA) with the IMF to solve Portugal`s problem of external imbalance, which is normally considered the first intervention of that organization in the country. Still, the author claims that the 1978 SBA represented the conclusion of three years of intensive interaction with the IMF, whose resources the country started to use as of July 1975, in addition to other international agents that helped to finance the Portuguese economy and the Government. The chapter explains the rationale behind this first IMF intervention in Portugal, the interactions between both parties between 1975 and 1979, but also other international loans received in that period, granted by the Bank of International Settlements, the World Bank or the European Investment Bank; and concludes that the 1978 SBA shouldn't be, in reality, considered as an intervention but instead the conclusion of a long effort of stabilization to restore external balance while keeping the economy growing with controlled inflation.

Yet, the country continued to struggle, at the end of 1982 recorded the largest current account deficit in the OECD, and the progressive worsening of the situation made international financing very limited. All combined, they contributed to an IMF intervention that occurred between 1983 and 1985, with Portugal resorting to several conditional IMF financing programs, such as the Stand-By Arrangement of 1983, its revision of 1984, and the Compensatory Financing Facility. João Zorrinho`s chapter provides an overview of the political and economic context which lead the country to this intervention and of the negotiations held between the Portuguese authorities and the IMF, and deals specifically with the implementation of these programs, which led to a rapid external adjustment of the economy, but with high social and political costs. The successful adjustment allowed it to be abandoned early, nonetheless with serious consequences for the external balance in the long term.

After almost twenty years of a near stagnation performance, the shock of the financial crisis of 2007–2008 deeply affected the Portuguese economy. A first response based on public spending substantially increased the level of sovereign debt, then a serious problem common to other Eurozone Member States. In the difficult scenario of that period, and due to structural weaknesses, political and economic tensions rose to a break point, and, in April 2011, the Portuguese government officially asked for an international bailout (IMF/EC/ECB). Joaquim Ramos Silva addresses this topic, in concrete the IMF intervention in Portugal from 2011 to 2014. The author focuses on the Memorandum of 2011 and its specificities, including the political context, the implementation of said memorandum, its results, and also the legacy of the program, and concludes that, despite the process led the Portuguese economy to a more balanced State, several major issues over 2011–2014 remain to be fully explained and understood.

In the article entitled "the impact of the 2011 Troika intervention in Portugal on the national legal framework", Nuno Cunha Rodrigues explains how was implemented the Memorandum of Understanding signed between the Portuguese Government, the European Commission, the International Monetary Fund and the European Central Bank on 17 May 2011 and how it stands as an example of consolidation of the Washington consensus policies by the European Union. It concludes that the effects of fiscal consolidation caused by the economic and financial adjustment programme were recessive as there was an increase in unemployment rates, tax revenues decreased, transfers increased and there was a deterioration of the budgetary balance and an increase in public debt. Furthermore, it is concluded that the Troika intervention left a legacy of several changes in the national legal framework that have remained until the present day.

In another chapter, the importance of EU pre-accession aid is analysed. Here, Paulo Alves Pardal concludes that pre-accession aid proved to be a valuable element for both Portugal – as it allowed the financing of important projects for economic and social development (e.g. infrastructures, equipment, companies, professional training) – as well as for the EU as it allowed to successfully expand to countries with different experiences and economic and social structures. Furthermore, it provided the EU with knowledge that would be useful, in 2004, at the time of the major enlargement to the Central and Eastern countries. This track-record can still be used, in the future, for other candidate countries.

José Renato Gonçalves's paper, entitled "the international monetary and financial system and the right to assistance from the International Monetary Fund" explains the evolution of IMF's types of financial assistance and how these have been changing over the years. It is concluded that there is a need to review and fine-tune the Fund's set of instruments for monitoring and advising members, within the necessarily interdependent but complex and asymmetric current and future framework of the international economic, financial and monetary order, which is constantly being reformulated.

The last chapter, jointly written by Guilherme Waldemar d'Oliveira Martins and Joana Graça Moura, explains the connections between EU funds and taxation and how both can be used to tackle financial crises, namely the one caused by Covid-19. Here, the

Portuguese experience is used as a case-study that can be followed by other EU Member States and pre-accession counties.

In the final chapter, Ricardo Paes Mamede presents the conclusions of this book, in an exceptional text that starts from a theoretical framework on the different types of impact that external financing can produce on national economies proceeding to an analysis of the historical Portuguese external financing interventions and finishing by a commentary on all the articles included in the book.

At the end, this book aims to present a panoramic view over external funding of EU countries, looking closely at the Portuguese case, from different sciences perspectives, specially an historic, economic and legal ones. Doing so, this book can be used not only by scholars but also by anyone involved that is interested in learning the history and the future of EU, IMF and other international organizations external funding.

Reference

Medeiros Ferreira, J. 2010: Um século ainda pequeno. *Relações Internacionais* 28, 43–49.

CHAPTER

1

Portugal and the Marshall Plan

MARIA FERNANDA ROLLO

The Marshall Plan had its origin in the speech given by George Marshall, U.S. Secretary of State, on 5 June 1947, at Harvard University. The speech made public the USA's intention to support European countries impoverished by World War II in their endeavours to achieve economic recovery. Once the proposal contained in the speech was accepted, only for those West European countries that acknowledged this as an indispensable resource for their economic recovery, it was implemented in a vast and complex program (the European Recovery Programme, ERP, or, adopting the name by which it commonly entered history, the Marshall Plan). A programme with an expected duration of four years that was going to encourage participating countries to break the impasse in which they were mired, and accomplish the rebuilding and recovery process to which they had committed.

At the same time, due to a condition previously imposed by the Americans, European countries would have to accept managing the aid programme jointly among themselves and together with the USA. This "imposed" solidarity led to the creation, on 16 April 1948, of the Organisation for European Economic Cooperation (OEEC), within which the details were discussed, the first measures were agreed upon and American aid, in the meantime approved by the U.S. Congress, was decided. Over the four years that the ERP lasted, the United States channelled approximately 13 thousand million U.S. dollars to Europe, representing something like 1.2 percent of the total American Gross National Product, every year, between 1948 and 1951.

Portugal took an active and full part in the Marshall Plan: it was present at the European Economic Cooperation Conference that brought the countries that had agreed to join the programme together, in Paris, and where, in response to the suggestions of the U.S. Secretary of State, their common needs were weighed and a recovery programme for participating countries was drafted; Portugal shared the various mechanisms created and developed within the framework of the ERP; it was a founding member of the OEEC and benefited from U.S. financial aid, even though initially it declined to do so.

1 Portugal's response to the launch of the Marshall Plan and participation in the Paris Conference

The Portuguese Government's official reaction to the speech given by George Marshall came on 21 June 1947, when Portugal's ambassador to Washington, João de Bianchi, conveyed to the American State Department the spirit of moral and material solidarity that moved the Portuguese Government, emphasising the fact that its willingness to participate in the aid to European countries was embedded in the thoughts and practices that had already been steering its actions.

By that time, France and Great Britain had already taken the reins of the events. The Foreign Ministers of their respective governments, Georges Bidault and Ernest Bevin, agreed to jointly invite their Soviet counterpart, Viatcheslav Molotov, to a meeting. The Conference that brought the Foreign Ministers of these three countries together took place in Paris, between 27 June and 2 July, without however being able to reach an understanding. In view of the Soviet refusal to participate in drawing up any plans before the USA gave any guarantees regarding their future collaboration, and the fact that, consequently, Molotov abandoned the Tripartite Conference, the French and English ministers invited the rest of the European countries, excepting Spain, to a conference in which they would be able to implement the plan that General Marshall's suggestion called for. It was at that time that both fields took opposite stances, since all the countries in the Soviet orbit refused the invitation. These events contributed decisively to aggravating the climate of the Cold War, markedly widening the East–West split and etching more sharply the outlines that defined the two blocks that opposed each other in the European and world areas.

Extending the matter to the rest of the European countries included inviting Portugal to formally attend the talks intended to implement the suggestions implicitly contained in the American Secretary of State's speech. The importance of this invitation must be emphasised, since it meant that Portugal was tacitly accepted and integrated within the "western" European community, especially if we bear in mind that the Portuguese request to join the United Nations, in September 1946, had been refused. In addition, Portugal was offered the opportunity to take an active part in the management of international problems. This effective involvement took the country out of its condition of mere observer, giving it, in the international arena, a privileged status, to a certain extent. Therefore, the readiness with which Portugal officially responded to the Franco-British invitation was understandable; it was second among the 22 invited countries.

However, Portugal's expression of solidarity, making its national resources available to the U.S. government, the satisfaction with which it accepted the Franco-British invitation and its subsequent participation in the Conference did not imply the Portuguese Government's unconditional adherence to the plan to rebuild the European countries, let alone to the principle of European cooperation. In this matter, Portugal's attitude remained initially faithful to a posture of undisguised scepticism and disinterest towards the prospects of international cooperation, in accordance with the beliefs that the President of the Council, Oliveira Salazar, held on this issue, and also in accordance with the key principles that were supposed to guide the country's actions in that context, among which prevailed the so-called "national principle". However, in spite of the fears and mistrust raised by the possible development of international cooperation schemes, the Portuguese Government always made available the necessary means and made the compromises indispensable to avoid Portugal being sidelined in the context of post-war international relations. The experience of Portugal's relationship with the Marshall Plan was pioneering and paradigmatic: in a time when the Cold War was setting in and economies were increasingly internationalised, the indispensability of getting closer to European economic cooperation overruled principles and superseded anti-European beliefs and prejudices.

After some perplexities and contradictory assessments had been overcome, the Portuguese Government decided to decline the offer of U.S. financial assistance. The Portuguese decision was made known by the Minister of Foreign Affairs, José Caeiro da Mata, in the speech he gave on 22 September 1947, during the signing ceremony, by the respective delegates, of the general report on the economic and social situation in which the 16 signatory countries found themselves, a report meant to be presented to the U.S. Government so that Marshall aid could be allocated: "The happy internal conditions of Portugal allow me to declare that my country does not need external financial aid"[1] – the decision of the Portuguese Government was translated into this emphatic statement issued by people who had no doubts and who intended to definitively close the matter. Costa Leite, Minister of

Finance, was even more adamant. In one of his reports, which formed a convincing component of the Portuguese decision, he stated: "if we manage our foreign trade properly, we will not lack credits in dollars, and I do not believe that it is in the country's interest, vis-à-vis North America and even Europe itself, to unnecessarily line up with those who are hungry for dollars ".[2]

Until then, all negotiations had been heading towards this stated rejection, even though the Foreign Minister himself, along with a few diplomats inside the structure of the future OEEC, had contemplated, with no great conviction, it is true, the opposite decision. Emphasising the favourable Portuguese economic and financial situation, Caeiro da Mata did not fail to point out, however, the existence of a few commercial constraints that might jeopardise that situation, in the short term. It was believed that although Portugal did not need credit, it did need supplies from other countries, in order to overcome the general and international scarcity of goods. Therefore, it tried to create conditions that would ensure the difficult flow of Portuguese exports, of limited interest, due to their non-essential nature.

Portugal was taking a peculiar stance, not because it adhered to the Marshall Plan without requesting financial aid, but because it persisted in this decision even though Portuguese political leaders were clearly aware of the growing frailty of the country's economic situation. However, until then everything seemed to coalesce into confirming that decision, made at a juncture in which principles, as well as political and ideological beliefs, clearly seemed more important than the new realities.

Observed from the perspective of the Portuguese authorities, the decision to dispense with the financial aid provided by the Marshall Plan, but still keep, with no great commitment, the country's presence and cooperation with the programme and its institutional framework, made perfect sense and followed a well laid-out strategy, particularly in European terms.

In the foreign policy field, this decision corresponded to a sort of compromise between fidelity to the fundamental principles upheld by Portuguese authorities and the need to avoid the country's marginalisation from international affairs. In the light of the perspectives of that time, Portugal's participation in the Paris Conference and in preparing the U.S. aid programme for Europe conformed to the prevalence of Portuguese sovereignty and autonomy and was reconcilable with the fundamental pillars of the country's foreign policy: Atlanticism, privileged relations with Spain and Brazil, the defence of the colonial Empire or, more explicitly, the defence of the essential unity of the Metropolis (*i.e.*, Metropolitan Portugal, in Europe) and the colonies –

as long as the country was able to maintain an acceptable degree of autonomy and commitment which, in fact, was apparent in the limited way that Portugal took part in the Paris Conference. Furthermore, the political thinking of the regime's main leaders was marked by a visceral anti-communist feeling and by a poorly disguised anti-Americanism, in addition to strong scepticism about the prospects of European cooperation.

There were a number of somewhat peripheral aspects that influenced the behaviour and the initial decision of Portuguese authorities concerning U.S. aid: the way the strategic importance of the Azores was valued, as well as the corresponding compensations that might be obtained; and the negotiations for the return of German gold, in an amount assessed by the Allies, thought to be deposited inside the vaults of the *Banco de Portugal*. The way that the Cold War and the international situation developed ended up de-dramatising the expression of that strong anti-Americanist feeling, especially noticeable in the events that surrounded Portugal's participation in the Marshall Plan. The evolution of the international context eventually recommended and imposed a closer and reinforced bilateral military and economic relationship between Portugal and the USA, formally translated into the signing of the Lajes agreement, on 2 February 1948, the Portuguese participation in the Marshall aid itself and the signing of the North Atlantic Treaty, on 4 April 1949.

From another perspective, the assessment of the country's economic and financial situation and the definition of future strategies, particularly in terms of foreign trade, were also in line with the decision presented in Paris, especially insofar as they matched the wish to dispense with any commitment that might involve somewhat sophisticated forms of external dependence.

In addition to the haughtiness and genuine optimism with which Portugal's favourable economic and financial situation was displayed at the end of the War, underlining its capacity to surmount, independently, any difficulties that might affect it, the statement made in Paris unveiled the reason for Portugal's presence at that meeting of 16 European countries, and for the country's involvement in the American programme: Portugal needed imports, indispensable for public consumption and for the electrification and industrialisation programmes launched at the end of the War (Law no. 2002, 1944, of the Electrification of the Country, and Law no. 2005, of Industrial Development and Reorganisation, 1945). Portugal also needed to find markets for its own exports; moreover, the country had to preferably find solutions that would allow it to save dollars and take advantage of other monetary reserves, more specifically, the chance to use its credit in pounds sterling. In practice, if we will, national economy was characterised by how far it was willing to acknowledge its own external dependence. The Portuguese Government wished to keep the country economically autonomous, but depended noticeably on foreign supplies to "live" and become self-sufficient. For this reason, although it really abhorred the economic consequences of cooperation, having closer relationships with its main trading partners was an inexorable imperative. Obviously, its considerable external dependence imposed strict limits on the desired autarchy.

The decision to decline American financial aid did not imply any change in Portugal's position as a participating country. Portugal continued to take part in the meetings and activities of the "16 Europeans", inserting itself, like other countries, in the mechanisms created under the Marshall Plan, and shortly afterwards, on 16 April 1948, signing the OEEC Convention. Through this signature, the Portuguese Government formally committed to taking part and actively adhering to the fundamental principles and objectives that governed the new organisation, thus joining a movement of economic cooperation promoted among European countries and strongly supported by the USA.

2 Crisis and pragmatism: From rejecting to requesting American financial aid

However, it did not take more than a year for the situation to change significantly, and Portugal found itself forced to request Marshall financial aid.

Under the pressure of a crisis that had persisted since 1947, and despite its scepticism regarding the solutions found internationally, its ideological principles and the voluntarism that the country had shown during the difficult post-war years, the Government ended up yielding and changing its position in one of the most important reversals of foreign policy which occurred during the New State.

Having tried, to the limits of its capacity, to avoid resorting to Marshall financial aid, the Portuguese Government pragmatically changed its attitude, requested aid and fought for Portugal to be included in the distribution of American credit.

Once the new position was assumed, there was the expectation that American aid might not only help overcome the country's financial deficit and surmount the serious economic crisis with which it was struggling, but also foster Portugal's economic development.

During the first months of 1948 there was, for the first time in several years, a marked deterioration in Portugal's commercial position, dragging the country's finances down with it, a fact that, leaving aside more structural reasons, had as its main causes: (i) the generalised increase in imports, both in quantities and in values (induced by the growing demand caused by the restrictions of the War and the conditions of international scarcity); (ii) the sharp decrease in exports of several products and goods, abnormally valued during the war; (iii) the increase in imports of agricultural products, due to the scarcity of grain production, strongly affected by the poor agricultural years of 1946 and 1947; and (iv) the increase in imports of industrial equipment, needed for the industrialisation programme launched after the end of the war. In fact, Portugal's economic and financial situation had been showing signs of precariousness since 1947 and, already at that time, everything pointed to a probable worsening of the situation. As a result of all this, gold and currency reserves decreased significantly, especially in the years 1947 to 1949, "breaking" the financial balance of the country, and "endangering" the strongest principle that presided over the financial politics of the New State's governments.

On the other hand, once set in motion, the programme of economic cooperation between European countries, supported by the USA, triggered adverse effects on the Portuguese economic and financial situation. Sharing resources in a scenario of widespread and world-wide scarcity was difficult and subject not only to the availability of dollars, but to the relative position of the countries in terms of hardships and needs. Moreover, and in practice, sharing depended increasingly on the only country that, being in a position to provide supplies and credit, had a political and economic hegemonic position in the Western hemisphere.

The clash with reality ended up being even worse than could have been foreseen in those circumstances. The truth is that the deterioration of the Portuguese commercial and financial situation, expected in light of the nature and difficulties of the country's economy, suffered an accelerated and profound decline following the economic policy recently pursued by the Minister of the Economy, Daniel Barbosa, since its effects on the financial and exchange rate were stronger than expected. Daniel Barbosa was called to the Government in February 1947, assuming the eminently political task of solving the issue of public supply. Growing social unrest, with feared political effects, ended up forcing the reversal of the strategy pursued since the end of the War and provided the new minister with permission to use large financial resources, in order to solve the supply problem. The policy of stabilising supply led by Daniel Barbosa, based on the massive purchase of foreign goods, effectively solved the most pressing public supply problems, alleviating the growing social instability and putting an end to the scenario of a wartime economy which had been dragging on since the end of the conflict. Daniel Barbosa, however, would go far beyond the pragmatic and conjunctural nature of this initial political design. Although his actions were more visible on the matter of public supply, falling short of the same level of accomplishment in other areas, the new minister had ideas and principles and advocated practices and strategies that contradicted the orthodoxy used to address economic and financial issues. The decrease in gold and currency reserves recorded at the time and, in particular, the deficit in public accounts, although consented to as an instrument used by Daniel Barbosa to finance the economic activity, were unsustainable in light of the thinking and practices that Salazar had imposed since the beginning of the New State. All this only triggered the reaction of the Portuguese Government on several fronts, seeking to remedy a situation of which it was already aware and had been trying to counter, in vain (namely through guidelines contained in diplomas meant to regulate external trade, but also by adhering to the OEEC). From then on, it was only a matter of time until Portugal reconsidered its position and, reversing its initial decision, asked the Americans for financial aid, setting aside the principles and prejudices that had shaped the position initially assumed. In the end, economic and financial factors prevailed and that was enough to move Portuguese authorities, in less than a year, from an initial position of declining help to another, radically opposed, one of "rushing" for American financial aid.

Even then, the Government still tried to resist. Setting aside the arrogance of people who did not want to join the "hungry for dollars", the Government made one last effort to avoid asking for Marshall aid, trying, under the same American programme, to transfer to the USA 40 million pounds of Portugal's outstanding credit with England. However, the attempt was unsuccessful.

Finally, due to a coincidence or intentionally, on the eve of signing the Luso-American cooperation agreement, drafted on the assumption that Portugal did not receive financial aid, on 27 September 1948, the Portuguese representative at the OEEC informally put forward, in Paris, the Portuguese Government's intention of requesting financial aid under the ERP.

3 The Portuguese Programme

From then on, the Portuguese Government engaged in intense activity in order to create favourable conditions for obtaining and applying the aid that it now deemed essential. During August 1948, legislation was prepared that would lead to the creation of the Technical Committee for European Economic Cooperation (*Comissão Técnica de Cooperação Económica Europeia* – CTCEE). A few months later, with functions that complemented those of the Technical Committee, the National Development Fund (*Fundo de Fomento Nacional* – FFN) was created, primarily to manage Portugal's use of American aid.

In November 1948, at the OEEC, with the assistance of officials from the Economic Cooperation Administration – ECA (the body that, in the USA, was in charge of managing the Marshall Plan and was the connection link to Europe), Portugal presented a long term programme which, according to OEEC guidelines, consisted of a general outline of national production and consumption goals, a detailed report on public works or economic objectives to be carried out until 1952–53, and an estimate of the trade and payment balances with the various monetary zones.[3] The amount of aid to be provided to Portugal depended on the presentation of this data. The programme assessed the capital it needed to be 625 million dollars, and that was the amount requested. Portugal was looking for American aid to finance a large-scale economic development plan, extrapolating the basic purposes of the ERP: helping European reconstruction.

The second part of the Portuguese application for Marshall aid consisted of the specific programme for 1949–50, which tried to show the increasing deterioration to which the Portuguese economy was being subjected. In this document, more technical and heavily quantified, the Portuguese Government resumed the general lines of the long-term programme, placing emphasis on the purchase of equipment abroad, intended for five major areas: energy, irrigation and the iron mining industry; transportation; the manufacturing industry; agriculture; health and education. In all, these acquisitions amounted to around 90 million dollars and represented 28 percent of the full sum requested for that purpose in the global programme. The remaining 300 million dollars were intended, during the years of the Marshall Plan (1949–52), to create the enterprises where that equipment was to be incorporated.

The "master plan", which was to undergo multiple adjustments, imposed by both Europeans and Americans, was, it should be noted, made mainly in the name of Portuguese economic and social structure, meaning, in this sense, going back in relation to the proposals for industrial modernisation approved at the end of World War II. The programme put forward and advocated by the Portuguese Government took for granted the essentially rural nature and features of the country, stressing a "renewed" focus on agricultural specialisation that tried to take into account a new international division of labour; in fact, this plan not only highlighted self-sufficiency in terms of food, but also emphasised an industrialisation process applied mainly to agricultural industries, leaving behind the purposes announced in the Law of Industrial Development and Reorganisation, confirming, in this plan as well, the focus granted to agriculture as the central element of the economic policy that the country sought to pursue.

The plan was confirmed and approved by the Council of Ministers, and accepted, recognised and defended before the OEEC and the ECA as the master plan for the Portuguese economy for the 1949 to 1952 period. Ironically, it was the use of Marshall aid that forced the Portuguese Government to formally structure a four-year economic development programme. Although with some adjustments, this was the economic programme that the Government adopted and pursued until the First Development Plan (1953–58).

Portugal would end up receiving Marshall financial aid, in an amount, however, far below what had been asked for by the Portuguese authorities, a fact that surprised and disappointed them. The truth is that, once the financing was requested, great expectations had been generated, and these were eventually frustrated; hopes had even been raised that Marshall aid would not only restore balance to the national economic and financial situation but also assist in financing the long-awaited industrial take-off. This is why the most disillusioned people were the President of the Council and the Minister of Finance, Costa Leite (Lumbrales), who, a few months earlier, had both been vehemently against any possibility of American aid.

4 Nature and values of Marshall aid to Portugal

Between 3 April 1948, and 30 June 1952, the period during which the ERP was formally in operation, the American administration made available to European countries a total amount of 13 thousand million dollars.

The features of the ERP changed gradually during those years, reflecting the trends and objectives of U.S. foreign policy, established according to the evolution of the international context and adjusted to the set-up and interests of the political forces present within the

American administration. The consensus that, in April 1948, had permitted the approval of the Economic Cooperation Act quickly became compromised, due to the different understandings and perspectives on how the aims of American aid to foreign countries ought to be handled. Soon, the beginning of the Korean War would become a factor in favour of the reasons and arguments of so-called "military diplomacy", gradually subsuming the "economic diplomacy" of which the Marshall Plan was the most visible component.

According to the procedures imposed by the American administration, the ERP could grant two kinds of aid: direct aid and indirect aid.

Direct aid was granted in dollars and was meant to pay for goods and services coming from the USA and, exceptionally, from other countries (off-shore payments), and took on three different forms: loan, conditional aid and grant (donation). Determining how much aid was received as grants or loans (within the sum allocated to each country) depended entirely on the American administration.

Indirect aid was provided as bilateral or multilateral drawing rights, expressed in the currencies of the participating countries that granted them for the payment of trade deficits of the participating countries that received them. Countries that were granted drawing rights, as mentioned above, received from the USA conditional aid in dollars; countries that used the drawing rights had to set up a corresponding counterpart fund, the same as with donations. Unlike direct aid, which was applied to specific operations, indirect aid was meant to be used by the central banks of participating countries in order to settle their mutual positions, trying, in the end, to facilitate payments between participating countries without spending gold and through coverages made in ERP dollars (just as with their reciprocal conditional aid). It was an important instrument to facilitate and stimulate intra-European trade exchanges before the creation of the European Payments Union (EPU). Once the EPU was created, indirect aid was, of course, no longer used.

During the four years that the ERP was active, initially under the administration of the ECA and, as of December 1951, of its successor, the Mutual Security Agency (MSA), Portugal benefited only from aid corresponding to the two interim financial years: 1949–50 and 1950–51. Concerning 1949–50, Portugal was allocated 31.5 million dollars in direct aid and 27.2 million dollars in indirect aid (drawing rights); as for 1950–51, Portugal received only direct aid in the amount of 11,051 million dollars. In the last Marshall year, 1951–52, in view of the fact that the Portuguese balance of payments had attained a balance, and taking into account that the programme had changed into almost exclusively military aid, the Portuguese

Government accepted with the American administration's decision to suspend direct aid to Portugal, and returned to its initial position of "non-beneficiary" of ERP aid.

Allocating funds did not necessarily mean these were actually granted; it was more of a case of general information of the amount that, in principle, was to be made available to the beneficiary country. On the one hand, the American administration reserved the right to introduce adjustments that might increase or decrease the amounts of loans and grants; on the other hand, the evolution of the actual use of drawing rights also had a decisive effect on establishing the global amounts of conditional aid and indirect aid.

In addition to financing, granted as direct and indirect aid during the two ERP years 1949–50 and 1950–51, Portugal benefited from three special loans, taking advantage of an extra-aid fund specifically intended for colonial projects, and received aid granted under the Technical Assistance and Productivity programme.

American aid granted and used in Portugal under the Marshall Plan was globally divided, as follows in Table 1.1.

Table 1.1 Marshall Plan aid granted to Portugal

	000 dollars				*escudos**
I – Direct aid:					
	1949-50	1950-51	Total		
Loan	27 500	8 551	36 051		
Donation	3 000	2 500	5 500		
	30 500	11 051	41 551		1 194 591
Conditional aid	8 256		8 256		237 360
(drawing rights granted)				49 807	1 431 951
II – Indirect aid (drawing rights) (counterpart in dollars)			1949-50		
Bilateral (obtained)	20 400	Of which were used	14 810		
Multilateral (obtained)	6 800	Of which were used	3 371		
	27 200		18 181	18 181	522 704
III – Special loans:					
Beira harbour (Mozambique)			2 065		
Meat industry (Angola)			663		
Limpopo railway			17 000	19 728	567 180
IV – Technical assistance (donation):					
In dollars					
With a counterpart in *escudos*			1 532		
Without a counterpart in *escudos*			385		
In *escudos*			303	2 220	63 825
Total (with conditional aid)				89 936	2 585 660
Total (without conditional aid)				81 680	2 348 300

* 1 US dollar = 28.75 *escudos*.

Direct aid was the most visible side of this Marshall aid, corresponding, in general terms, to the way found to finance the importation programme essential to carrying out the economic programmes approved by the OEEC and the ECA.

Portugal received from the USA a global amount of 49.807 million dollars as direct aid: 36.051 million as loans, 5.5 million as donations and 8.256 million in exchange subsidies or conditional aid by means of drawing rights granted to other participating countries.

The loans were granted, on behalf of the ECA, by the Export-Import Bank, with an annual interest rate of 2.5 per cent, and could be repaid in the long term through annual instalments. These were intended to finance the purchasing of goods and services previously authorised by the ECA administrator. Portugal contracted two loans with the Washington Export-Import Bank, one related to the 1949–50 financial year and the other related to the following year, respectively for the amounts of 27.5 and 8.551 million dollars, in accordance with the provisions of Decree-Laws no. 37 792 and no. 38 413, dated 24 March 1950, and 8 September 1951, respectively. These diplomas gave the Government authorisation to contract those loans with the entity designated by the ECA, pending approval of the respective draft contracts by the Council of Ministers. It was also approved that the funds required to pay the interests on those loans were to be included in the Portuguese State Budget, while the sums that the FFN (National Development Fund) was going to pay to the Treasury would be considered as revenue.

The funds obtained in this way could be used (i) to grant loans (medium or long term) in *escudos*, equivalent to the dollars used, and in accordance with the rules established by the national programmes, to the importers of goods and services provided by the USA, or (ii) to finance (in the medium or long term) productive undertakings carried out with the *escudos* that resulted from the sale of lent dollars to the national importers of goods. In other words, the Government could transform the American loan into national credit operations, creating new creditors whose debts, depending on the type of merchandise imported from the USA, were settled immediately (as was the case with most consumer goods), or were instead turned into medium or long term debts, letting the loan, in the end, become an internal means to finance national economic activities, since it was freely used by the beneficiary country. With the *escudos* that resulted from the sale of dollars, medium or long-term loans were granted through the FFN (National Development Fund). In any case, the Portuguese Government was always responsible for the debt to the USA. Naturally, this kind of financing was only available for entities that gave the State safe assurances for the repayment of capital and corresponding interest. Another important factor was the Portuguese Government's preference for the sort of financing that might conceivably increase national production and, desirably, lead directly or indirectly to a decrease in imports; in principle, this way of acting generated savings in foreign exchange, letting the Government compensate for the expenditure of dollars to which it was compelled due to the amortisation of capital and interests stemming from loans contracted with the Export-Import Bank.

In addition to the loans granted to Portugal through the Export-Import Bank, the country benefited from direct aid from the Marshall Plan in the form of donations. This kind of aid was provided almost free of charge and, taking into account the foreign exchange reserves of the beneficiary country, depended essentially on its deficit vis-à-vis the USA. Dollars obtained this way were sold to national importers, and required a counterpart fund in national currency (with the *escudos* received from the said importers), which were then credited to the Portuguese Government in a special *Banco de Portugal* account, after deducting a percentage for expenses incurred by the local ECA Mission, or 10 per cent in the days of the MSA. Portugal received 5.5 million dollars as donations, 3 million during the 1949–50 financial year and 2.5 million during the following year.

Finally, Portugal also obtained 8.256 million dollars in direct aid in the form of conditional aid, resulting, therefore, from bilateral drawing rights granted in *escudos* to other participating countries, so they could settle their deficits with Portugal. Of this amount, one million dollars came from the coverage of drawing rights granted by Portugal to Greece (for the sale of cork); the remaining 7.256 million dollars were received according to multilateral drawing rights used in Portugal by other participating countries (basically corresponding to an unforeseen increase in Portuguese exports). See Table 1.2, overleaf.

In spite of the efforts and interest shown by the American administration, only 4 per cent of total direct aid was applied in the Colonies. However, equipment and raw materials for industry were primary; the amount of 224 thousand dollars, allocated to the purchase of consumer goods, was essentially due to an "imposition" from the Metropolis (*i.e.*, Metropolitan Portugal, in Europe), forcing the colonial territories to buy flour. In any case, when observed individually, the funds linked to the energy production projects of Lourenço Marques and Mabubas and those reserved for colonial aerodromes represent undertakings of a significant size, when compared to the majority of investments made in the Metropolis.

Table 1.2 Direct aid granted to Portugal

	000 dollars	%	
Metropolitan Portugal (Europe)			
Equipment and raw materials for industries	16 052	33	
Consumer goods	30 556	63	
Freightage	2 003	4	
Total	48 611	100	96
Portuguese colonies			
Equipment and raw materials for industries	1 696	88	
Consumer goods	224	12	
Total	1 920	100	4
Total equipment Metropolis + Colonies	17 748	35	
Total consumer goods Metropolis + Colonies	30 780	61	
Total freightage	2 003	4	
Total Metropolis + Colonies	50 531	100	100

As for the Metropolis, the weight represented by consumer goods or, more exactly, by wheat imports, was of note. These imports represented more than two thirds (68 per cent) of total metropolitan purchases in this category and 41.4 per cent of total direct aid (Metropolis + Colonies). There was no other product that came close, in terms of value; in all, oil ranked second, representing 16.6 per cent of the total.

Among beneficiary entities, the most significant amounts were those used by the *Companhia Portuguesa de Celulose*, those allocated for the purchase of locomotives for CP (the railway company) and those used to buy equipment destined for the Sorraia project. At a secondary level, the amounts that stand out were those attributed to A. J. Oliveira & Filhos, to Grémio dos Armadores da Pesca do Bacalhau and to the factory owned by Campos, Melo & Irmão. It is also worth mentioning the value represented by the purchase of tinplate (itemised as various goods) for the fish canning industry. In fact, on the whole, the relative weight represented by the private industrial sector as a beneficiary of American aid should be noted.

Contrary to the initial expectations of the American administration, consumer goods ended up predominating in Portuguese purchases provided by the Marshall Plan, representing, in 1955, a percentage of 61 per cent, compared to the 35 per cent recorded for the purchase of industrial equipment and raw materials. A further note should be made to highlight the small weight of State services in the use of aid: about 10 per cent of the total. Most direct aid was used by the business sector (private or mixed capital) and by corporate bodies, notably the National Federation of Industrial Milling (*Federação Nacional dos Industriais de Moagem* – FNIM), the entity with official permission to buy grain.

In addition to direct aid, Portugal received 27.2 million dollars of indirect aid, consisting of drawing rights over other OEEC countries, intended to cover Portugal's expected balance of payments deficits with those countries, which, in return, were entitled to the corresponding amount of conditional aid, in dollars, which they could use to buy American goods and services.

The estimates of the balances of payments were established within the OEEC and negotiated bilaterally with the countries concerned. Experts from each country discussed bilaterally, with delegations from other countries, the terms and limits under which drawing rights would be granted. As a general framework, and depending on what was established and agreed upon, European countries, with the support of the ECA, signed a payment and compensation agreement, with the firm purpose of contributing to the development of intra-European exchanges. Portugal, of course, only participated actively in this process in the year 1949–50.

In 1950–51, the third year of the ERP, Portugal did not receive any indirect aid. The system abolished aid given as drawing rights following the creation of the European Payments Union – EPU. Henceforth, intra-European settlements were made through the EPU, periodically compensating the bilateral surpluses and deficits of each contracting party.

It should be noted that indirect aid was only effectively usable providing that the International Bank of Payments, in its capacity as the agency that settled accounts between the issuing institutions of participating countries, and after all possible multilateral compensations had been carried out, paid off the existing debits, by means of the available drawing rights.

Of the total of 27.2 million dollars allocated to Portugal in 1949–50, around 70 per cent (20.4) consisted of bilateral drawing rights (which could only be used with those countries to which they had initially been granted), and only the remaining 30 per cent were multilateral drawing rights (which, therefore, could be used as a reinforcement of bilateral drawing rights and, under certain conditions, with any country, in case the results of the balance of payments did not correspond to the initial estimates).

However, of the total amount of 27.2 million dollars' worth of drawing rights obtained, corresponding to the 1949–50 financial year, Portugal only used 18.2 million during that period, and eventually renounced the use of the rest. See Table 1.3, below

Table 1. 3 Drawing rights obtained by Portugal

(000 dollars)

		Allocated	Used
Bilateral			
Austria		525	242
Belgium		9 450	9 450
Denmark		825	0
France		3 075	3 035
Italy		1 500	991
Holland		2 250	0
Norway		1 125	1 092
Sweden		1 650	0
	Subtotal	**20 400**	**14 810**
Multilateral			
Germany		6 800	
Belgium			3 371
Denmark			
Greece			
Norway			
	Subtotal	**6 800**	**3 371**
Total		**27 200**	**18 181**

Source: CTCEE Archives, "The use of Marshall aid in 1949-1950 and perspectives for 1950-51", a report by the Minister of the Presidency, 11 November 1950.

Chances opened up to Portugal through indirect aid which allowed the country to improve its general position in relation to the countries with which it held a trade deficit position. More specifically, 20.4 million dollars of Portugal's estimated balance of payments deficits with the above-mentioned OEEC countries were assuredly covered and, in addition, the country was able to use 6.8 million dollars to cover possible deficits with any participating country.

In addition to the total of 67.988 million dollars granted to Portugal under the Marshall Plan, as direct and indirect aid, the country also benefited from American aid via a set of three special loans and the use of the technical assistance and productivity programme.

Portugal got three special loans, granted by the American administration as extraordinary aid, with a view to supporting the development of colonial projects. The first loan, equivalent to 2 065 000 dollars, contracted with the ECA, was meant for the construction of a new pier for the Beira harbour, having been authorised by Decree-Law no. 37 988, dated 2 October 1950. The two other loans were contracted with the Export-Import Bank. The first, authorised by Decree-Law no. 38 323, dated 28 June 1951, on the eve of the entry into force of the contract signed between the Portuguese Government and the American bank, amounted to 663 000 dollars for the acquisition of equipment and materials, and payments for services, needed to install a meat processing industry in Angola. The last special loan, and also the largest, was the subject of Decree-Law no. 39 139, authorising the Portuguese Government to contract a loan of up to 17 000 000 dollars with the Export-Import Bank in order to build and outfit the Limpopo Railway.

American aid granted under the TA&P programme continued until 1957, assisting 54 projects which benefited from financing in the amounts of 1 916 852.04 dollars and 8 716 770.40 *escudos*, and having a significant impact on Portuguese economy as a whole, involving 98 Portuguese and 74 foreign technicians. Altogether, these projects represented American financing in the amounts of 1 916 852.04 dollars and 8 716 770.40 *escudos* (part of the American contribution applied to agricultural productivity projects was applied in Portuguese currency). Of the total sum in dollars allocated to Portugal under the TA&P programme, 1 531 835.10 dollars originated a corresponding deposit in *escudos*. This counterpart fund was meant to be invested in national projects, meaning that the TA&P programme, in addition to the benefits it generated directly, was also important for its co-participation in investments later used in national development projects.

The Technical Assistance and Productivity programme was the most innovative and stimulating feature of Portugal's participation in the Marshall Plan. See Table 1.4, overleaf.

Adopting the exchange rate used by the Portuguese administration at the time (1 dollar = 28.75 *escudos*), the TA&P programme in Portugal consisted of American aid of 64 thousand *contos* (1 *conto* = 1000 *escudos*).

Table 1.4 American aid for the TA&P programme

	Dollars	*Escudos*
Financing in dollars	**1 916 852.04**	55 109 496.15
Projects with counterpart	**1 531 836.10**	44 040 259.13
Projects with no counterpart	**385 016.94**	11 069 237.03
Financing in *escudos*	303 192.01	**8 716 770.40**
Total American TA&P financing	**2 220 044.05**	**63 826 266.55**

In addition to this donation, made under the auspices of American technical assistance, there was a contribution made by Portuguese beneficiary entities either by paying expenses related to the projects in which they participated or by depositing in the counterpart fund a sum in *escudos* (required by some projects), corresponding to expenses incurred in dollars by the American administration. The expenses in national currency were the direct responsibility of participating entities, which, in each case, while accounting for them, did so outside the control of the CTCEE (the Technical Committee for European Economic Cooperation). However, there is an estimate, made later by the CTCEE, indicating that in Portugal the technical assistance programme amounted to 100 000 *contos*[4], allowing us to infer that the expenses assumed by Portuguese entities must have been in the order of 36 000 *contos*.

The implementation of the TA&P programme in Portugal, only partly embodied in specific projects, took place in four phases, between 1949 and 1957, and naturally reflected the various ongoing changes in terms of design and management which affected the programme itself during the ten years the American administration kept it operational. The first phase began in 1949 and ended in mid-1950, when an important shift happened in the general concept that guided the TA&P programme, which then evolved towards giving greater attention to matters of defence and military production in European countries. It was mostly a preparatory phase, in which the implementation of the programme had to face, apart from its specific difficulties, the complex process of defining and starting the general use of Marshall financial aid in Portugal. Therefore, the attention and priority of Portuguese authorities concentrated on the scope and adaptation needed to implement the financial aid programme from which the country sought to benefit, almost two years later than the rest of the participating countries.

Although, at first, the position of the Portuguese authorities concerning the acceptance of technical assistance provided by the USA wavered between apathy and disinterest, partly due to a mixture of ignorance and distrust regarding the aims and mechanisms incorporated within the programme, this did not mean that they made light of the importance that such technical assistance might have for both the metropolitan and the colonial economies. The Portuguese authorities understood the value of such technical support and of the chance to take advantage of it concerning specific and already pressing national issues, such as the study of the potential uses of the Douro river basin or the undertaking of mining prospecting in the colonies. In addition to the hesitations of the Portuguese Government to formally embrace the TA&P programme, and the timidity of private initiative, Portuguese authorities did, directly or indirectly, limit the use of technical assistance they actually deemed important for the country. The reasons for this were mainly financial imperatives, explained by a financial policy guided by a typical aversion to spending money that escaped budget projections.

Two more aspects should be noted, still within the context of how this first phase unfolded. The first has to do with the way technicians from the ECA Mission, and other American and European specialists, introduced themselves into the Portuguese economic and social sphere, and their subsequent performance. They identified and promoted contacts with the public and private technical elite, looking for partners that they embraced and to whom they provided new international contacts, particularly in the USA, although the spirit of initiative and nature of their Portuguese interlocutors also deserve being mentioned. The second aspect concerns the diffusion of ideas and concepts contained in the TA&P programme, whether these were theoretical and general ideas or practical concepts, which later became technical assistance projects. Among other things, it is worth noticing how the evolution and the changes that took place within the general philosophy of the TA&P programme, putting the spotlight on the analysis and improvement of productivity levels in European countries, arrived in Portugal slowly, as the actual concept of productivity gradually permeated Portuguese logic and vocabulary.

The second phase unfolded between mid-1950 and the end of 1951. The use of American technical assistance really took off, as well as the country's growing involvement in initiatives developed within the scope of the OEEC, in collaboration with the ECA. Some of the most important projects were launched, namely the study of the Douro river and aerial reconnaissance and geological surveys in Angola and Mozambique. However, the largest number of projects belonged to the agricultural sector, both metropolitan and colonial, involving learning missions to the USA by Portuguese technicians, and others, by

American specialists, in Portugal and its colonies, in order to study specific aspects.

Generally speaking, following the start of the Korean War, in August 1950, the TA&P programme and other ERP programmes were reorganised and reoriented, becoming subordinate to the priority objective of increasing European military production and reinforcing a policy of defence and rearmament. To this goal, however, was added the concern to increase productivity levels in European countries, namely through the implementation of management practices and industrial relations according to the American model, within the framework of a genuine productivity campaign which included the goal of stimulating the creation of productivity centres in beneficiary countries. In Portugal, defence-related projects would only acquire any significance during the following phase, but in the meantime the productivity campaign took off and was prolonged, involving, among other things, the diffusion of the concept, the dissemination of American management methods and organisational practices and the attempt to create a productivity centre.

The third phase unfolded between mid-year 1951 and mid-year 1953, a period during which the programme was under MSA administration. In 1951, its last year of existence, the ERP witnessed the elimination of part of the ECA-launched programmes. The TA&P survived under the management of the MSA, formally created in late 1951, but was once again reconverted to stimulate increase in European military production, acknowledging at the same time the need to carry on the assistance to European civilian production. During this third phase, several projects were launched, including six in the defence area, but the numerical predominance of agricultural-related projects remained. However, the productivity campaign was stepped up. According to the new moulds that shaped the future of American assistance abroad, two main objectives were pursued: on the one hand, launching the new programme to increase productivity and industrial production in Portugal; on the other hand, preparing a similar programme in the agricultural sector with a view to identifying the sector's main needs in terms of technical assistance. At the same time, creating a productivity centre remained a priority. Simultaneously, in compliance with the recent impositions by the ECA/MSA, extra care was given to the strict monitoring of activities involving strategic materials, an issue closely related to the development of colonial territories, for, according to the new guidelines, this was included in the productivity programme.

In June 1953, the MSA was replaced by the Foreign Operations Administration (FOA), followed by the International Cooperation

Administration (ICA) in July 1955. However, the technical assistance programme stayed operational. Therefore, the fourth phase of the TA&P programme in Portugal began in 1953 and continued until 1957, the year of the last expenses related to technical assistance projects developed in our country. The philosophy that guided the programme was already very different from the one that had been present at the time it was launched. Portugal kept the emphasis given to the productivity side, presenting specific programmes to increase production and productivity levels in the agricultural and industrial sectors, and insisting on the creation of a productivity centre. In addition to members of the Government, Portuguese industrial and commercial associations were involved in this matter. Concerning technical assistance projects, Portuguese technicians were still sent to the USA on learning missions, but the bulk of the projects were included in the Programme for Agricultural Promotion and Provision (also known as the Agricultural Demonstration Programme), which the American administration decided to support through the Undersecretariat of State for Agriculture. Thanks to the initiative of a small group of agricultural engineers, this programme ensured the predominance of the use of American technical assistance. Apart from agriculture, only two projects were carried out, both consisting of Portuguese technicians being sent to the USA on learning missions: a Portuguese engineer attended a course on reactors and four of the most distinguished Portuguese surgeons attended a course organised by the FOA, in collaboration with the American College of Surgeons.

Finally, the counterparts in *escudos* deposited in the *Banco de Portugal* account were meant to be used in national investments, pending the agreement of the American administration. In all, since the date the first counterpart funds generated by American aid were released until June 1958, a total of 655 180 898.80 *escudos* were committed to projects aiming at promoting the Portuguese economy, most of them through the FFN (National Development Fund).

Portugal's involvement in the Marshall Plan, in the context of the European economic cooperation that surrounded it, formed a significant part of the process in the late 1940s to recover the Portuguese economy, paving the way and introducing a few decisive traits for the cycle of economic growth and development that marked the following decades.

When analysing Portugal's participation in the Marshall Plan, there are three main dimensions to consider: (i) the reinforcement of the internationalisation of the Portuguese economy during the post-war period; (ii) the impact of American financial aid and technical assistance on the construction of infrastructures and on the effort to reorganise and modernise the Portuguese productive system; (iii) the definition of new options regarding economic development policies, with effects during the 1950s, and the adoption of the principles of economic planning.

As for the significance of the Marshall Plan in Portugal and the assessment of its impact on the Portuguese economy, the following aspects hold special significance:

☐ Portugal's involvement in the Marshall Plan played an important role in structuring a controlled process of economic development. The application for Marshall Plan financing forced the Portuguese Government to engage in an effort to analyse and think about the Portuguese economy in order to explain and substantiate the reasons for its request. Furthermore, presenting a four-year economic programme forced the government to: (i) expound on its ideas concerning the development strategy it wanted to apply in the country; (ii) agree on the objectives of a set of measures and sectorial plans that were being implemented in a more or less dispersed manner; (iii) identify and prioritise specific projects, framing them within global guidelines and allocating resources; (iv) envisage investments and estimate their expected results in the national accounts and, more specifically, as far as the projects included in the programme were concerned, describe their effects on the national economy and in the international sphere.

In practice, the Marshall Plan was the reason and the opportunity to formulate an economic programme for the post-war period, condensing the main aspects of the Government's perspectives for its economic policy and guiding its actions until the implementation of the First Development Plan; a kind of intermediate plan between the Economic Reconstitution Law of 1935 and the First Development Plan, if we concede the continuity that the New State ascribed to those two laws in terms of their economic framework.

In this context, it is also worth pointing out how Portugal's involvement in the Marshall Plan helped the country adhere to new ways of dealing with economic policy through economic planning, consubstantiated in successive medium-term plans that went on to guide Portuguese economic activity until the end of the New State;

☐ the presentation, defence and discussion of Portuguese programmes before the American administration and the OEEC meant that Portugal had to share decisions, applied to the implementation of

Portuguese projects that depended on the approval of both the OEEC and, especially, the Americans. In other words, the path of the Portuguese economy was no longer an exclusively Portuguese matter and was instead inserted within a framework of intra-European relationships, or, including the USA, Western relationships;

☐ participation in the Marshall Plan provided motives to reinforce a focus on the colonies; those territories formed part of Portuguese programmes and their projects were clearly considered, even receiving more focus, in raising and using American aid;

☐ since it constituted a source of external financing and also involved the raising of Portuguese capital, the Marshall financial aid granted to Portugal was incorporated and adapted to the guidelines of Portuguese economic policy and to the very evolution of the country's economy, providing it with additional resources;

☐ in context, American aid was important in terms of containing and surmounting the multidimensional crisis that, at the time, was affecting the Portuguese economy and society. ERP aid triggered mechanisms that helped eliminate the balance of payments deficit and expedited the supply of essential goods, needed to overcome the crisis and mitigate its economic and social effects. Equally, it enabled the acquisition of equipment for several projects that required this to start or carry on their activities. The impact of direct aid and counterpart funding for building infrastructures and on the effort to reorganise and modernise the national productive system, especially the industrial sector, are worth mentioning. As far as agriculture was concerned, and in spite of its primary position, in the end American aid dodged structural and structuring issues.

In general, indirect aid gave Portugal the chance to improve its position in relation to OEEC countries, with which it had a commercial deficit;

☐ if the Marshall Plan was used, to a large extent, to achieve scattered economic policy objectives, it is also true that it introduced important changes in certain implementations. It is worth mentioning the importance of studies carried out by foreign technical specialists, especially Americans, concerning specific aspects of the Portuguese economy, even when undertaken outside the TA&P programme. In addition, there were more opportunities to discuss ideas and share knowledge. In general, Portugal benefited from technical assistance insofar as it was able to explore its resources under better technical conditions, allowing the country to devise new ventures;

☐ globally, the TA&P programme contributed to expanding and developing the Portuguese scientific and technical system. Through the various initiatives promoted in the context of exchanging experiences, undertaking learning missions, providing training courses and carrying out technical assistance programmes between European countries and the United States of America, the TA&P programme also brought about developments in several areas within Portuguese economic activity;

☐ the TA&P programme also produced a cultural mix that extended its influence to a part of the Portuguese elite, an effect that was to become more intense during the following years, even compensating, in a way, for the frustration of certain opportunities lost along the way. Furthermore, it allowed the Portuguese to intensify contacts and get to know new international realities, the same way that it unexpectedly opened the country to the presence of foreign specialists, contributing to gradually opening up the New State, a process that, once opened, could hardly go back.

The full use of the programme was conditioned, to some extent, by the general guidelines and principles that steered the attitude of the Portuguese authorities, by the State's economic and financial policy, by the constraints of the country's economic and social structure and by its modest scientific and technological infrastructures. The level and features of the Portuguese economic fabric at the time placed limits on the amount and type of use that could be reaped from technical help given by foreign sources, either under the TA&P programme or within the framework of inter-European technical assistance, sponsored by the OEEC and, from 1953 onwards, by the AEP.

Teaching and introducing new concepts and application methods, and being a platform for the transfer and sharing of knowledge and technologies, the programme had a qualitative importance in the context of Portugal's economic and social development.

Even though it was one of the more "invisible" aspects of Portugal's participation in the Marshall Plan, making the most of the TA&P programme yielded some of its most important and lasting benefits. In other words, as a general balance, what was achieved in terms of technical assistance surpassed what is measurable, and had beneficial overall effects, in the short and medium term, with lasting positive impact.

As examples, we may mention the reorganisation of national accounting, the radical reform of higher education in the field of economics, started at the Higher Institute of Economic and Financial Sciences (Instituto Superior de Ciências Económicas e Financeiras – ISCEF) in 1949, or the progressive assimilation of the concept of productivity, with the resulting influence it exerted upon the management of Portuguese companies. Even considering the resistances underlying the failed attempts to set up and put into operation a "national productivity centre", the idea slowly took root; somewhat belatedly, it was eventually institutionally acknowledged, both through the creation of the Productivity Committee (COPRAI) of the Portuguese Industrial Association (Associação Industrial Portuguesa), and within the scope of the National Institute for Industrial Research (Instituto Nacional de Investigação Industrial – INII), created in 1959. This latter productivity service, in collaboration with the OEEC and the AEP (in the meantime closed in September 1961), launched an awareness campaign targeting industries and, soon afterwards, started producing a set of studies, regarding direct and indirect productivity measures, industrial spectrograms, methods and techniques of organisation and business management, all applied to the most important sectors of our manufacturing industry.

Furthermore, Portuguese participation in the TA&P programme forced the authorities to produce many works, namely studies, diagnoses, and global and sectorial projections, which significantly improved the knowledge of micro and macroeconomic reality. This participation, therefore, turned out to be a sort of general rehearsal to establish a new way of conceiving economic policies, which, thus, made their way into development plans. It was precisely within the framework of the Third Development Plan (1968–73) that productivity emerged as an important objective of economic policy.

☐ Portugal's participation in the Marshall Plan contributed to accelerating the country's immersion in a process of growing internationalisation and opening up to the outside. Portugal had taken the first steps in its "European adventure". By being involved in the Marshall Plan, and by joining the OEEC and the EPU, the country made sure it was part of the post-war trading and payment systems, and was actively present in the emerging movements of European economic cooperation. Let us note the meaning of this cooperation: one of the aspects that influenced the performance of the various European market economies over the "golden 30 years" was the economic cooperation platform created and its effects, namely in terms of liberalising and stimulating exchanges, a platform of which Portugal was also a part, reaping first-hand benefits;

☐ the changes introduced to Portuguese public administration should also be noted, caused either by imperatives arising from the design of the ERP or by the presence of a number of technicians trained through contacts and works carried out within the various national and international organisms. In this context, the meaning and importance assumed by the creation and activities of the CTCEE and the FFN should be emphasised.

Portuguese participation in the Marshall Plan, within the OEEC, created opportunities and opened up vast fields of learning, which was important in the sense that Portuguese technicians were able to acquire the skills and training they needed, namely in the areas of national accounting and statistics, as well as carry out multiple studies, diagnoses, and global and sectorial projections that significantly improved the knowledge of our own micro and macroeconomic reality;

□ Portugal's participation in the Marshall Plan was also important because it forced Portuguese public and private capital participation in investments made in "national development" projects, meaning that the ERP had a dual effect. Setting up and using the counterpart value of the aid granted in dollars was particularly significant, since it directed national capital towards development ventures, via the FFN, thus creating the opportunity to develop thinking on how to finance economic activity and make it happen through the increase in resources brought about by the Marshall Plan.

It should be noted that the Portuguese Government saw these financial resources as "extra" or "additional" means to invest in promoting and even boosting the country's economic activity. Thus, Marshall aid made for more animated investment in the Portuguese economy, a task left to the FFN. The part that resulted from taking part in the Marshall Plan represented practically 50 per cent of the funds that the FFN managed during its first years of activity, even taking into account the progressively broader functions and forms of financing that the FFN was allocated, especially following the launch of the First Development Plan;

□ as a whole, Portugal's participation in the Marshall Plan provided the country with financial assistance in the amount of approximately 90 million dollars (more than two and a half million *contos*), affecting a significant number of Portuguese economic agents, including the State itself. To this sum must be added the Portuguese counterpart funds, in the order of 650 thousand *contos* (100 to 120 million *contos* in current values, *i.e.*, 600 million euros).

Although these are modest amounts, especially when compared to the sums allocated to other beneficiary countries, their impact, even if evaluated in merely quantitative terms, was significant in the national context, corresponding to about a quarter of the Portuguese gross fixed capital formation (GFCF)) in 1950 and 1951.[5]

□ Let us point out that even though the grants and the ways to use the aid were widely publicised, economic and social agents did not always understand the sometimes discreet way in which Marshall money penetrated the realities of entrepreneurship, particularly when it was channelled through the FFN. Despite the vast collective neglect, the Marshall Plan did touch a significant part of the Portuguese population;

☐ for Portuguese authorities, who decided that resorting to American financial aid and involving the country in the Marshall Plan was indispensable, the balance was frankly positive. They got a portion of the aid that was meant for countries impoverished by World War II, a conflict in which Portugal did not even take part; and although the amounts received fell far short of what had been "ambitiously" requested, Portuguese authorities were able to benefit from useful and timely financing. They succeeded in managing it in a way to meet the goals and accomplishments of their choice. Fears of the American model and "imperialism", of "interference" in national and colonial affairs or of any threatening attempts at national sovereignty were, in practice, circumscribed to mere rhetoric or reasonably diluted within the benefits of American aid.

Notes

1   José Caeiro da Mata, "Conferência Europeia de Cooperação Económica. I. Em Paris, em 22 de Setembro de 1947", in *Ao Serviço de Portugal*, 1951, pp. 163–164.

2   Historical Archives of the Ministry of Foreign Affairs, 2nd floor, M 53, A 39, Proc. 41, 2, A Report by the Ministry of Finance, Minister's Office, Costa Leite Lumbrales, 27 August 1947.

3   The general outlines of the program were published later, by Araújo Correia, in his book *Estudos de Economia Aplicada*, 1950.

4   Comissão Técnica de Cooperação Económica Externa, *"Resumo do Aproveitamento da Assistência Técnica Americana em Portugal"* (Technical Committee for External Economic Cooperation, "Summary of the Use of American Technical Assistance in Portugal"), April 1958 (typed), p. 11.

5   See GFCF data published in *Statistics of National Product and Expenditure 1938, 1947 to 1952, O.E.C.E.*, Paris, 1954.
(million *escudos*)

1938	1947	1948	1949	1950	1951	1952
Gross Fixed Capital Formation						
1 921	4 988	5 334	5 416	5 759	6 038	6 095

References

Rollo, M. F. 1994: *Portugal e o Plano Marshall*. Lisbon: Editorial Estampa.

Rollo, M. F., 2004: O Programa de Assistência Técnica: o interesse americano nas Colónias portuguesas. *Ler História* 47, 2004, 81–123.

Rollo, M. F. 2004: Inovação e produtividade: o modelo americano e a assistência técnica americana a Portugal no pós-guerra. In J. M. Brandão de Brito, M. Heitor and M. F. Rollo (ed), *Momentos da Inovação e Engenharia em Portugal no Século XX*, 3 vols. Lisbon: Publicações Dom Quixote.

Rollo, M. F. 2007: *Portugal e a Reconstrução Económica do Pós-Guerra. O Plano Marshall e a Economia Portuguesa dos anos 50*. Lisbon: Ministério dos Negócios Estrangeiros.

CHAPTER 2

Financing the Portuguese Democracy: The International Monetary Fund and Other Creditors (1975–1979)

Luciano Amaral

On 9 May 1978 the second constitutional Government of the Portuguese democracy signed a Stand-by arrangement (SBA) with the International Monetary (IMF) (Nunes, 2011, Lopes, 1982 and 1996, Pinto, 1983, Schmitt, 1981, Mateus, 2013, Zorrinho, 2018, and Amaral *et al.* 2020). However, this did not correspond to a sudden need for financing nor the first time Portugal had made use of IMF assistance in the immediately preceding years: in fact, the 1978 SBA represented the conclusion of three years of intensive interaction with the IMF, in a context where many other international agents helped finance the Portuguese economy and Government. Portugal had started using IMF resources in July 1975 and following policies to control the external deficit that were concordant with IMF principles and techniques, since December of the same year.

What was new in the 1978 SBA was the inclusion of conditionality with performance criteria. That the use of IMF resources did not imply, until then, strictly monitored conditionality had to do with the fact, firstly, that some of this had been undertaken within the first tranches of Portugal's IMF quota, something that did not imply conditionality (or only mildly) according to IMF rules; and, secondly, that another part of that use had been channelled through special facilities created by the IMF in the context of the 1970s crisis that were also granted with no conditionality attached. What is more, the Portuguese authorities had started following austerity policies concordant with IMF principles since 1976, in the context of the use of the second special Oil Facility. The stance of the Portuguese authorities was interesting: as the facility did not require strong policy commitments on the part of the receiving countries; the Portuguese authorities seem to have started following those policies largely on their own, or at least in tandem with the IMF, rather than constrained by it. Similar policies continued to be adopted in the following year, in the context of the negotiation of an SBA, which already implied conditionality, although only of a mild kind: the Government had to present a policy plan to be approved by the IMF, but no performance criteria to be closely monitored. The reason for this was that the resources used were still within the first tranche of the Portuguese quota. However, the country's authorities nevertheless adopted an adjustment programme in association with the SBA: many of the most important policies adopted in the context of the 1978 SBA had been in use since 1977.

The apparently overzealous attitude of the Portuguese authorities seems to be related to their internalisation of the need to adopt austerity measures in order to deal with the combined effects of the 1973 oil shock and the 1974 Portuguese revolution, something that coincided with a change in the political cycle in the country, as the initial socialist-communist inclinations of the revolution gave way to capitalist moderation, from late 1975 onwards. The relationship with the IMF and the kind of policies followed from then on were an integral part of that change. Once the idea of keeping the Portuguese economy within the capitalist mould had prevailed among the political class, something that was not clear from the beginning, as many political agents fought for the instauration of a communist/socialist regime, the various governments from 1976 onwards felt the need for two things: one was to fight the economic crash of the two previous years, and the other was to provide the population with those sorts of social services that most European democracies had been developing since the end of World War II, something the previous authoritarian regime had generally neglected. Both created difficulties for the economy's external balance, helping to explain the persistent need for financial assistance. A return to external balance would only be achieved in 1979, and was short-lived, as in 1980 an international payment imbalance reappeared, eventually leading to a new SBA between 1983 and 1985. But that is a different story.

A highly significant aspect of the 1978 SBA is that Portugal failed to comply with some of its performance criteria and, consequently, did not receive any IMF assistance throughout its duration. The explanation for this lies in the fact that Portugal was then using other, much larger, sources of external financing: preeminent among these was a $750 million loan granted by a syndicate of countries led by the US, but there were many other loans with different origins. This points to one further dimension of the process, namely that IMF assistance was only a small fraction of the external assistance received by Portugal in the period: the IMF was only responsible for 8 percent of that assistance, the remaining 92 percent coming from other sources, such as the Bank of International Settlements (BIS), the European Economic Community (EEC) and individual countries, for instance the US, the Federal Republic of Germany or the UK. The reason for Portugal being such a large recipient of foreign assistance had to do with the international political context of the time: Portugal at that time had become a pivotal element of the Cold War, as the possibility of it becoming the first Western European country to adopt a communist regime was seen as highly probable, with some probable contagion effects also on Spain, France, Italy or Greece. Therefore, Western countries contributed with significant amounts of assistance to keep the country firmly within the capitalist side of the divide.

The remainder of this paper is organized as follows. The first section describes the economic context explaining the need for an IMF intervention in Portugal. The second addresses the transformations the IMF itself was passing through at the time, especially due to the 1970s international crisis. This affected its relationship with Portugal, namely with respect to conditionality. The third section provides a thorough description of the different interactions between the Portuguese authorities and the IMF between 1975 and 1979 and the fourth section describes the other international loans received by Portugal in the period.

1 The Economic context

The need for the Portuguese economy to obtain major external financing between 1975 and 1979 resulted from the combination of the 1970s international crisis and a political revolution in the country. Two major shocks affected the world economy in the early 1970s: the end of the so-called "Bretton Woods system" (the fixed-exchange rate mechanism created in 1945), following the Nixon administration's decision to terminate the convertibility of the US dollar into gold in August 1971; and the decision by the Arab countries of the Organisation of Petroleum Exporting Countries (OPEC) to embargo oil exports to various Western countries in October 1973 (Hamilton,

2011). The latter, especially, had a huge impact on the Portuguese economy (Amaral, 2019).

To these, a series of internal challenges having to do with the over-throwing in 1974 of an authoritarian regime (the *Estado Novo*), which had ruled the country since 1933, were added. The events leading to the toppling of the regime were initiated by a movement of junior military officers, the starting point for which was a general dissatisfaction with their career prospects and combat conditions in the Colonial War, a military conflict in which Portugal was involved in its African colonies. The main point of these officers was to terminate the war, but they associated this with the overthrowing of the authoritarian regime. On 25 April 1974, together with some senior officers, they orchestrated a military coup. The old authoritarian regime fell but there was no consensus among the revolutionaries over what the new regime should be. From 1974 to 1976, they split over the issue, together with political stakeholders and society in general. The division followed a typical Cold War pattern, with some favouring a democracy of the Western type and others an outright socialist/communist regime (Reis, 1994a, and Ramos *et al.* 2009). Between September 1974 and March 1975, the latter obtained control of the political levers of the country.

This political evolution had crucial economic consequences. One of them was the eruption of a vast wave of labour unrest, with the occurrence of various strikes and episodes of occupation of firms by workers. The purpose of much of this activity was to obtain higher pay and shorter working hours. With the revolutionary authorities abstaining from repressing labour, workers were generally successful in their demands: wages increased 7 percent and 14 percent in real terms in 1974 and 1975, respectively (Mateus, 2013). The various governments approved legislation highly favourable to labour: a national minimum wage was introduced, striking became legal, a general system of unemployment benefit was created, the old corporatist unions were extinguished, unionisation became free, and a new Labour Code was approved, making individual firing almost impossible and collective firing also difficult (Amaral, 2019).

While this was taking place, the labour market was rocked by a massive shock deriving from the process of decolonisation. Getting out of Africa was the main objective of the revolutionaries. Panic spread among the colonists of Angola and Mozambique (the two territories with sizable white populations) from mid-1974 onwards, and they started an exodus in the direction of mainland Portugal, in a process that corresponded to one of the largest population movements ever in Portuguese history: about 600,000 to 700,000 people (or something close to 8 percent of the mainland's population), most of them economically active, entered the mainland between late 1974 and early 1976 (Pires *et al.*, 1984). What is more, this was not the only shock to the labour market. The slowing down of emigration, as the other European economies were also at the time dealing with the effects of the international crisis, and the demobilisation of the soldiers involved in the Colonial War, were other major contributing factors. The labour supply expanded massively, as the active population grew by about 400,000 persons between 1973 and 1975 (Amaral, 2009). Given this, exactly when both the international crisis and the increase in the supply of labour should have led wages to fall, the exact opposite happened, thanks to the political environment of the country.

In the extremely volatile political environment of the period, the difficulties felt by firms to keep up production levels were understood by the revolutionary authorities as "economic sabotage". Pressures thus started growing for many companies to be nationalised and taken away from their owners. Eventually, in March 1975, these pressures were translated into policy, and one of the largest nationalisation programmes ever in modern European history unfolded. By the end of the process, in early 1976, 550 firms had passed into the hands of the Government, which totally or partially controlled a wide variety of sectors: money emission, banking, insurance, basic metals, naval construction and repair, cement, paper and paper pulp, chemicals and petrochemicals. The Portuguese entrepreneurial public sector became one of the largest in the Western world, being responsible at that time for about 20 to 25 percent of GDP, 30 percent of investment, and 8 percent of the workforce (Baklanoff, 1996).

This series of events led to a rapid deterioration of the balance of payments, as shown in Figure 2.1. Portugal had got used to a comfortable international payments position during the Post-war period. The persistent trade deficit, of about 5 to 7 percent of GDP in the 1960s and early 1970s, was normally compensated for by income obtained from emigrant remittances and tourism. Emigration accelerated in the 1960s, involving both rural and urban workers heading in the direction of the then fast growing north European economies, especially France and Germany, with more than one million persons leaving the country between 1961 and 1974 (Baganha, 1994). These emigrants were then responsible for an extraordinarily high influx of remittances, which grew in the late 1960s and early 1970s to reach a peak of 9 percent of GDP in 1972, as shown by the item Transfers in the balance of payments displayed in Figure 2.1. Tourism also grew in the 1960s, as Portugal became a favourite beach destination for many north Europeans (mostly from the UK but also the Netherlands,

Germany and Scandinavia) and, in 1973, the number of tourists visiting Portugal reached the number of four million (Marques, 2000). Foreign exchange originating in tourism grew in the 1960s until reaching a peak of 5 percent of GDP in 1966; it declined slightly afterwards but still remained at a level of about 3 percent until 1973 (Figure 2.1). Because of this, the current account stayed roughly in balance, even displaying some surplus years of significant size (3 percent of GDP).

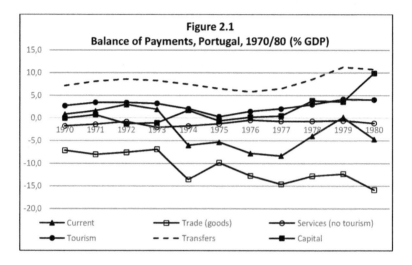

It was this structure of international payments that the mid-1970s crisis destroyed. The trade deficit without tourism passed from 5–7 percent of GDP to 10–15 percent in the second half of the 1970s. The traditional amount from tourist payments and emigrant remittances would not have been enough to compensate for such a deficit, but the situation became even worse as both declined in these years, as both tourists and emigrants feared the revolutionary environment of the country (Figure 2.1). All of this was compounded with the collapse of the economy. The last thirty years of the authoritarian regime had been the best in terms of economic growth in all of Portugal's History. However, from 1974 onwards there was a significant slowdown: as Table 2.1 shows, the economy crashed during the transition from one period to the other – the remaining Western economies also had a slowdown, but the process was much more pronounced in Portugal. In the words of Schmitt (1981: 1), "the problem of managing economic growth with a balance of payments constraint was new to Portugal".

Table 2.1

GDP per capita, Portugal and former EU-15

(annual growth rates), 1970-1980

	Portugal	EU-15
1970	9.21	4.12
1971	11.07	2.93
1972	10.29	4.89
1973	4.87	4.94
1974	0.24	2.04
1975	-9.18	-0.19
1976	-0.24	3.48
1977	7.18	2.20
1978	5.43	2.77
1979	6.71	3.24
1980	4.44	1.43

Source: Portugal Amaral (2009);
Former EU-15: The Conference Board.

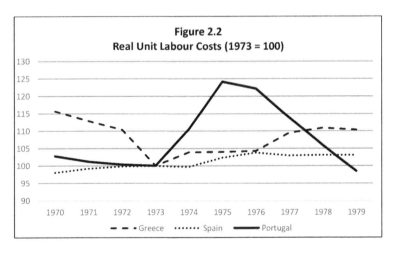

Figure 2.2
Real Unit Labour Costs (1973 = 100)

Source: AMECO.

The initial policy reactions were largely uncoordinated. The first measures taken consisted of a return to capital controls and protectionism: in September 1974, the Government limited the amount of foreign exchange for travel purposes to be sold by the banks to 20,000 escudos per adult for trips longer than three days and to 6,000 escudos for trips shorter than three days, with other amounts being dependent on authorisation by the Bank of Portugal (BoP); and in May 1975 it introduced a surcharge of 20 to 30 percent over a large number of imported goods (for all these measures, see Amaral *et al.*, 2020). At the time, the authorities opted for not depreciating the exchange rate and relied mostly on the vast amount of foreign exchange reserves at the BoP to buffer the impact of international payment needs. The lack of action on the exchange rate, together with the wage shock described above, made unit labour costs rise considerably (Figure 2.2) (Amaral, 2019).

Portugal was in desperate need of external financing, but had no access to private international markets, due to its volatile political and economic situation. This is the context explaining the country's long involvement with the IMF and other creditors in the second half of the 1970s.

2 The IMF context

The IMF interventions in Portugal in the 1970s occurred in a period in which the organisation was in a state of flux, having to deal with major shocks to the world economy that implied an important redefinition of its functions. With the collapse of the fixed-exchange rate system the IMF lost its function as "guardian of the international monetary system" (Polak, 1994: 2) as designed at Bretton Woods, and "several critics intimated that the Fund had outlived its usefulness" (de Vries, 1985: 3). The IMF had, thus, to reinvent itself, and the main direction it took was that of "developing into an important lending institution" (de Vries, 1986: 118). Rather than being the instrument for the smooth functioning of a no-longer existent system of fixed exchange rates, the Fund started accepting different exchange rate arrangements. And with the development of its lending function to ailing countries, it increased its monitoring activities of the policies followed by the member countries (more details in Amaral *et al.*, 2020). This links with another crucial issue associated with IMF activity, that of so-called "conditionality".

"Conditionality" is Fund parlance for the set of conditions imposed on the countries borrowing from its resources. Conditionality principles became clearly defined during the 1950s. As was stated in the Fund's 1955 Annual Report: "access to the gold tranche is almost automatic; and requests for drawings within the next 25 percent (the so-called 'first credit tranche') are also treated liberally but, even so, such requests will be approved only if the country asking for assistance can show that it is making reasonable efforts to solve its own problems. For drawings beyond that tranche (i.e. beyond the first 50 percent of the quota), substantial justification is required" (quoted in Diz, 1984: 222). Finally, on September 20, 1968, the hallmarks of conditionality were defined in a clear way by an Executive Board decision (de Vries, 1976: 347). In 1969, the principle of conditionality was given full legal force by its inclusion in the first amendment of the IMF's Articles of Agreement. From then on, countries having signed an SBA with the IMF had to present an "economic programme" to be approved by the Executive Board and be subject to frequent "consultation" by the IMF staff (Diz, 1984).

Just when the IMF was perfecting these concepts and techniques the world economy entered a dramatic period that forced it to relax conditionality. Between 1966 and 1975, the IMF made access to its resources easier. In 1966, it liberalised access to the Compensatory Financing Facility, a scheme that had been created in 1963 to help primary producing countries deal with sudden shortfalls in export receipts (de Vries, 1976). Between 1966 and 1971, the Executive Board introduced a buffer stock financing facility, especially dedicated to developing countries facing wide price fluctuations for their exports (de Vries, 1976). In 1974, the IMF introduced a temporary Oil Facility, focused on countries having difficulties in dealing with the oil shock. The facility did not involve conditionality. This was followed by a new temporary Oil Facility in 1975, involving some conditionality but of a mild kind: countries were only asked to make a statement on the policies they were intent on following to deal with their balance of payments difficulties but no performance criteria or phasing applied. The facility was discontinued in 1976 (de Vries, 1985, and Diz, 1984). Also in 1974, the Fund created an Extended Fund Facility, which implied conditionality similar to that used in SBAs but involving larger loans and longer periods (Diz, 1984).

3 The interactions between the IMF and Portugal and the programmes adopted (1975–1978)

3.1 1975–1976

The first moment of financial assistance from the IMF to Portugal after the revolution took only about one year to occur: on 29 July 1975, the Portuguese authorities asked for the purchase of 22.28 million Special Drawing Rights (SDR, the IMF's "currency", so to speak) from its gold tranche in order to meet balance of payments needs, a request that was accepted the following day by the IMF's Executive Board.[1] The

Table 2.2
Portugal purchases with the IMF

Gold tranche: 28th July 1975	22.28 million SDR	19% of Portugal's quota	0.14% GDP
Oil Facility: 15th December 1975	73.12 million SDR	62.5% of Portugal's quota	0.48% GDP
Remainder Gold tranche: 24th December 1975	7 million SDR	50% of Portugal's access to the facility	0.05% GDP
Oil Facility: 11th March 1976	41.64 million SDR	Remaining 50% of Portugal's access to the facility	0.27% GDP
Compensatory Financing of Export Fluctuations: 23rd June 1976	58.5 million SDR		0.36% GDP
Stand-by arrangement 12th April 1977	42.4 million SDR	36.2% of Portugal's quota	0.26% GDP
Compensatory Financing of Export Fluctuations: 22nd July 1977	29.25 million SDR	25% of Portugal's quota	0.18% GDP
Stand-by arrangement 5th June 1978	57.3 million SDR		0.36%

Sources: "Portugal – Staff Report and Proposed Decision for the 1976 Article XIV Consultation", SM/76/186, 20 August, 1976, IMF Archive ref. 181178; "Minutes of Executive Board Meeting" EBM/76/91, 23 June, 1976, IMF Archive ref. 185012; "Portugal – Stand-by Arrangement", EBS/77/100, 27 April, 1977, IMF Archive ref. 226306; "Portugal – Use of Fund Resources – Compensatory Financing", EBS/76/280, 18 June, 1976, IMF archive ref. 182138; "Portugal – Stand-by Arrangement", EBS/78/228, 6 June, 1978, IMF Archive ref. 220136.

purchase represented 19 percent of the Portuguese quota in the organization and 0.14 percent of Portugal's GDP (Table 2.2) and the financial conditions were those associated with SDR drawings at the time: an interest rate of 3.75 percent per year, close to half the US dollar market rates, plus charges raised by the Fund of 2 percent per year as remuneration for the service provided (de Vries, 1985). Since this purchase was made well within the Portuguese quota, no conditionality was associated with it. However, Portugal's transactions with the IMF continued until the end of the year. On 24 December, the Portuguese authorities asked to purchase the remainder of the country's gold tranche, in an amount of 7 million SDR, again to cover a balance of payments deficit, which was accepted by the Executive Board on 31 December.[2] The amount represented 6 percent of the Portuguese quota and 0.05 percent of its GDP (Table 2.2), this time with an interest rate of 3.5 percent per year. Again, no conditionality was associated with the purchase.

Roughly two weeks before the latest transaction, on 15 December, Portugal made one further and larger request for assistance, this time under the 1975 Oil Facility, in an amount of 73.12 million SDR, corresponding to 50 percent of the country's access to the facility and to 0.48 percent of GDP, accepted by the Executive Board on 22 December, with the financial conditions associated with the facility (which were different from those of SBAs): a 7.25 percent a year interest rate for a period between 3 and 7 years, with charges payable to the Fund of 7.625 percent up to 3 years, 7.750 percent between 3 and 4 years and 7.875 percent between 5 and 7 years (Table 2.2).[3] These rates were close to market rates obtained in good conditions: in the case of the Oil Facilities the role of the IMF was to raise the funds in the market and then lend to the country requesting them.

The way the Portuguese authorities formulated this request is very interesting. As we have seen in the previous section, the 1974 and 1975 oil facilities had been created by the IMF as instruments to help countries in external distress without imposing much conditionality. Receiving assistance under the heading of the 1975 facility implied only a statement on the policies to be followed. The Portuguese authorities, however, presented a relatively detailed package of measures. The nature of the package was somewhat mixed in terms of incentives, with both expansionary and restrictive measures, but included many aspects of the kind of "financial programming" typical of IMF adjustment programmes, such as ceilings on total credit and on credit to the public sector (see Table 2.3). This ambiguous stance of the programme corresponded to the dilemma of Portuguese economic policy at the time, where a collapse of production in 1974 and 1975 was associated with an enormous deterioration in the balance of payments as well as the need to increase public spending on social items. As a matter of fact, the various governments from 1976 onwards felt the need to provide the population with those sorts of social services that most European democracies had been developing since the end of World War II.

Table 2.3 Oil Facility Measures, 1975

Net domestic credit of the banking system (until June 1976):
Ceiling: 421 billion *escudos*
Rate of expansion: 31.15% (predicted growth of nominal GDP: 25%)
Actual: 392 billion *escudos*
Rate of expansion: 22.12%
(actual growth of nominal GDP: 22.9% - December)
Bank credit to the public sector (until June 1976):
Ceiling: 81,66 billion *escudos*
Rate of expansion: 58.07%
Actual: 85.3 billion *escudos*
Rate of expansion: 65.12%
Price increases:
Foodstuffs: various pieces of legislation for different goods between late 1975 and the year 1976;
Petrol: between 36% and 54% depending on the type of fuel (Order 29 December 1975, Order 5 March 1976, and Declaration 9 November 1976)
Public transportation: between 20% and 60% (Ordinance 783-A/75, 30 December 1975, and Ordinance 595-A/76, 8 October 1976)
Taxes:
Various: Decree-law 768/75, 31 December 1975 (Government budget for 1976): Rental income tax, increase from a flat 12% rate to a progressive range from 13% to 20%; Rates on dividends raised from 6.5% to 10%, tax on interest reduced from 15% to 10%; Transaction tax: rates were increased from 7%, 12% and 20% to 10%, 20%, and 30%, with a new 40% rate being created; Various excise taxes, including petrol, cigarettes and beverages;
Car registration and sales: Decree-law 81/76: tax rates on car registration raised between 20% and 40% depending on type of car, and tax rates on car sales raised from a range of 18-57% to a new one of 26-90%
Wage limits:
Cancelation of wage negotiations (Revolutionary Council decision, 27 November 1975 and Decree-law 783/75, 31 December 1975)
Balance of payments objective:
Keeping the same deficit of the current account; Not achieved: deterioration current account from 5.34% of GDP in 1975 to 7.82%

Sources: "Portugal –Purchase under the Oil Facility", EBS/75/467, 15 December 1975, IMF Archive ref. 185208; "Portugal – Staff Report and Proposed Decision for the 1976 Article XIV Consultation", SM/76/186, 20 August, 1976, IMF Archive ref. 181178; Portuguese legislation; Schmitt (1981).

The plan allowed prices to increase, as a way of restoring profit margins and stimulating investment. The way of doing this was by stopping the subsidy of certain consumption goods, as had been undertaken in previous years. A similar effect would be obtained by raising indirect taxation as well as directly limiting wage growth. Accordingly, a wage freeze was introduced until the end of 1975. The Portuguese authorities, and the IMF together with them, believed there was room for an expansion of credit, in order to accommodate the predicted expansion of the economy. Consequently, they proposed to allow credit to grow above the estimated nominal GDP, although introducing a ceiling, so that the process was not entirely devoid of any discipline (Table 2.3). Even if the Portuguese authorities and the IMF believed that the expansion of credit would contribute to the deterioration of the balance of payments, they expected the price and tax measures to compensate for this, by increasing the demand for exportables and decreasing that of importables. All of this also explains why the Portuguese authorities and the IMF accepted the possibility of a deterioration of public accounts, with credit to the public sector allowed to grow by 58 percent, largely to accommodate the growth of social programmes (Amaral, 2019, and Amaral *et al.*, 2020).

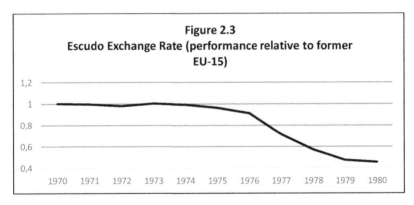

Figure 2.3
Escudo Exchange Rate (performance relative to former EU-15)

Source: AMECO.

Despite the strong reliance on the substitution of imports and the expansion of exports, no clear measures were taken at this time concerning exchange and interest rates. The Portuguese authorities had depreciated the escudo only mildly until the end of 1975 (7 percent throughout the year) and, rather than making a strong commitment in this respect, they proposed to continue to have "a flexible approach to exchange rate policy".[4] The practical result of this "flexible approach" was a depreciation of the escudo's effective rate by 9 percent during 1976, with the efforts at the beginning of the year being interrupted in July and resumed in December (Figure 2.3) (Pinto, 1983 and Dornbusch, 1981). The same kind of flexibility applied to interest rates: in late 1975, the BoP reduced its discount and rediscount rates by 1 to 1.5 percent and raised commercial bank lending rates

(Pinto, 1983). Also forming part of the strategy of substituting importables with exportables were measures clearly not appreciated by the IMF but somehow tolerated in view of the exceptional Portuguese circumstances: the non-removal of the import surcharge introduced in May 1975 and of capital controls introduced in 1974, namely the amount of escudos Portuguese citizens could exchange into foreign currencies for travelling purposes (details in Amaral *et al.*, 2020). Most of the measures presented to the IMF were not required by it. Instead, they were part of a general change in policy stance after the 1974–75 revolutionary wave, corresponding to the more moderate sixth interim Government (after the failed coup d'état of 25 November 1975) and the first constitutional Government, resulting from the 25 April 1976 elections (see Amaral *et al.*, 2020).

As the balance of payments problems appeared to continue, the Portuguese authorities asked for new assistance on 10 March 1976, again under the heading of the 1975 Oil Facility, approved by the Executive Board on 18 March (Table 2.2).[5] With this purchase, of 41.64 million SDR, representing 0.27 percent of GDP, Portugal exhausted its Oil Facility quota. In order for the request to be accepted by the IMF, the Portuguese authorities simply stated that they were "broadly implementing the economic and financial policies which were outlined in connection with the request for the first purchase under the 1975 oil facility".[6] However, just a few months after this, on 18 June 1976, the Government made a new purchase request, this time under the heading of the Compensatory Financing Facility, of 53.5 million SDR, amounting to 0.36 percent of GDP, approved by the Executive Board of the IMF on 23 June; financial conditions were the same as for regular SDR drawings (de Vries, 1985) (Table 2.2).[7] Conditionality associated with this facility was light, essentially implying an assessment on the part of the Fund if the shortfall on export earnings was due to reasons beyond the member's control, and a verbal commitment on the part of the member that it would apply the appropriate measures to correct the balance of payments need.

The interactions between Portugal and the IMF mentioned above show that for the whole of 1976 Portugal tried to follow policies in part co-ordinated with the IMF having the purpose of combining external rebalance and economic growth. The results, however, were far from outstanding, on both counts: Table 2.1 shows that growth continued to be negative in 1976, although rising from the extreme depths of the previous year, and Figure 2.1 shows that the current account continued deteriorating. Private consumption failed to significantly reanimate in 1976, but public consumption grew strongly. The reason for this was the radical transformation of the structure of public

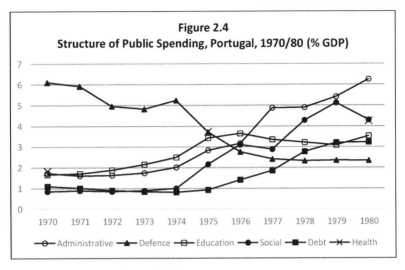

Figure 2.4
Structure of Public Spending, Portugal, 1970/80 (% GDP)

—○— Administrative —▲— Defence —□— Education —●— Social —■— Debt —✕— Health

Source: Mata (2001) and Carreira (1994).

accounts, with military spending passing from being the largest in proportional terms in Western countries in 1974 (on account of the Colonial War) to reach levels common in Europe from 1975 onwards, and with social items growing very quickly (Figure 2.4). Not surprisingly, the budget deficit deteriorated (Figure 2.5). The growth of exports failed to materialize, despite the reliance on policies intent on substituting importables with exportables. Imports, on the contrary, resumed at a high pace. Deterioration of the current account was due to a combination of a growing trade deficit and an even stronger reduction as in previous years of the influx of emigrant remittances and tourism (Figure 2.1) (Amaral *et al.*, 2020).

3.2 The April 1977 Stand-by arrangement

It is not surprising that, under these circumstances, Portugal continued to need external assistance, and 10 months after having had recourse to the IMF, it asked for further assistance. This time, it was difficult for Portugal to continue using the special facilities created by the IMF to deal with the 1970s international crisis and so the country signed its first SBA with the Fund. A request was made on 12 April 1977 for the amount of 42.4 million SDR for one year, corresponding to 36 percent of Portugal's quota with the Fund and 0.26 percent of GDP, and was accepted by the Executive Board on 25 April 1977 (Table 2.2).[8] The financial conditions associated with SBAs were a charge of 4.38 percent per year for the first year (growing yearly to 4.88, 5.38, 5.88, and 6.38 percent up to five years) plus a service charge of 0.5

percent per year (as remuneration for the service provided by the Fund) (de Vries, 1985). In most of the literature, this SBA is barely mentioned. But in fact, it turned out to be a pivotal moment, or at least the policies associated with it became pivotal in the inversion of the external imbalance stemming from 1975. The SBA itself did not imply conditionality, as it was still within Portugal's quota. However, it came associated with a policy package, which was designed autonomously from IMF assistance but which included the policies that became a hallmark of the 1977–1979 period.

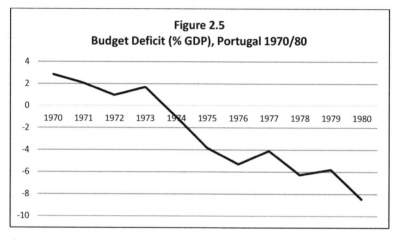

Source: Pinheiro (1997).

The policy was implemented in two "austerity packages", as they were commonly named at the time, put in place by the first constitutional Government. One was adopted in February, the other in August, with the actual SBA being signed in April. The February measures covered many aspects: wages, prices, taxes and exchange and interest rates (Table 2.4). Wage increases were capped at 15 percent for 1977, first for public servants and then for all dependent workers. The prices of public transportation, public services (electricity, water, and telephone) and foodstuffs were raised in various proportions. The sales tax was raised by 20 percent. The exchange rate was depreciated by 15 percent and pegged to a basket of currencies, consisting of those more relevant for Portuguese external payments (Figure 2.3). Interest rates (the rediscount rate and the banking rates) were raised in variable proportions. Furthermore, the Government not only kept the import surcharge introduced in 1975 and aggravated in 1976, but introduced quantitative import quotas for about 4 percent of imports as well. It also kept the restrictions on the amount of foreign exchange for travel purposes (details in Amaral *et al.*, 2020).

In April the SBA was signed. Even if this implied no conditionality, the Portuguese authorities presented the February measures as part of a programme to deal with balance of payments and economic growth problems. To these, the SBA added the typical IMF financial programming measures, such as ceilings on domestic credit and credit to the public sector. The programme would be completed in August-September with a new depreciation of the escudo of 4 percent and mostly the introduction of a crawling peg mechanism for depreciation to start operating from 15 September onwards. Under this regime, the escudo would depreciate at the rate of 1 percent per month in relation to the currencies of the most relevant international partners (Dornbusch, 1981). Interest rates were again raised on a variable basis, to limit pressure on the external value of the escudo and control inflation (Table 2.4) (details in Amaral *et al.*, 2020).

Table 2.4 Stand-by arrangement Measures 1977

Net domestic credit of the banking system (until December 1977):
      Ceiling: 651.2 billion escudos (excluding uncollectible debt)
      Rate of expansion: 28.63% (predicted growth of nominal GDP: 27.7% - year)
      Actual: 645.7 billion *escudos* (702.6 including uncollectible debt)
      Rate of expansion: 27.42% (39.96%)
      (actual growth of nominal GDP: 28.53%)

Bank credit to the public sector (until December 1977):
      Ceiling: 123.3 billion *escudos*
      Rate of expansion: 52.22%
      Actual: 123.3 billion *escudos*
      Rate of expansion: 52.22%

Exchange rate:
    1) 15% depreciation (February 1977) and pegging to basket of currencies
    2) 4% depreciation (September 1977)
    3) Crawling peg (1% month depreciation from 15 September on)

Interest rates:
    1) Rediscount: 6% to a progressive scale 8%-12% (February 1977); 13%-18% (August 1977)
    2) Deposit rates:
       30-90 days: 4.5% to 5% (February 1977); 6% (August 1977)
       180 days-1 year: 9.5% to 11% (February 1977); 15% (August 1977)
       1-2 years: 10.5% to 12% (February 1977); 16% (August 1977)
    3) Standard lending rates:
       Up to 90 days: 8.75% to 10.25% (February 1977); 14.75% (August 1977)
       180 days-1 year: 10.5% to 12% (February 1977); 16.5% (August 1977)
       2-5 years: 12.25% to 13.75% (February 1977); 17.75% (August 1977)

Despite the adoption of these measures, the current account deficit reached the record level of 8.4 percent of GDP in 1977 (Figure 2.1). This time, however, the economy boomed, as GDP per capita passed from a negative rate of -0.24 percent in 1976 to a positive one of 7.2 percent (Table 2.1). Deterioration of the current account resulted from trade, the deficit of which went from 13 percent in 1976 to 15 percent in 1977 (Figure 2.1). This shows that depreciation, combined with wage control, was not enough to restore the competitiveness of Portuguese exports: exports did grow at an interesting pace but were more than offset by imports. This time both remittances and tourism improved their performance, but the problem was that their contribution was not enough to compensate for the trade deficit (Figure 2.1). As for growth of the economy, the largest contributors were public spending and investment, the latter also explaining the large increase in imports, as raw materials and intermediate goods were necessary to reactivate this (Amaral *et al.* 2020).

3.3 The June 1978 Stand-by arrangement
The record of the economy after two years of policies to recover from the chaos of the 1973–1975 period was somewhat mixed: growth had returned but the external balance had worsened. Portugal therefore had recourse to another SBA on 9 May 1978, this time signed by the second constitutional Government, a Government formed in January basically for that purpose (Reis, 1994b, and Ramos *et al.*, 2009). However, the new agreement did not bring a radical change of policy, as the essence of the measures adopted did not differ from those stemming from 1977. The origin of the 1978 SBA seems to have resulted from the fact that a group of countries willing to make Portugal a giant loan of 750 billion US dollars (agreed in the Summer of 1977) made its disbursing conditional on the country signing a new SBA with the IMF (see below) (Schmitt, 1981, Lopes, 1982 and 1996, and Pinto, 1983). The amount negotiated under the new SBA was 57.3 million SDR, or 0.36 percent of GDP, quite similar to that which had been obtained in the previous interactions with the Fund, and was approved on 5 June 1978.[9] The financial conditions were the same as in the 1977 SBA, with only a slight increase in the Fund's service charge. The main difference between this SBA and the previous interactions with the Fund was that, as Portugal was now delving beyond its quota, heavier conditionality was required. However, the conditions associated with the SBA very much went along the lines of policies from previous years, especially the February-August 1977 package.

Most measures of the stabilisation programme were taken right before or around the time of the signing of the SBA. The prices of various goods and services (foodstuffs, public transportation, electricity, gas and water) were raised in March, to become effective in April, in an amount between 30 and 50 percent – the price of fuel would only be raised in October, although in a similar proportion. Taxes were raised in variable proportions (between 10 and 15 percent) in April, when the Government's budget for the year was approved by parliament; a cap on wage increases at 20 percent for the year was also introduced. The exchange rate was depreciated 6 percent in May while the monthly depreciation under the crawling peg was increased from 1 to 1.25 percent (Figure 2.3). At the same time the various interest rates were increased in variable proportions, with some exceptions for activities that were considered to be of exceptional relevance (agriculture, exports and certain priority investments) (details on all these aspects in Table 2.5).

Table 2.5 Stand-by arrangement Measures 1978

Net domestic credit of the banking system (until March 1979):
Ceiling: 698.8 billion *escudos* in June 1978; 735.8 billion *escudos* in September 1978; 792.9 in December 1978; 808.6 in March 1979 (all excluding uncollectible debt)
Rate of expansion yearly: 19.92% (predicted growth of nominal GDP: 26.79%)
Actual: 705.5 billion *escudos* in June 1978 (782.8 including uncollectible debt); 738.7 billion *escudos* in September 1978 (821.5 including uncollectible debt); 784.6.9 in December 1978 (874.9 including uncollectible debt); 808.8 in March 1979 (874.9 including uncollectible debt)
Rate of expansion: 21.33% (23.97%, including uncollectible debt)
(actual growth of nominal GDP: 27.30%)
Bank credit to the public sector (until March 1979):
Ceiling: 137.3 billion *escudos* in June 1978; 142.3 billion *escudos* in September 1978; 160.3 in December 1978; 177.3 in March 1979
Rate of expansion yearly: 30.01% (predicted growth of nominal GDP: 26.79%)
Actual: 142 billion *escudos* in June 1978; 156.6 billion *escudos* in September 1978; 171.7 in December 1978; 188.6 in March 1979
Rate of expansion: 39.25%
Informal ceiling for the money base (until March 1979):
Ceiling: 143.6 billion *escudos* in June 1978; 143.6 billion *escudos* in September 1978; 151.0 in December 1978; 149.2 in March 1979
Actual: 197.3 billion *escudos* in June 1978; 210.9 billion *escudos* in September 1978;
Exchange rate:
1) 6% depreciation (May 1978)
2) Crawling peg (1.25% month from May 1978 onwards)
Interest rates:
1) Rediscount: from a range of 13%-18% to 18%-23% (May 1978)
2) Deposit rates:
Interest rates on time deposits raised by 4% (May 1978)
3) Standard lending rates:
increased by 3.5% except for housing, only 1%-2%, and agriculture, exports and priority investments, only by 2%-3% (May 1978)

Positive results finally started to appear in 1978 and 1979. The current account passed from a deficit of more than 8 percent of GDP to 4 percent in 1978 and an actual positive balance in 1979 (Figure 2.1) while GDP per capita grew at the quite respectable rates of 5 and

7 percent in each of those years, considerably above the average of Western countries (Table 2.1). Moreover, these results were obtained without respecting some of the most important performance clauses of the SBA set out by the IMF, namely both credit ceilings (Table 2.5) – this determined that Portugal would end up not receiving financial assistance from the Fund. Interestingly, the external positive balance was achieved while the budget deficit deteriorated, from 4 percent in 1977 to 6 percent in both 1978 and 1979 (Figure 2.5). Inflation also exceeded expectations, as, despite some moderation, it continued to display quite high rates (from 33 percent in 1977 to 27 percent in 1978 and 24 percent in 1979) (Figure 2.6).

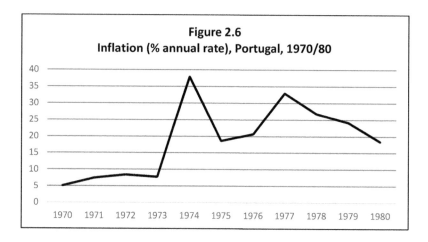

Figure 2.6
Inflation (% annual rate), Portugal, 1970/80

The positive evolution of the current account seems to have depended on various developments: exports of goods finally grew strongly, not being offset by imports (which also grew strongly, but less than exports). All of this happened while the import surcharge fell from 30 to 20 percent in October, as had been negotiated with the IMF. Consequently, public and private internal demand (consumption and investment) could grow at a relatively high pace without jeopardising the external balance. Investment grew especially quickly and the Government budget deteriorated even more, as the authorities continued expanding the most important social programmes: spending on Health and on Education, which corresponded to just 2 percent of GDP each in 1970, doubled to 4 percent from 1975 onwards; as for pensions and unemployment benefits, the jump was equally clear, from roughly 1 percent of GDP in 1973 to close to 4–5 percent in 1978 (Figure 2.4) (for more details, Amaral, 2019, and

Amaral *et al.*, 2020). Thus, despite all the difficulties, the Portuguese governments of the time were still able to introduce the basics of a modern Welfare State in Portugal.

In Lopes' (1982) opinion, the existence of a high volume of unused capacity in the export sector meant that the combination of the exchange rate depreciation and the wage restraints (nominal wage increases remained below the legal limits established by legislation: Schmitt, 1981) were especially effective. Real unit labour costs were very significantly reduced (Figure 2.2). As a consequence of all this, the trade balance for goods improved. However, it still remained at the very high negative level of 12 percent of GDP. This is where other elements entered the picture: tourism reanimated, and exchange entries associated with this in 1979 returned to levels close to those before the revolution, at about 4 percent of GDP; but the most important contributor to the external balance were emigrant remittances, which started recovering in 1977 and reached their highest level in 1979, with 11 percent of GDP. Schmitt (1981), Lopes (1982) and Pinto (1983), again, attribute great importance to the interest rate policy in explaining this positive behaviour.

The second constitutional Government, which had signed the SBA, fell in August 1978, being replaced by three technocratic Governments organised by the President of the Republic, meaning that the implementation of the 1978 SBA was mostly achieved through this special political solution not resulting directly from parliamentary elections. The Portuguese authorities implemented practically all aspects of the stabilisation programme. They reduced the 30 percent import surcharge to 20 percent (also making the bureaucracy associated with imports less stringent) and respected the limit of the net foreign liabilities of the banking system, but they failed to comply with two other performance criteria: those relative to the ceilings both for overall credit and for credit to the public sector (Table 2.5).[10]

4 Other foreign assistance

The IMF was far from being the main source of financing of the Portuguese external imbalance. Quite the contrary, as its weight was relatively small among those various sources. At its highest point, in 1976, it accounted for only 17 percent of Portuguese financing needs (see Table 2.6; for the detailed data see Amaral *et al.* 2020, and also Mateus, 1982, and Bruneau, 1982). Until 1978, by far the most substantial amount of financing came directly through the BoP. On 9 May 1975, amid the most turbulent period in the Portuguese revolution, the Bank of International Settlements (BIS) approved a 250 million US dollar loan, 72 percent of the yearly external debt resources in that year and explicitly earmarked to finance the external deficit. By contrast, the resources coming from the IMF in the same period (July 1975) accounted for 8 percent of the Portuguese external debt. The BIS performed the most critical role in mobilising financial resources for filling in the current account deficit, both on its own and in conjunction with other European central banks. For instance, in 1975, and besides the BIS, the Swiss National Bank lent 50 million US dollars to Portugal on a short-term basis, in an instrument that could be rolled out for 3 years and in that year represented much more than the annual transactions with the IMF (Amaral *et al.* 2020).

Table 2.6
Portuguese external debt as a percentage of current GDP (1975-1979)

	(1) Loans to BoP	(2) Loans to Government	(3) IMF loans	(4) Market	(5) Total	(6) Total debt, M USA$
1975	1.63	0.07	0.19	–	1.90	348.8
1976	4.03	0.98	1.08	0.27	6.36	1182.3
1977	2.22	1.66	0.44	0.73	5.05	952.2
1978	2.21	1.45	0.36	3.15	7.17	1458.6
1979	1.16	1.65	–	3.49	6.30	1463.0

Sources: Columns (1) and (2): Amaral *et al.* (2020); Column (3): tables II, III, V, and VI; Column (4): Mateus (1982).

The decrease in the importance of loans through the BoP and having the BIS as the pivotal institution only receded below other sources of funding in 1978, but even then, they amounted to just below 1/3 of the total external debt. The direct financing role of the IMF and its SBA arrangements disappeared then. Slowly, in 1976, and decisively after 1977, the Portuguese government was receiving higher amounts of funding through external debt. The World Bank (38 percent), the US government, through AID (19 percent), the European Investment Bank (EIB) (12 percent), the KfW (German state-owned development bank, 10 percent) and the Council of Europe (7 percent) were the main agents of this mostly institutional funding to the Portuguese Government (Amaral *et al.* 2020). For instance, the Resettlement Fund for Refugees within the Council of Europe financed aid for returning Portuguese citizens from the former African colonies. AID, the EIB, and KfW funded a series of infrastructure projects (in education, housing, sanitation, irrigation, electric power, ports, roads, airports and communications), as well as small and medium-sized firms, and the restructuring of state-owned firms (Petrogás, Quimigal, Empresa Polímeros de Sines) (Amaral *et al.* 2020).

Market-driven external debt became significant only after 1978, coinciding with the 750 million US dollar loan to Portugal organised by the consortium mentioned above and which lay at the origin of the second SBA with the IMF. One small bond issuing had already taken place in 1977, but the most significant operations referred to the use of the Eurodollar market to obtain 641.2 million dollars in 1978, increasing to 811 million in 1979. This return to the debt market had much to do with the increased confidence in the credibility of the Portuguese government, thanks to the process of political moderation described above.

These results raise the question of why the BIS played such a critical role in the first years after the revolution. The role of the BIS needs to be understood considering the Bretton Woods institutional framework, even after the general move to floating rates in 1973. There was from the beginning some division of labour between the BIS and the IMF (Bordo and James 2000): the former provided immediate assistance when there was the risk of an imminent collapse of the financial system or under severe short-term shortages of funds, while the latter acted mostly as an agent to restore confidence, backing domestic economic policies aimed at regaining credibility and persuading the financial markets that the sources of financial imbalances would be overcome. By doing so, the IMF provided a sort of "seal of approval" in relation to such policies. This division of labour reinforced the IMF role as rule setter. A loan from the Fund provided borrowers with more than just money. In fact, in relative or absolute terms, the amounts received from the IMF were much less than from other institutions, such as the BIS, the consortia of central banks, or the World Bank. However, getting IMF assistance through an SBA signalled to financial markets and the international community a mark of credibility. The Portuguese authorities, as they tried to move away from the revolutionary imprint of 1974–1975 and acquire a "respectful" capitalist one, strongly valued such a signal.

Conclusion

This chapter has shown that the SBA signed with the IMF by the Portuguese authorities in 1978 should not be seen in isolation from a string of interactions between the two entities since late 1975. This means that the 1978 SBA should not really be seen as an "intervention" but rather the conclusion of a long effort at stabilisation that started in 1975 and was progressively adjusted until 1979, in order to restore external balance while keeping the economy growing with inflation controlled. The effort included the use of various IMF instruments: the buying of foreign exchange within the country's quota, the use of different special facilities created by the IMF to help countries deal with the 1970s crisis, and the signing of two SBAs. The fact that the 1978 SBA was the first to include explicit conditionality did not have to do with the country using IMF resources for the first time (which it was not) but rather with the circumstance that it had already exhausted all means including moving from no to weak conditionality. This long relationship between the Portuguese authorities and the IMF was an integral part of the process of change in the Portuguese political cycle, from socio-communist revolution in 1974–1975 to capitalist moderation after late 1975.

The importance of the IMF for the process of rebalancing the Portuguese current account was never much linked to the amount of financing provided by the Fund but rather in applying a sort of "seal of approval" on the policies followed by the Portuguese authorities in order to restore a certain international confidence in the Portuguese political and economic situation. Other sources were much more significant, such as the BIS, the EEC and individual countries (for instance the US, the Federal Republic of Germany or the UK). The reason for Portugal being such a large recipient of foreign assistance in this period had to do with the international political context of the time, as the country became a pivotal stage of the Cold War, thanks to the possibility of it becoming the first Western European country to adopt a communist regime. Therefore, Western countries contributed with significant amounts of assistance in order to keep the country firmly within the capitalist side of the divide.

Despite the adoption of many measures designed in coordination with the IMF, the results in terms of external rebalancing and economic growth took a relatively long time to come about. By 1977, growth returned at a relatively quick pace but not a positive external balance. The joint return of external imbalance and economic growth only appeared in 1979. All this happened while the country was also able to transition to a high volume of social spending within the context of a nascent Welfare State. A series of circumstances would make this external rebalance short-lived, as in 1980 imbalance reappeared, eventually leading to a new SBA in 1983–1985. But that is a story for another time.

Notes

1 "Portugal – Gold Purchase Transaction", EBS/75/267, 29 July 1975, IMF Archive ref. 187074, and "Executive Board Minutes", EBM 75/134, 30 July 1975, IMF Archive ref. 187064.
2 "Portugal – Gold Tranche Purchase of Special Drawing Rights", EBS/75/491, 24 December 1975, IMF Archive ref. 184978, and "Executive Board Minutes", EBM 75/208, 31 December 1975, IMF Archive ref. 184900.
3 "Portugal – Purchase under the Oil Facility", EBS/75/467, 15 December 1975, IMF Archive ref. 185208, and "Executive Board Minutes", EBM 75/203, 22 December 1975, IMF Archive ref. 185012.
4 "Portugal – Purchase under the Oil Facility", EBS/75/467 . . . , p. 5.
5 "Portugal – Purchase under the Oil Facility", EBS/76/105, 10 March 1976, IMF Archive ref. 183860, and "Executive Board Minutes", EBM 76/47, 18 March 1976, IMF Archive ref. 183692.
6 "Portugal – Purchase under the Oil Facility", EBS/76/105, p. 5.
7 "Portugal – Use of Fund Resources – Compensatory Financing", EBS/76/280, 18 June 1976, Archive ref. 182138, and "Executive Board Minutes", EBM 76/91, 23 June 1976, IMF Archive ref. 185012.
8 "Portugal – Request for Stand-By Arrangement", EBS/77/100, 12 April 1977, Archive ref. 226616, and "Executive Board Minutes", EBM 77/61, 25 April 1977, IMF Archive ref. 226352.
9 "Portugal – Request for Stand-By Arrangement", EBS/78/228, 9 May 1978, Archive ref. 220586, and "Executive Board Minutes", EBM 78/81, 5 June 1978, IMF Archive ref. 220168.
10 "Portugal – Review of Stand-By Arrangement", EBS/78/707, 26 December 1978, Archive ref. 216774.

References

Amaral, L. 2009: New series of Portuguese Population and Employment, 1950–2007: Implications for GDP per capita and Labor Productivity. *Análise Social* XLIV (193), 767–791.
Amaral, L. 2019: *The Modern Portuguese Economy in the Twentieth and Twenty-First Centuries.* Cham: Palgrave Macmillan.
Amaral, L., Ferreira da Silva, Á. and Simpson, D. 2020: A Long International Monetary Fund Intervention: Portugal 1975–1979. *FEUNL Working Paper Series 635.*
AMECO:
   http://ec.europa.eu/economy_finance/ameco/user/serie/SelectSerie.cfm
Baganha, M. I. 1994: As correntes emigratórias portuguesas no século XX e o seu impacto na economia nacional. *Análise Social* XXIX (128), 959–980.
Baklanoff, E. N. 1996: Breve experiência de socialismo em Portugal: o sector das empresas estatais. *Análise Social* XXXI (138), 932–935.
Bastien, C. 2001: Preços e salários. In N. Valério (ed.), *Estatísticas Históricas Portuguesas*, Lisbon: INE, pp. 615–655.

Bordo, M. and James, H. 2000: The International Monetary Fund: Its Present Role in Historical Perspective. *NBER Working Papers* 7724, June.

Bruneau, T. C. 1982: As dimensões internacionais da Revolução Portuguesa: apoios e constrangimentos no estabelecimento da democracia. *Análise Social* XVIII (72–73–74), 885–896.

Carreira, Henrique Medina (1996), "As políticas sociais em Portugal", in António Barreto (ed.), *A Situação Social em Portugal, 1960–1995*, Lisbon, ICS.

The Conference Board, https://www.conference-board.org/data/economydatabase/index.cfm?id=27762

De Vries, M. G. 1976: *The International Monetary Fund 1966–1971 – The System Under Stress*, Washington DC: International Monetary Fund.

De Vries, M. G. 1985: *The International Monetary Fund 1972–1978. Cooperation on Trial*. Washington DC: International Monetary Fund.

De Vries, M. G. 1986: *The IMF in a Changing World 1945–1985*. Washington DC: International Monetary Fund.

Diz, A. C. 1984: The Conditions Attached to Adjustment Financing; Evolution of the IMF Practice. In AAVV, *The International Monetary System: Forty Years after Bretton Woods*, Boston: Federal Reserve Bank of Boston.

Dornbusch, R. (1981), "Portugal's Crawling Peg", in John Williamson (ed.), *Exchange Rate Rules: The Theory, Performance and Prospects of the Crawling Peg*, London and Basingstoke, The Macmillan Press, pp. 243–251.

Hamilton, J. D. 2011: Historical Oil Shocks. *NBER Working Paper* 16790, February.

Lopes, J. S. 1982: IMF Conditionality in the Stand-By Arrangement with Portugal of 1978. *Estudos de Economia*. III (2), 141–166.

Lopes, J. S. 1996: *A Economia Portuguesa desde 1960*. Lisbon: Gradiva.

Marques, H. T. 2000: Turismo. In A. Barreto and M. F. Mónica (eds.), *Dicionário de História de Portugal*, Suplemento P/Z, Vol. XV, Porto: Editora Figueirinhas.

Mata, Maria Eugénia (2001), "Finanças públicas e dívida pública", in Nuno Valério (ed.), *Estatísticas Históricas Portuguesas*, Lisbon INE, pp. 657–712.

Mateus, A. (1982), *Crescimento Económico e Dívida Externa. O Caso de Portugal*, Lisbon, Instituto de Estudos para o Desenvolvimento.

Mateus, A. 2013: *Economia Portuguesa: Evolução no Contexto Internacional (1910–2013)*. Lisbon: Principia.

Nunes, A. B. 2011: The International Monetary Fund's stand-by arrangements with Portugal. An ex-ante application of the Washington Consensus? *Instituto Superior de Economia e Gestão – GHES Documento de Trabalho/Working Paper* 44.

Pinheiro, M. (ed.) 1997: *Séries Longas para a Economia Portuguesa, Pós-II Guerra Mundial, Vol. I – Séries Estatísticas*. Lisbon: Banco de Portugal.

Pinto, A. J. M. 1983: A economia portuguesa e os acordos de estabilização económica com o FMI. *Economia* VII (3), 555–606.

Pires, R. P. *et al.* 1984: *Os Retornados. Um Estudo Sociográfico.* Lisbon: Instituto de Estudos para o Desenvolvimento.

Polak, J. J. 1994: *The World Bank and the IMF: A Changing Relationship. Brooking Occasional Papers.* Washington DC: The Brookings Institution.

Ramos, R., Vasconcelos e Sousa, B. and Monteiro, N. G. 2009: *História de Portugal.* Lisbon: A Esfera dos Livros.

Reis, A. 1994a: O processo de democratização. In A. Reis (coord.), *Portugal, 20 Anos de Democracia,* Lisbon: Círculo de Leitores.

Reis, A. 1994b: O poder central. In A. Reis (coord.), *Portugal, 20 Anos de Democracia,* Lisbon: Círculo de Leitores.

Schmitt, H. O. 1981: Economic Stabilization and Growth in Portugal. *International Monetary Fund Occasional Papers* 2, April.

Zorrinho, J. 2018: O Processo de Intervenção do FMI em Portugal entre 1975 e 1985, Masters Dissertation, Lisbon: Faculdade de Ciências Sociais e Humanas da Universidade Nova de Lisboa.

3

The IMF Intervention Process in Portugal between 1983 and 1985

JOÃO ZORRINHO

1 Background, 1979–83

The application of the IMF stabilisation programmes, between 1975 and 1979, contributed to the fall of the 2nd Constitutional Government, inaugurating an era marked by political instability, with successive Presidential Governments. The dichotomy between the austerity requested by the IMF and a Parliament opposed to more austerity created enormous difficulties for those Governments. The 4th Constitutional Government saw the 1979 State Budget fail, and had to present a new, less restrictive budget, in a process that culminated in the dismissal of the then Prime Minister Carlos Alberto da Mota Pinto (Nunes, 2011). In this context, many of the stabilisation measures started to be reversed by the government.

The IMF admitted that the success of the stabilisation programme had put the country in a better position to face the difficulties resulting from the international economic crisis that emerged. However, as early as 1980, it warned of the progressive worsening of the Portuguese situation, predicting that without a quick correction, the economy would quickly fall into an external imbalance.

The IMF also recommended a set of short-term measures, in line with the ones previously applied, intending to reverse this trend. Despite this warning, the 6th Constitutional Government, led by Francisco Sá Carneiro, maintained and even reinforced expansionist measures throughout 1980. The favourable external performance in 1979, the anti-inflationary strategy, and the electoral calendar contributed to this option. Only in the second half of 1981, because of the clear worsening of the external position in 1980, did the 7th Constitutional Government, under the leadership of Francisco Pinto Balsemão, adopt corrective measures. The corrective actions taken were in line with the recommendations made by the IMF in 1980. The application of these measures may be related to the negotiations undertaken with the Fund in 1981 to enter a new Stand-by Agreement. However, they were not effective, and the programme never materialised.

The poor results that occurred in 1981, with the current account deficit reaching 11 per cent, proved the weaknesses of the measures applied, which was reaffirmed by the IMF in the 1982 report that insisted on the urgency of the government implementing measures to reverse this trend. The IMF also warned of the dangers of the substantial growth in foreign debt for the country's future development. With the current account deficit higher than that of 1977 and 1978 and without significant foreign currency reserves, the postponement of the Portuguese adjustment was only possible given the availability of external credit, which was made available to Portugal after the success of its IMF adjustment.

Governments led by Pinto Balsemão postponed as much as they could the necessary adjustment of the economy, with or without the support of the IMF, using external credit to finance the imbalances, which resulted in a vast increase in external debt. This statement does not invalidate the fact that certain measures were applied. However, these fell far short of what was necessary to reverse the increase in demand or loss of competitiveness that continued to increase throughout the period. Frictions within governments and the concern to create the required consensus for the approval of the 1982 constitutional review seem to have contributed to this (Amaral, 2018; Bento, 2018).

At the end of 1982, the country recorded the largest current account deficit in the OECD. The progressive worsening of the situation made international financing extremely limited. Portugal had to resort once again to gold reserves at the beginning of 1983. Faced with this reality, in December 1982, Prime Minister Pinto Balsemão asked for his resignation and scheduled early elections for 25 April 1983. While resigning, the 8th Constitutional Government applied more significant measures for externally rebalancing Portugal, as exemplified by the 1983 State Budget and the increase in interest rates. The application of these measures on the eve of elections resulted from the lack of alternatives created by the dragging on of the situation.

The IMF report under article IV in 1983, faced with the emergency in Portugal, already contained the bases for a stabilisation programme, which the Fund considered inevitable, and the technical conclusion indirectly recommended the implementation of a new adjustment programme with the IMF.

This Stabilisation programme would start to be applied shortly after the inauguration of the 9th Constitutional Government in June, beginning a new phase of intervention by the IMF in Portugal.

2 The assistance period, 1983–85: The second rescue

2.1 The Portuguese government takes the initiative

Shortly after taking office on 9 June 1983, the 9th Constitutional Government, made up of a post-electoral coalition consisting of the Socialist Party and the Social Democratic Party and headed by Mário Soares, faced with the seriousness of the external situation of the country and the lack of alternatives to adjustment, introduced a package of financial and economic stabilisation measures and purchased the reserve tranche of the quota[1] from the IMF. This purchase placed Escudo reserves at 100 per cent of the quota, which at that time corresponded to 258 million Special Drawing Rights[2] (SDR), inaugurating a new period of intervention by the IMF in Portugal.

The withdrawal of the reserve tranche was unconditional. However, the stabilisation plan applied by the government, which included a 12 per cent devaluation of the escudo, the freezing of the public investment programme, a substantial and generalised increase in the price of subsidised goods, the introduction of a new tax on corporate profits and a rise in interest rates on deposits by 2 per cent and loans on 2.5 per cent followed the previous recommendations of the Fund which had been holding periodic talks with the Portuguese authorities (Cardoso, 2018). These measures formed the basis for the Portuguese adjustment, with the Government having applied for a new Stand-By Arrangement[3] before the start of official negotiations with the IMF (Ter-Minassian, 2011), with this constituting the first step for these to occur.

Negotiations between Portugal and the IMF for this agreement took place in Lisbon between 18 July and 8 August 1983. On 9 September, the talks materialised (IMF, 1983) with the letter of intent sent by the then Minister of Finance and Planning, Ernâni Rodrigues Lopes, and by the Governor of the Banco de Portugal, Manuel Jacinto Nunes. The Portuguese request was officially accepted by the IMF on 9 October. The Stand-by arrangement lasted 16 months, covering the period between 7 October 1983, and 28 February 1985, and provided for the purchase of 445 million SDR, equivalent to 172 per cent of the quota, increasing the allocation of Escudos from the IMF to 272 per cent of the quota. Simultaneously, in October 1983, Portugal requested a Compensatory Financing facility[4] in the amount of 258 million SDR, 100 per cent of its quota.

2.2 Stand-By Arrangement of 1983

The programme stipulated by the Stand-by Arrangement had as its primary objective to reduce the current account deficit in the balance of payments, which reached 3.2 billion dollars in 1982 (13.2 per cent of GDP), to 2 billion dollars in 1983, 9.3 per cent of GDP, and about 1.25 billion dollars in 1984, 6 per cent of GDP.

The programme aimed to reduce and stabilise asset losses in foreign currency by the banking sector, to reduce the value of inflation from 29 per cent at the date of the agreement, to 20 per cent at the end of 1984, and to reduce the public sector deficit from 12.6 per cent of GDP in 1982 to 6 per cent of GDP in 1984.

The fulfilment of these objectives would allow Portugal to reduce the financing difficulties of the economy in the short term and, at the same time, to gradually reduce the debt service charges, essential factors for sustained growth of the economy in the future.

This programme included financing with purchases in higher credit tranches and, according to the IMF conditionality rules (Polak, 1991), with the funding being staggered, and performance criteria to access it.

The staggered financing established in the Stand-by Agreement was 96.75 million SDRs until 31 January 1984, 78, until 30 April, 166.40, until 31 July, 236.05, until 31 October, 305.70 and 375. 50 until 31 January 1985.

Regarding the performance criteria, objectives were defined in the arrangement to be reached by 31 December 1983, and provisional objectives to be achieved by 31 December 1984. The established objectives defined limits to the credit expansion of the national banking system at the domestic level and the public sector. It also set maximum limits on the total external debt contracted from the non-monetary sector, maximum limits on the short-term external debt pledged, and a test of liquid foreign assets for the period from the beginning of the agreement until 29 February 1984.

Domestic credit in the banking sector, based on the value of 2 148.9 billion Escudos at the end of 1982, could not exceed 2,786.5 billion until 31 December 1983, and 3,416.5 billion until 31 December 1984. Within domestic credit, credit to the public sector, which was 462.3

billion Escudos at the end of 1982, could not exceed 629.3 billion as of 31 December 1983, and 779 billion as of 31 December 1984.

The maximum limits of the total external debt contracted from the non-monetary sector, starting at the value of 12,864 million dollars, verified at the end of 1982, were 13,800 million until 31 December 1983, and 15,000 million until 31 December 1984. Within these limits, the sub-limits for short-term external indebtedness, based on the value of 3,752 million U.S. dollars verified at the end of 1982, were 3, 800 million up to 31 December 1983 and 4,000 million up to 31 December 1984.

Regarding the test of net foreign assets, which was intended to account for the accumulated loss of foreign currency assets in the banking sector, which since the beginning of 1983 amounted to 981 million dollars, the Stand-By arrangement established that they could not exceed 1.6 billion between 7 October 1983 and the end of February 1984. Negotiations would be held in the future to set new limits for the rest of the period.

The agreement provided for the limits established as performance criteria to be regularly reviewed during the development of the programme, with changes and adjustments to them, if necessary. Included as a performance criterion was the need to reach an agreement on the establishment of quarterly ceilings, referring to 1984, for the expansion of domestic and public sector credit until 31 March 1984, under penalty of Portugal being prevented from making new purchases from that date on.

Performance criteria also included Portugal's commitment not to aggravate or introduce new restrictions on trade and payments and the obligation to reduce the import surcharge from 30 per cent to 10 per cent in the 1984 budget, applying this change until 31 March 1984.

The agreed stabilisation programme aimed to achieve an improvement in the current account, combining measures that simultaneously sought to reduce domestic demand and allocate more resources to the export sector. As we saw earlier, certain measures were introduced before the signing of the Stand-by Agreement but constituted a first effort by the Portuguese government to recover stability, serving as a basis for the introduction of the new measures provided for in the agreement.

This programme placed a great emphasis on the public sector. One of the objectives set was to reduce the public sector deficit. A wide range of measures was agreed, such as increasing the tax burden through new indirect taxes created in September 1983, raising prices administered by the supply fund, in particular for certain goods such as oil and oil products, and greater control of public expenditure.

The control of public expenditure included restraining salary increases for civil servants by 17 per cent, freezing contracts, and the investment programme, reducing transfers from the Central State for other public entities and the change in the mechanism for calculating interest rates paid to the Banco de Portugal.

The IMF saw the Portuguese tax system as being too complicated, full of exceptions, and with several application deficiencies, which resulted in an unfair distribution of the tax burden and very significant evasion. As a result, the programme supported the renewal of the Portuguese tax system and the strengthening of its application.

Another essential aspect of this programme was the strengthening of the financial situation of the state's business sector and, above all, the reduction of the recourse to internal and external indebtedness. Portugal would achieve this objective throughout cutting investment programmes and increasing self-financing capacities by setting realistic prices, containing wages, increasing productivity, and, where necessary, adjusting the workforce.

The debt limit extended to including the government and debt ceilings were created for the expansion of domestic credit to central State administration, which implied a decrease in the growth rate of this credit from the 33.3 per cent verified in 1982 to 18.8 per cent in 1984.

Domestic credit control was a central feature in this programme, which aimed at reducing the rate of expansion from 29 per cent in 1982 to 21.5 per cent in 1984. To this end, beyond the limits to the expansion of credit included in the agreement as performance clauses, further contributing would be the improvement in public finances, a better application of the credit limits imposed by the Banco de Portugal, through the increase of penalties for banks that defaulted, and a rise in credit interest.

The price and wage system was another aspect considered by the programme. The prices of subsidised goods, which had already undergone significant increases in June, were expected to further increase in early 1984.

Prices would be revised throughout the year to reflect the evolution of prices in the international market, allowing for an improvement in the financial position of the supply fund.

Expected wage increases in 1983 and 1984 were to be significantly below inflation rates, meaning wages were to decrease in real terms. The agreement also established that salary increases for workers in public companies were limited to 20 per cent. On the other hand, significant increases in unemployment benefits were foreseen, to face the foreseeable rise in unemployment resulting from the adjustment programme.

The increase in interest rates on deposits and credit, as part of the package of stabilisation measures applied by the Portuguese government *a priori*, raised them to positive values in real terms. However, the programme underlined the importance of flexible interest rate management, to adapt them to inflation figures and the evolution of rates in the foreign market. The programme also required that existing export interest rate subsidies be eliminated by the end of 1983 and the other incentive systems reviewed.

The 12 per cent devaluation of the Escudo in June increased the country's competitiveness to values higher than those observed in 1979. However, the programme foresaw the continuation of the escudo sliding devaluation policy at a rate of 1 per cent per month. This devaluation was considered sufficient to maintain the country's competitiveness. However, a revision of the rate of depreciation could happen if the context required it.

The IMF hoped that realist interest and exchange rates, coupled with greater political stability, would lead to increased tourism revenues and emigrant remittances.

However, in terms of foreign policy, the agreement imposed greater control over the growth of external debt, particularly in the short term, to reduce the costs of servicing it, maintaining a system free of restrictions on international payments and transfers and the reduction of barriers to trade. The agreement included these objectives as performance criteria.

Like the previous ones, this stabilisation programme was of short duration and had as its main objective an immediate improvement of the Portuguese balance of payments imbalance. It used a policy of fiscal austerity, wage control, credit restriction, and exchange rate and interest rate flexibility, to decrease domestic demand and recover the external balance. However, this agreement also sought to initiate some medium-term reforms to resolve certain structural weaknesses such as the reform of the tax system, the control of public finances and the development of the financial market, and making the labour market more flexible.

The Portuguese government and the IMF recognised the consequences and social impacts of this programme. The fall in domestic demand caused a significant reduction in real household income and consumption, accompanied by a fall in public and private investment, resulting from the restriction of credit and public expenditure. The external balance, with the increase in exports, due to the rise of national competitiveness, and the reduction of imports, would contribute positively to the GDP, but not enough to avoid a reduction in it during the programme and the consequent increase of unemployment in a context of generalised price increases, including administered prices, increases in the tax burden and moderation of social transfers (Lopes, 2004; IMF, 1983).

2.3 Compensatory Financing Facility of 1983

As mentioned at the beginning of this chapter, together with the request for the Stand-by agreement, Portugal submitted an application for a Compensatory Financing Facility in the amount of SDR 258 million, 100 per cent of the quota. This request focused on the deficit in revenues from the exports of goods, remittances from emigrants and tourism, due to their underperformance in the 12 months preceding March 1983.

Since this request exceeded the value of 50 per cent of the quota, under the rules of conditionality, the IMF could only accept this if the cooperation and the efforts made to resolve the balance of payments imbalances were satisfactory to the Fund. The IMF considered that Portugal met this requirement by adopting the stabilisation programme established in the Stand-by arrangement.

Concerning the deficit in revenues from the exports of goods, remittances from emigrants and tourism, a fundamental criterion for accessing Compensatory Financing, the IMF calculated that, based on the results achieved between 1980 and 1982 and the estimates for the years 1983 to 1985, this would be 359 million SDR, that is, a value 40 per cent higher than the request in the programme. This deficit was subdivided into 121 million SDR in goods exports, 92 million SDR in tourism revenues, and 141 million SDR in emigrant remittances.

In March 1984, these figures were revised by the IMF based on the new data available. The real deficit was 354 million SDR. Since the amount required by Portugal remained below the deficit, there was no impact on the programme.

The main reason given for the verification of this deficit was the adverse effect of the global economic recession. The political and economic instability in Portugal, given the uncertainty caused by the 1983 elections, also had a significant impact.

According to the IMF, the recovery of revenues from the exports of goods, remittances from emigrants and tourism was dependent on the expected improvement in the economic situation in industrialised countries and the application of the stabilisation programme, namely with the growth of the competitiveness of the Portuguese economy and the adjustment of interest rates to positive values.

Together, the two programmes envisaged the provision of 703 million SDRs to Portugal by the IMF, equivalent to 272.5 of the national quota.

2.4 Stand-by arrangement revision of 1984

Portugal made the first purchase under the stand-by arrangement in the amount of 96.75 million SDR on 15 October 1983 and the second, in the amount of 69.95 million SDR, on 15 March 1984, after proof of fulfilment of the performance clauses for 31 December 1983.

In 1984, the Portuguese quota in the IMF went from 258 million SDRs to 376.6 million SDRs, changing the percentages of financing to the quota.

The Stand-by arrangement programme included a review in March 1984 for the establishment of new performance criteria for 1984. Although there had been negotiations between Portugal and the IMF during February and March, they could not set the criteria in the time determined due to deficiencies in the forecasts for the public enterprise sector borrowing requirements. The financial situation of public companies and the *Fundo de Fomento* (Stimulation Fund) was, throughout this period, very unclear due to weaknesses in the national accounting system, which made it challenging to establish adapted performance criteria.

These criteria, as well as a new schedule to stagger the financing, would eventually be established in the talks held in Portugal between May and June 1984 between the Portuguese government and the representatives of the IMF, T. Ter- Minassian, E. Spitaeller, T. Catsambas E. Kalter and C. Strayer, in the annual Article IV consultation and review of the stand-by arrangement.

The rescheduling of the financing for 1984 involved 166.4 million SDR by 15 September 1984, 259.3 million SDR by 15 November and 359.3 million SDR by 15 February 1985.

The fulfilment of performance criteria established in the Stand-by arrangement and the ones added in the review for 1984 conditioned these purchases. In particular, new quantitative performance criteria were introduced and to be attained on 31 July, 30 September, and 31 December 1984.

The limits set for the growth of domestic bank credit were of 2.875 billion Escudos until 31 July, 2.929 billion Escudos until 30 September and 3.106 billion Escudos until 31 December. For domestic bank credit to the public sector, including, for the first time, the business sector, the limits were 1.125 billion Escudos until 31 July, 1.110 billion Escudos until 30 September and 1.168 billion Escudos until 31 December.

The limits set for the growth of the external debt of the non-financial sector were, with the benchmarks, 616 million dollars up to 31 July, 1,113 million dollars up to 30 September and 1,250 million dollars up to 31 December.

The established short-term external debt objectives were 200 million through 31 July, 150 million through 30 September and 200 million through 31 December and for the accumulated loss of foreign currency assets in the banking sector, quantified at 450 million U.S. dollars through 31 July, 150 million through 30 September and 100 million through 31 December.

These talks also aimed to analyse the evolution of the Portuguese economy and negotiate the new policies to be implemented.

The talks culminated in the sending of a new letter of intent to the IMF, again signed by the Minister of Finance and Planning, Ernâni Rodrigues Lopes, and the Governor of the Bank Portugal, Manuel Jacinto Nunes, on 20 June 1984, which overlapped the previous letter.

In revising the arrangement, the IMF considered that the evolution of the Portuguese economy under the stabilisation programme, in 1983, had generally been satisfactory. Performance clauses established for 31 December were comfortably met with the public administration deficit at 9 per cent of GDP and with a significant reduction in the pace of credit growth, from 29 per cent in 1982 to 18 per cent in 1983. Public sector credit declined from 33 per cent in 1982 to 19 per cent in 1983.

This sharp reduction was due to difficulties in accessing credit in international markets, reinforcement of the application of credit limits, and the significant increase, by 6.5 per cent in 1983, in interest rates. This reduction of credit in the economy had a direct effect on businesses and households.

Companies adapted by reducing financing needs, draining existing stocks, and freezing planned investments, which led to a significant reduction in domestic demand. The IMF warned in its report that, due to the unavailability of foreign credit on which the state's business sector was extremely dependent, there would be an increase in pressure on national banks. Public companies demanded a large part of the available financing, which limited further access to credit by private companies.

Together with the reduction in available credit for households, there was a 10 per cent reduction in real wages, an increase in the tax burden, and reduction in emigrant remittances. These resulted in a drop of around 5 per cent in the income of families. However, consumption declined only 1 per cent, with families resorting to savings, which fell significantly, to maintain consumption patterns.

Overall, domestic demand fell by 7 per cent. The GDP only decreased by 0.5 per cent in 1983, not fully reflecting this decline, given the better than expected improvement in the balance of trade, because of the substantial increase in exports and the reduction in imports.

The balance of trade performance made it possible to compensate for the under-performance of other variables, such as the deterioration in terms of trade and emigrant remittances, which were negatively affected by the slow recovery of the European economy and the appreciation of the dollar.

In this context, the current account deficit, external debt, and, in particular, short-term debt, remained below the limits established in the agreement. The deficit of the current account was 1.7 billion dollars, significantly below the target set in the programme, and the position was the same with the balance of payments that recorded a deficit of 900 million dollars, compared to the expected value of 1,140 million dollars.

Despite these positive results, unemployment reached 10.5 per cent, and inflation reached 34 per cent at the end of 1983.

Carrying out this review, the IMF considered that the data for the first months of 1984 indicated the maintenance of the trend observed at the end of 1983. Domestic demand continued to decline with the maintenance of the wage policy and credit restrictions, which were reflected in a deceleration in inflation, which stood at 30 per cent in May.

There was an increase in domestic credit to the public sector compared to 1983, but it was offset by a more significant reduction in external credit, which resulted in a decrease in total credit to the public sector.

The current account continued on a positive development trend, with a deficit of 350 million dollars by May, less than half of the corresponding value in 1983, driven by an increase in exports and a decrease in imports and, in opposition to the end of the previous year, with the recovery of revenues from tourism and remittances from emigrants.

The balance of payments remained in deficit, recording in fact a deficit of 263 million dollars in May, due to the limitation of capital inflows from abroad, but at the time of the programme review, there were already signs of an increase in foreign capital inflows in response to the issuance of floating-rate bonds and the increase in private investments. The review reaffirmed the objective of reducing the current account deficit to less than 1.25 billion dollars by the end of 1984. To this end, Portugal maintained the strategy followed in 1983 with minor adjustments in the light of changes within the context.

Because of the sharp fall in imports, a progressive increase in demand was expected in the second half of 1984, compatible with the equilibrium of the balance of payments. Great importance was attached to reducing inflation, which remained above the average for the previous year, and the objective of reaching an inflation level close to 23 per cent at the end of 1984 was established.

Although the quantitative limits on external indebtedness and internal credit granted by the banking system had remained, there had been a liberalisation of interest rates on bank deposits with maturities over one year and a reduction of 1 per cent in interest on loans.

In this review, the IMF again was clear about the need for structural reforms in the Portuguese economy, without which sustained growth in the country would be impossible. In response, the Portuguese authorities committed to complementing the short-term measures agreed with an increased effort to solving the structural problems arising within the economy.

Public finances remained structurally problematic. Despite the improvements made in 1983, the IMF recognised that the rebalancing of public accounts was dependent on medium-term reforms, and the capacity for substantial improvements in 1984 was quite limited. However, the government had committed itself to implementing a wide range of measures to reduce expenditures further and simultaneously increase revenues.

Among the measures adopted, of note was the progressive elimination of consumption subsidies, the reform of the tax system, with the introduction of VAT in 1985, and its application, the review of existing tax incentives and exceptions, greater control over investment and a restructuring of the state's business sector.

For the restructuring of the public business sector, Portugal started negotiations with the International Bank for Reconstruction and Development (IBRD) for technical and financial support through a loan programme for the restructuring of public companies to be implemented also in 1984 and monitored by the IMF.

An interministerial commission was created, to coordinate public finance policy, with the participation of the Banco de Portugal with its mission being to review the evolution of the financial situation monthly and decide on the allocation of financing and define possible corrective measures necessary to meet the requirements established.

Given the success achieved with maintaining a competitive exchange rate, the Portuguese authorities committed themselves to maintaining this policy, making adjustments to the monthly rate of devaluation, where necessary. In March 1984, the surcharge on imports was reduced from 30 per cent to 10 per cent.

After the annual consultation provided in article IV to Portugal, the IMF executive committee praised the country for the results achieved so far in rebalancing the balance of payments and restoring confidence in international markets, underlining the fulfilment of all performance criteria.

The executive committee also approved the maintenance of the stabilisation policy and the new measures introduced. However, it considered that some of these could be more ambitious, and it was also clear in pointing out that problems such as the excessive burden of the external debt, the precarious competitivity and the imbalance in public accounts remained a concern, requiring continued effort and structural reforms.

2.5 Compensatory Financing Facility of 1984

Also within the scope of the annual consultation of article IV and the review of the Stand-by agreement, Portugal requested a new Compensatory Financing Programme in the amount of 54.6 million SDRs, 14.5 per cent of the new quota, corresponding to the deficit in the revenues of goods exports, emigrant remittances and tourism, due to their underperformance in the 12 months preceding March 1984. This request was made official on 25 July in a communication sent by the Banco de Portugal to the IMF.

The IMF considered that the Stand-by Arrangement and the good performance of Portugal in its application, were sufficient to satisfy the required cooperation criterion.

With this purchase, the IMF's assets in Escudos reached 771.3 million SDR, equivalent to 204.8 per cent of the quota in 1984.

Concerning the deficit in the export earnings of goods, in the remittances of emigrants and tourism, the IMF estimated that this would be 203 million SDR, that is, a value much higher than the request as part of the programme. The final deficit calculation, carried out in early 1985, slightly changed the figure to 218 million SDR, which did not influence the agreed programme.

As we saw earlier, although in this period the gains from exports exceeded the IMF's forecasts, tourism and remittance revenues from emigrants were substantially below expectations. The main reasons given for this situation were the slow recovery of European economies, the primary source of tourists in Portugal and countries of destination for the majority of Portuguese emigrants, in addition to the devaluation of European currencies against the SDR, which contributed to gains in SDR being lower than expected.

2.6 Waiver request: short-term external debt

On 5 December 1984, Portugal sent the IMF a request to waive the performance criterion related to the increase in short-term external debt on 31 July 1984, to be able to make further purchases. As part of this request, the Fund assessed the evolution of the Portuguese economy under the Stand-by programme. The technicians concluded that, excluding the criterion of increasing short-term external debt, all other limits determined, such as the performance criteria on 31 July 1984, were met, some with slack.

Regarding exceeding the limit of the increase in short-term external debt, which was 31 million, this was attributed, in line with that exposed by the Portuguese authorities, to a technical failure, derived from the preliminary data that served as the basis for calculating the limits having underestimated the increase in the external debt in the first months of 1984. The IMF predicted that given the efforts made by Portugal, the limit defined for 30 September would be respected.

The Fund further considered that the economy's performance was in line with the programme's objectives. The current account evolved in a more positive way than expected, with the target set for the deficit, 1.25 billion dollars in 1984, expected to be considerably exceeded as a result of the strong growth in product exports, enabled by the main-tenance of the monthly devaluation of the escudo and a consequent increase in revenue, and a sharp recovery in tourism revenues, together with a significant decline in imports caused by the 6 per cent drop in domestic demand.

The decline in real wages, which was over 10 per cent and the delay in applying administered prices led to a slowdown in inflation in the second half of 1984, with the intention to reduce inflation to 23 per cent by the end of the year being probable.

This positive trend extended to monetary and financial variables, with the IMF foreseeing that with the maintenance of credit control policies, Portugal would respect the limits of expansion for domestic credit.

However, the Fund anticipated that the ceiling established for domestic credit to the public sector, including public companies, could be slightly exceeded in September and January, due to the substitution of external debt for domestic credit in the public business sector, to delays in increasing subsidised goods prices and in reduced gold sales compared to those planned.

Because of this analysis, the Fund's technicians proposed the approval of the Portuguese request, which occurred on 12 December 1984.

2.7 Portugal abandons the Stand-by Arrangement in advance

As foreseen in the Fund's technical evaluation, Portugal would even-tually exceed the limits established for domestic credit to the public sector from September 1984 to 31 December 1984. Contrary to what had happened previously, Portugal did not request an exemption from meeting these criteria and was prevented from making further purchases from the IMF. Thus, Portugal did not use 185.7 million SDR made available in the Stand-by Agreement.

Given the improvement in external accounts verified in 1983 and 1984 and the consequent improvement in financing conditions, in January 1985, Portugal informed the IMF that it did not intend to request the renewal of the Stand-by Agreement for 1985. Despite this option, Portugal expected to maintain its consultations with the Fund and asked the Fund to review the country's performance concerning the programme between 1983 and 1984.

Given this, an IMF team, formed by T. Ter-Minassian and E. Spitaeller, came to Lisbon from 25 February 1985 to 1 March 1985.

In this review, the IMF concluded that the adjustment of external accounts implemented by Portugal under the Stand-by agreement had been very successful. The current account deficit, which had reached 13 per cent of GDP in 1982, was less than 2.5 per cent of GDP in 1984, showing an improvement which was much more significant than that foreseen in the programme.

The same happened with external debt for the non-monetary sector and with the short-term external debt, in which the results achieved far exceeded forecasts. The exception to this success was the imbalance of public finances and the disrespect for the credit limits for the public sector established in the agreement. Public sector deficit, including the business sector, surpassed 17.5 per cent of GDP in 1984, well above the 14.5 per cent target. The IMF also regretted the unsatisfactory progress in resolving the structural problems identified.

The document prepared after the Fund's technical visit to Portugal also included an analysis of the economic strategy for 1985 and a prospective analysis of the evolution of the Portuguese economy. This analysis highlighted the fact that 1985 was a year marked by its polit-ical calendar, with presidential elections at the end of the year and local elections at the beginning of 1986, which could increase tensions within the coalition that was supporting the government.

The Portuguese government, for its part, considered that given the improvement in the external position of the economy, there was room for a moderate increase in domestic demand and GDP. Thus, the 1985 economic strategy foresaw a relative rise in GDP of 3 per cent and 3.5 per cent in domestic demand. The driver of this growth would be investment, through an increase in credit available to the private sector, since consumption should increase only 1 per cent because of the maintenance of the real value of wages in 1985 when inflation was expected to be 22 per cent.

The government intended to maintain the monthly devaluation of the escudo at 1 per cent to maintain the competitive position of the economy. Imports were expected to recover, given the increase in domestic demand, with a deceleration in the pace of export growth, resulting in a worsening current account deficit that was projected at 850 million dollars, equivalent to 4.5 per cent of GDP. The government did not expect difficulties in finding financing for this deficit.

The economic programme foresaw the maintenance of the deficit to GDP ratio, unchanged in relation to 1984. A deceleration in the growth of domestic credit and public sector financing needs was expected, which should increase the credit available to the private sector, which would support the increase in productive investment.

The data available at the end of February did not show a recovery in private consumption, with domestic demand remaining depressed, but there was a modest increase in investment in the export sector. The Fund predicted that if this trend continued, Portugal would not achieve the objectives for domestic demand and GDP growth.

Given the lack of response from domestic demand, the current account deficit maintained a positive trend, improving compared to the same period in 1984, and was expected to remain so during the first half of the year due to the decline in imports.

Labour costs generally remained unchanged with the figures for increases and inflation staying within the target values. In this context, the IMF considered that the monthly devaluation of 1 per cent of the escudo would be sufficient to maintain the competitiveness of Portuguese exports.

The main concern expressed by the Fund was the failure to implement the planned measures, predicting the occurrence of falls in revenue and increases in expenditure, due to unforeseen factors. Although there was no data on the performance of public companies in 1985, the IMF pointed out the weakness of this sector. Administered prices remained well below real costs, and debt service costs continued to rise, pointing to a further significant increase in financing needs.

The final technical assessment made by the IMF, as part of this review, recognised that the success of the stabilisation programme had enabled a moderate recovery in domestic demand and GDP. However, sustaining this recovery, in the long run, would only be possible without creating a new external imbalance, through increased exports and productive investment. This need was reinforced by the future entry into the European Economic Community (EEC), investing in exporting industries, in the modernisation of infrastructure and the agricultural sector's essential priorities.

The Fund supported the Portuguese intention to maintain a flexible exchange rate and moderate labour costs and reinforced the importance of channelling adequate financial resources for productive investment. For the Fund, the foreseeable increase in public sector borrowing requirements undermined this objective, as it would limit the credit available to the private sector, within the framework of prudent monetary policy.

Another worrying aspect was the evolution of the public deficit, which reflected high levels of public consumption and subsidies, losses in the business sector, and the high costs with debt servicing. It was considered essential to apply short-term corrective measures in this area, such as further increases in administered prices, modernisation of the tax system, improved control over expenses, strengthening financial control over public companies, and implementing adequate restructuring programmes for these companies.

The Fund also warned that the weakness of domestic demand could mask the negative consequences of postponing the application of corrective measures in the short term, but stressed that these would be felt as soon as there was a recovery in demand, and could plunge Portugal into a new crisis that would mortgage the country's future development.

2.8 The 1985 Article IV Annual Consultation
The trends identified in this report were, to no small extent, confirmed in the annual consultation of Article IV conducted by IMF staff between 18 June and 2 July.

The available data showed an improvement in the Portuguese external position until the summer of 1985 with exports increasing by 12.5 per cent and imports decreasing by another 6 per cent.

The lack of dynamism in consumption and investment that occurred undermined the goals for GDP growth in 1985, with the Portuguese government admitting the possibility of GDP growing less than 2 per cent despite the country's external performance.

At the political level, the Fund's forecasts also materialised. The national congress of the Social Democratic Party, a member of the government coalition, held in May 1985, elected a new leadership led by Aníbal Cavaco Silva, who decided to withdraw from the coalition, ending the so-called central bloc. The inability of the Socialist Party to form a new government in Parliament led the President of the Republic, Ramalho Eanes, to dissolve Parliament after the ratification of the EEC Accession Treaty in July and to call parliamentary elections for October, followed by local elections and then presidential elections in early 1986.

To this climate of instability and political uncertainty was added the accession to the EEC in 1986, which would have enormous consequences in economic terms and the external balance, which made it impossible to establish a solid economic plan or make predictions with any degree of certainty for 1986, at the time of this consultation.

It was also in the summer of 1985, due to the improvement in the external balance and the continued weakness of domestic demand, that the Portuguese government began to reverse many of the measures implemented, adopting an expansionist policy to stimulate domestic demand thus ending, within the scope of our analysis, the period of macroeconomic adjustment.

The external adjustment of the Portuguese economy between 1983 and 1985 had been an undeniable success. The short-term measures implemented under the Fund's support programme had lifted the country out of an emergency. For the IMF, it was now necessary to carry out structural reforms that would prevent the cycles experienced between 1975 and 1985 from reoccurring.

Conclusions

The image of what happened in the periods previously analysed, that is, the evolution of the Portuguese economy between 1983 and 1985, was deeply influenced by the change in external and internal dynamics, which generated a unique context indispensable for the results achieved. Contrary to what had happened in the first redemption period between 1975–79, Portugal immediately resorted to a Programme with a high degree of conditionality, a Stand-by agreement in a superior credit tranche, complemented by two Compensatory Financing programmes.

In 1983, the Portuguese situation was critical, which limited the scope to resort to other types of programmes, with lower financing values, but this option also seemed to reflect the Portuguese government's commitment to adjustment and the awareness that this was inevitable. During this period, the implementation of an Extended Financing Facility,[5] with a duration of 3 years, which would focus on structural reforms, was proposed and discussed with the Fund. The government discarded the hypothesis because of the political costs of this type of long-term programme.

As we have seen, the measures that formed the basis of the macroeconomic adjustment programme were introduced before the start of official negotiations with the Fund. However, there was a visible influence from previous recommendations.

The Stand-by Agreement of 1978 added to the June package of measures, through performance criteria, the control of credit expansion, and the elimination of barriers to trade. In the agreement, reinforcement of measures in specific areas such as fiscal policy and a first effort to resolve structural blocks in the economy were also visible. In general, the stabilisation programme in 1983 did not differ much from that of 1978 (Nunes, 2015; Cardoso, 2018). Both were short-term programmes that, using the same type of instruments, sought to contract domestic demand, increase the competitiveness of exports, and the attractiveness of escudo assets to solve short-term balance of payments problems. However, in 1983, given the dragging of the unbalanced situation, the measures for the contraction of domestic demand were more severe and had higher costs for the quality of life and living conditions of the Portuguese.

In retrospect, given the rapid adjustment of the economy, the social costs of this programme could have been reduced. This adjustment period can be divided into two parts. A first phase in which Portugal made several purchases fulfilling the performance criteria or agreeing with the Fund with its non-compliance and a second phase, starting in September 1984, in which Portugal no longer met the performance criteria and did not renew the arrangement to 1985. However, it maintained cooperation with the IMF.

The first phase of the adjustment was very successful, with the results in terms of external balance largely outperforming forecasts. The current account deficit stood at 2.5 per cent of GDP in 1984 compared to the 6 per cent provided for in the Stand-by Agreement. An exception to this success was the balance of public finances. The IMF also regretted the unsatisfactory progress in resolving the structural problems identified.

This significant improvement in the external position of the Portuguese economy resulted from the stabilisation policies implemented and from contextual issues, not foreseen in the programme, which amplified the expected effects on the decline of domestic demand and the increase of the economy's competitiveness.

The Fund's intervention was necessary for the implementation of this austerity policy in two ways. In the first place, Portugal needed the financing and, therefore, to fulfil the conditionality criteria, legitimising these measures internally and, on the other hand, functioning as a scapegoat for the government.

In the second phase, the success of the external adjustment contributed to the early abandonment of the Stand-by Agreement. The

Fund's role was not only as a funder but above all as a guarantor of external funding through the legitimacy it attributed to the countries involved. The rapid success achieved allowed the government to resort to external financing before the end of the adjustment programme, choosing not to fully comply with the agreement, thus avoiding the political costs of a longer conditioned adjustment. However, these short-term political gains compromised the necessary long-term reforms (Bento, 2018; Cardoso, 2018).

Notes

1   The gold tranche or reserve tranche represents the unconditional right of Member States to purchase from the IMF, free of charge, having only to submit a statement demonstrating the need for withdrawal for balance of payments issues. It corresponds to 25 percent of the quota.
2   The SDR is an international reserve asset, created by the IMF in 1969 to supplement its member countries' official reserves.
3   An arrangement between the IMF and a member country under which the member country is entitled to borrow up to an agreed amount of foreign currency from the Fund to cover a possible deficit in its balance of payments.
4   Created in 1963, this was a short-term programme by the IMF that sought to respond to the balance of payments problems associated with exogenous shocks, either due to falling exports and/or financial remittances or due to increasing imports.
5   The Extended Financing facility, which was created in 1974, was a long-term programme, which sought to deal with payment imbalances resulting from structural imbalances in production and trade, due to serious and permanent cost and price distortions, and imbalances where the long-term balance of payments deficits have limited the implementation of growth policies, causing weak growth and causing structural imbalances.

References

Amaral, J. F. 2018: *A intervenção do FMI em Portugal entre 1975 e 1985*. In Zorrinho, J. 2018: O processo de intervenção do FMI em Portugal entre 1975 e 1985, Lisboa: Master's Dissertation in Political Science and International Relations, Faculty of Social Sciences and Humanities, NOVA University of Lisbon.
Bento, V. 2018: *A intervenção do FMI em Portugal entre 1975 e 1985. A intervenção do FMI em Portugal entre 1975 e 1985*. In Zorrinho, J. 2018: O processo de intervenção do FMI em Portugal entre 1975 e 1985, Lisboa: Master's Dissertation in Political Science and International Relations, Faculty of Social Sciences and Humanities, NOVA University of Lisbon.
Cardoso, T. 2018: *A intervenção do FMI em Portugal entre 1975 e 1985. A intervenção do FMI em Portugal entre 1975 e 1985*. In Zorrinho, J. 2018: O processo de intervenção do FMI em Portugal entre 1975 e 1985, Lisboa: Master's Dissertation in

Political Science and International Relations, Faculty of Social Sciences and Humanities, NOVA University of Lisbon.

IMF 1983: *Portugal – Request for Stand-By Arrangement.* Retrieved from archivescatalog.imf.org: archivescatalog.imf.org

IMF 1983: *Portugal – Use of Fund Resources – Compensatory Financing Facility.* Retrieved from archivescatalog.imf.org: archivescatalog.imf.org

IMF 1983: *PRESS RELEASE NO. 83/69.* Retrieved from archivescatalog.imf.org: archivescatalog.imf.org

IMF 1983: *Stand-by Arrangement – Portugal.* Retrieved from archivescatalog.imf.org: archivescatalog.imf.org

IMF 1984: *Compensatory Financing Facility – Early Drawing – Final Calculation of the Shortfall.* Retrieved from archivescatalog.imf.org: archivescatalog.imf.org

IMF 1984: *Minutes of Executive Board Meeting 84/186.* Retrieved from archivescatalog.imf.org: archivescatalog.imf.org

IMF 1984: *Portugal – Purchase Transaction – Compensatory Financing Facility.* Retrieved from archivescatalog.imf.org: archivescatalog.imf.org

IMF 1984: *Portugal – Use of Fund Resources - Compensatory Financing Facility.* Retrieved from archivescatalog.imf.org: archivescatalog.imf.org

IMF 1984: *Portugal – Waiver of Observance of Performance Criterion Under Stand-By Arrangement.* Retrieved from archivescatalog.imf.org: archivescatalog.imf.org

IMF 1984: *Staff Report for the 1984 Article, IV Consultation and Review Under the Stand-By Arrangement.* Retrieved from archivescatalog.imf.org: archivescatalog.imf.org

IMF 1985: *Compensatory Financing Facility – Early Drawing – Final Calculation of Shortfall.* Retrieved from http://archivescatalog.imf.org: http://archivescatalog.imf.org

IMF 1985: *Portugal – Report on Staff Visit.* Retrieved from archivescatalog.imf.org: archivescatalog.imf.org

IMF 1985: *Portugal – Staff Report for the 1985 Article IV Consultation.* Retrieved from archivescatalog.imf.org: archivescatalog.imf.org

IMF (1985, September). *The Chairman's Summing Up at the Conclusion of the 1985 Article IV Consultation with Portugal Executive Board Meeting 85/133.* Retrieved from archivescatalog.imf.org: archivescatalog.imf.org

IMF 1987: *Portugal – Staff Report for the 1986 Article IV Consultation.* Retrieved from archivescatalog.imf.org: archivescatalog.imf.org

Lopes, J. S. 2004: *A Economia Portuguesa desde 1960.* Lisbon: Gradiva.

Lovato, G. 1983: *Statement by Mr. Lovato on Portugal.* Washington: IMF.

Nunes, A. B. 2015: *The Portuguese Economy in the 1980s: Structural change and short-term upheavals.* Lisbon: ISEG-GHES.

Nunes, M. J. 2011: Orçamento de 1979, o primeiro debaixo do FMI, foi o único a ser chumbado, Lusa, Interview

Ter-Minassian, T. 2011: Prefácio. In H. Piriquito, *FMI Os Acordos Com Portugal 1977.1983.1984.* bnomics.

4

The European Communities Pre-accession Aid to Portugal: A Dynamic Process

Paulo Alves Pardal

"On 7 October 1980 the European Economic Community decided to agree to the Portuguese Republic's request for financial aid in order to undertake, with a view to Portugal's accession to the European Communities, measures of common interest to prepare and facilitate the harmonious integration of the Portuguese economy into the Community economy".[1] This was not the first time that the Community had provided financial aid to Portugal. But this time was different. The aim of special aid was precisely "to facilitate the harmonious integration of the Portuguese economy into the Community after Portugal's accession to the European Communities".[2] In effect, Portugal had submitted an application to join the Community, to which the latter had responded favourably.[3] However, the process of negotiating Portugal's accession to the Communities was a long one, lasting about eight years (Cunha, 2019). It was during this long and difficult negotiation process that the pre-accession financial assistance for Portugal was agreed upon between both parties. But how was the concept of pre-accession aid for Portugal born? How was this aid implemented? And how important was this financial aid for the Portuguese economy?

1 Overview of relations between the European Communities and Portugal prior to 1980

Portugal joined the European Communities in 1986. Indeed, the

Treaty of Accession was signed on 12 June 1985 and came into force on 1 January 1986.[4] However, the relations between both sides had begun much earlier. The first interaction was through the European Free Trade Association, an organisation founded by the Stockholm Convention in 1960. The original members were the United Kingdom, Norway, Denmark, Austria, Portugal, Sweden and Switzerland. Therefore, Portugal was one of the founding members of the European Free Trade Association (EFTA).[5] Trade relations with EFTA countries, especially with the United Kingdom, were very important for the Portuguese economy. This was the main reason why the Portuguese Government could not remain indifferent when the United Kingdom, followed by other EFTA countries, asked to join the European Communities.[6]

The first Treaty of Accession was signed in January 1972.[7] Thus, the United Kingdom, Ireland and Denmark became members of the European Communities on 1 January 1973, the date on which the Treaty of Accession came into force. Before this, the Portuguese Government had expressed to the European Communities its desire to participate in an arrangement regarding trade, technological and scientific cooperation.[8] The Portuguese Government took into consideration three essential and very important objectives: to maintain all the advantages gained in the Danish and British markets, to guarantee access of Portuguese agricultural products within the European Community market, and to maintain protection for Portugal's industry.[9] The negotiations between both sides were opened in December 1971, and completed in July 1972.[10] Consequently, an agreement was signed on 22 July 1972 by Portugal and the European Communities.[11] A "Joint Committee" was set up to administer this Agreement. [12] This committee would later play an important role in the negotiations on pre-accession aid.[13]

A new page was turned when the dictatorship regime fell in April 1974. The new Portuguese authorities asked the European Communities for a new relationship.[14] But following the fall of the dictatorship, the transition to democracy was turbulent (Royo & Manuel, 2003). Meanwhile, in the turbulent period following the fall of the dictatorship and in view of the difficult political and economic situation, the Communities granted Portugal special emergency financial aid. On 11 June 1975, the European Commission presented a communication to the Council "on action to be taken for Portugal's benefit", proposing that this State should be granted special financial aid.[15] And on this basis, on 7 October 1975, the Council of the European Communities decided to grant Portugal special emergency financial assistance totalling 150 000 000 units of account in the form of loans from the European Investment Bank for investment projects. These loans would be subsidised by a 3 percent interest rate from the Community budget, representing 30 million units of account[16] Therefore, to enable Portugal to overcome a period of economic difficulty, the European Investment Bank was to finance these projects.[17]

In addition, the negotiations for the conclusion of an Additional Protocol and the Financial Protocol were completed on 9 June 1976.[18] Thus, an Additional Protocol to the 1972 Agreement was signed, as well as the Finance Protocol of 20 September 1976.[19] Within this framework of financial cooperation, the Economic European Community would participate in financing projects designed to contribute to the economic and social development of Portugal, namely to increase productivity and to diversify the Portuguese economy, promoting industrialisation and the modernisation of agriculture.[20] Thus, an amount of up to 200 million European units of account (EUA) was able to be committed in the form of European Investment Bank loans from its own resources, including 150 million EUA with an interest rate subsidy of 3 percent p.a., although the cost for the Community to finance these subsidies could not exceed 30 million EUA.[21]

In the second half of the 1970s, Greece, Portugal and Spain asked to be admitted to the European Communities.[22] More specifically, on 28 March 1977, Portugal requested membership of the European Communities.[23] On 19 May 1978, the European Commission transmitted to the Council its favourable opinion on Portugal's application for membership.[24] This European Institution had formerly considered that candidate countries, namely Greece, Spain and Portugal, could receive financial assistance.[25] The official negotiations for Portugal's accession to the European Communities started in October 1978.[26] Following the Commission's position, the Council also considered that the Community could examine additional measures with the Portuguese Government in order to ease Portugal's integration into the Community.[27] At that time, the disparity between Portugal's level of development and that of Community countries suggested that several models of development should be envisaged within the EEC.[28] On this basis, the Portuguese Government requested special Community aid, namely to support small and medium-sized industrial and artisanal enterprises.[29] The purpose of this financial support would be different to the previous ones. In fact, the main objective was to prepare the Portuguese economy for integration into the Community economy.

2 The SMIE Agenda

Concerning Portugal's request, in September 1979, the European Commission submitted a proposal to the Council introducing special aid for small and medium-sized industrial enterprises in Portugal.[30] With the goal of accession in mind, both the Portuguese authorities and the Community officials converged on the need to promote adjustment to Portugal's economic structures and improve the basic conditions needed for growth in employment. The Portuguese Government focused its attention on small and medium-sized industrial enterprises because, according to OECD criterion, at the end of the 1970s about 15 000 of these enterprises existed in Portugal, responsible for more than 60 percent of industrial employment and contributing to more than 50 percent of industry's gross added value. Nonetheless, they were very weak in the export sector and so, in January 1979, the Portuguese Government requested special Community aid to create a programme to exclusively support the development of small and medium-sized industrial and artisanal enterprises. More precisely, the request was submitted through the "Joint Committee" that was established by the Agreement between the European Economic Community and Portugal, in 1972.[31]

The Portuguese Government presented the following estimates: for a period of three years, the programme should cost about 57 million and the Community should contribute about 47 million. The idea was to establish a special Fund to finance the operations managed by the Institute for Support for Small and Medium-Sized Enterprises (*Instituto de Apoio às Pequenas e Médias Empresas* – IAPMEI), that was a single public body.

Therefore, the European Commission presented a proposal to introduce special aid for small and medium-sized industrial enterprises, hereinafter referred to as SMIE.[32] Four types of operations could benefit from the special Community aid, i.e.: training operations to improve SMIE; operations to improve the quality of the services available to SMIE; operations to restructure, modernise and develop the activities of SMIE; advance training periods abroad for experts responsible for implementing the outline programme and its various operations. Each of these types of operations could involve sub-categories.

The Economic and Social Committee expressed its favourable opinion in November 1979, acknowledging "the principle that special aid should be granted to facilitate the entry of Portugal into the Community".[33] Nevertheless, this Community advisory body emphasised what seems controversial, namely that "the granting of aid to

Portugal cannot be regarded as a precedent for giving Community aid to other applicant countries".[34]

Following the reports issued by the committees,[35] in March 1980, the European Parliament adopted a resolution "on the proposal from the European Communities Commission to the Council, regarding a Decision to introduce special aid for small and medium-sized industrial enterprises in Portugal".[36] Despite approving the Commission's proposal and agreeing on the importance of SMIE within the Portuguese economy, the European Parliament also approved some amendments.[37] The Commission accepted the Parliament's amendment proposals and submitted these amendments to the Council.[38] Thus, it was accepted that the Community should grant Portugal special aid in the amount of 40 million EUA to help SMIE to progressively adjust to the consequences of accession. However, given that the difficulties of the Portuguese economy were not limited to SMIE and that other sectors needed to be modernised, the special aid for SMIE was replaced by a more comprehensive programme, *i.e.* pre-accession aid for Portugal.

3 The adoption of the pre-accession aid Agreement

Although the Portuguese Government requested special Community aid for small and medium-sized industrial enterprises in 1979, preference was given to organising general financial aid during the year of 1980. Thus, it was decided by both Parties to negotiate an Agreement in order to grant financial aid not only for small and medium-sized industrial enterprises, but also to other sectors of Portugal's economy.[39] Portuguese authorities were concerned with its vulnerable economy, particularly in view of accession to the Communities. Simultaneously, the European Communities were looking for successful expansion in both political and economic terms. Indeed, it emphasised the connection between political and economic success for expansion. In essence, there was a convergence of views regarding the need to prepare the Portuguese economy for smooth integration into the Communities' economy.[40]

On 7 October 1980 the European Economic Community (EEC) decided to agree to the Portuguese Republic's request for financial aid to prepare and facilitate the harmonious integration of the Portuguese economy into the Community economy.[41] A rapid succession of events followed. On 17 November of the same year the delegations from the EEC and the Portuguese Republic agreed on the terms and detailed arrangements for the implementation of pre-accession aid for

Portugal.[42] On 19 November the Commission for the European Communities transmitted the draft Agreement to the Council in order to implement pre-accession aid for Portugal, indicating that this could enter into force on 1 January 1981.[43]

On 3 December 1980, the Agreement was signed in the form of letters exchanged between the European Economic Community and the Portuguese Republic concerning the implementation of pre-accession aid for Portugal. On the one hand, the Council of the European Communities approved this Agreement on behalf of the European Economic Community,[44] and on the other hand, the Portuguese Government also approved this Agreement.[45] The Agreement, previously approved by the European Parliament, was designed to grant financial aid to Portugal prior to accession.[46] After the instruments of notification were exchanged, the Agreement entered into force on 1 January 1981.[47] Portugal was the first State to benefit from pre-accession financial aid (Cunha, 2019).

4 The pre-accession aid regime

The text of the Agreement for pre-accession aid for Portugal was attached to Council Regulation (EEC) No. 3323/80 of 18-12-1980.[48] In the same way, for the Portuguese legal order, the text was attached to Decree No. 143-A/80, of 26-12-1980.[49] Subsequently, other legislative acts were adopted by both Parties.

What was the main goal of the pre-accession aid? It was the participation of the European Economic Community in the financing of specific operations undertaken by the Portuguese Government in order to ease the integration of Portugal's economy into the Community.[50] The total amount of pre-accession aid was 275 million European units of account.[51] This sum was allocated as follows: 150 million European units of account in the form of loans from the European Investment Bank, granted from its own resources; and 125 million European units of account in the form of grant aid.[52] As a consequence, there were basically two sources of financing: the European Investment Bank and the budget of the European Communities. However, there were connections between these two sources of financing, whereby, from the amount of 125 million European units of account in the form of grant aid, 25 million were to be applied towards financing the interest rate subsidies of European Investment Bank loans. In other words, the European Communities' budget contributed to reducing the cost of funding the European Investment Bank loans.[53]

It is worth mentioning that at this time the European Investment Bank specialised Community body had already accumulated considerable experience in Portugal and Mediterranean countries, hence the accession aid for Portugal did not present a major technical problem.[54] Thus, the amount of 150 million European units of account was to be "used for financing or contributing to investment projects which, with the objective *inter alia* of encouraging regional development in Portugal, would help to increase productivity and strengthen the Portuguese economy, namely promoting and improving the country's industrial structures, the modernization of its agriculture and fisheries and infrastructure development".[55] The granting of loans had to follow the rules, conditions and procedures laid down by the European Investment Bank's Statute.[56] Such loans could be granted through the intermediary of the Government or by the appropriate Portuguese bodies, on condition that they onlend the amounts to the recipients on the terms decided, in agreement with the European Investment Bank.[57]

In reference to the grant aid, 25 million European units of account were to be used for financing the interest rate subsidies for the European Investment Bank's loans,[58] and the other 100 million European units of account should finance or contribute towards cooperation projects or programmes and technical assistance operations.[59] There was a finance regime distinction between cooperation projects or programmes and technical assistance operations.

Therefore, when selecting the cooperation projects or programmes, special attention would be given to projects or programmes aimed at encouraging: the restructuring, modernization and development of small and medium-sized businesses; improving production and marketing structures in agriculture and fisheries; creating infrastructures aimed at facilitating a more balanced development between regions; and establishing an integrated national vocational training policy based on a network of vocational training centres. However, in these cases, the Community's financial contribution could not exceed 50 percent of their total cost.[60] The selection of technical assistance operations, however, was to give particular attention to operations that would prepare or complement the projects or programmes as well as to more specific operations aimed at facilitating Portugal's adoption of the *acquis communautaire*. And in these cases, the Community's financial contribution might cover the full cost.[61] Be that as may, the financial Community aid might be used to cover costs necessarily incurred in carrying out approved projects, programmes, including expenditure on studies, the services of consulting engineers and technical assistance, or operations, but not to cover administrative, maintenance or operational expenditure.[62]

The requests for European Investment Bank loans or the Commission of the European Communities grants would be submitted by the Portuguese Government or, with the latter's agreement, the other beneficiaries (such as public or private undertakings having their registered place of business or a place of business in Portugal, as well as individuals within the framework of cooperation projects or programmes and technical assistance operations).[63] The Community then proceeded with the examination of eligible projects, programmes and operations.[64] However, the responsibility for the execution, management and maintenance of schemes remained with Portugal and the other beneficiaries.[65] The European Investment Bank could require a provision of guarantee if the beneficiary was an entity other than the Portuguese Government.[66] In any event, the Portuguese authorities were to provide assistance to the Community representatives.[67]

According to the Agreement, the interest and all other payments due to the European Investment Bank were exempt from any national or local taxes or levies, on the one hand, and, in addition, the fiscal and customs regime applicable to contracts awarded for the execution of projects, programmes or operations should be at least as favourable as those applied in respect of other international organizations.[68]

At that time, the currency used in Portugal was the Portuguese Escudo. So, throughout the duration of the loans accorded pursuant to the Agreement for pre-accession aid, Portugal had to undertake to make available to debtors enjoying such loans or to the guarantors of the loans, the foreign currency necessary for the payment of interest, commission and other charges and the repayment of the principal.[69]

A special status was given to the "Joint Committee" referred to in the Agreement between the European Economic Committee and the Portuguese Republic signed on 22 July 1972.[70] Indeed, the implementation of the pre-accession aid might be examined by this "Joint Committee".[71] Last but not least, the financial accession aid was to cover the period from 1 January 1981 until the date when the Treaty governing Portugal's accession came into force. In this regard, it was specified that no financial commitment might be made after the date of accession.[72] This emphasised the characteristic of this being pre-accession aid. Nevertheless, due to various delays, there were projects which were executed after Portugal joined the European Communities, *i.e.* after January 1986.[73]

5 Financial pre-accession aid implementation

During 1981, the Portuguese authorities started to present funding projects to the European Communities (*e.g.* SMIE and road construction). There were also several technical meetings between Portuguese and European Commission officials. Portuguese officials sought to obtain more precise knowledge about how Community procedures and processes worked. And the European Commission officials sought detailed information about the projects submitted by Portugal.[74] At the same time, the Portuguese Government adopted legal, administrative and other measures.[75] Consequently, special legislation was approved that created an autonomous financing fund and provided guarantees by the European Investment Bank loans. Therefore, in compliance with the pre-accession agreement, the Portuguese Government laid down specific tax rules.[76] Thus, tax benefits, exemptions from customs duties and other taxes were approved for contracts concluded for the implementation of projects, programmes and actions financed by the European Economic Community pre-accession aid.[77] Furthermore, it was necessary to adapt the Public Administration by restructuring ministries and services to manage the financial funds coming from the Community (Magone, 2017).

5.1 Pre-accession grant aid implementation

In December 1981, a "financing agreement" was signed in Brussels in connection with pre-accession aid concerning the financing of a 10 million ECU grant programme for the restructuring, modernization and development of small and medium-sized businesses.[78] Indeed, once projects had been approved, "financing agreements" were concluded. A "financing agreement" was considered a technical-legal instrument that regulated how the aid should operate. Normally a "financing agreement" would be divided into two distinct parts: general clauses, which were normally the same for all projects, and particular clauses that related specifically to each project.[79]

In addition to financial aid from the European Community, the public financial aid plan also involved contributions from the Portuguese State Budget (co-financing regime). In this context, the Portuguese Government approved special national legislation with a view to defining the internal channels for the movement of funds intended to finance actions aimed at preparing and facilitating the smooth integration of the Portuguese economy into the Community economy. Thus, in order to simplify the administrative process of the financial execution of actions of common interest and to facilitate its control, the Portuguese Government decided to create an autonomous financing Fund directly dependent on the Minister of Finance and Planning.[80] The official designation of this Portuguese Financing Fund was the "*Fundo de Financiamento das Ações Pré-Adesão Portugal-*

CEE".[81] The operation of this Portuguese Financing Fund was subject to simpler and more flexible rules regarding public accounting and the movement of funds, without prejudice to the indispensable precautions that should surround the application of public money.[82]

This Portuguese Financing Fund was essentially intended to fulfil two tasks: firstly, to administer the funds allocated to Portugal under the agreement between Portugal and the European Economic Community on pre-accession aid granted by the Community to Portugal to finance actions of common interest aimed at facilitating the smooth integration of the Portuguese economy into the Community, and secondly, to provide financial support for the implementation of cooperation and technical assistance projects and programmes which were able to apply for funding within the framework of that aid.[83] This Portuguese Financing Fund was managed by an Administrative Board, but the bureaucratic and administrative support was provided by the General Directorate of the Treasury (Ministry of Finance and Planning).[84]

It was considered that the Portuguese Financing Fund should also act as the "authorizing officer" (*payeur délégué*) in order to pay in national currency (Portuguese escudos at that time) aid to project beneficiaries.[85] So, in accordance with the Convention signed on 17-09-1982 between Portugal and the European Economic Community, the Portuguese Financing Fund also acted as the "authorizing officer" of the Commission of the European Communities.[86] The Portuguese Financing Fund effectively paid the sums corresponding to Community aid, as well as the sums from the Portuguese State Budget to finance the national contribution for each of the projects.[87] In practice, the Fund began its operations in December 1982.[88]

5.2 The European Investment Bank's loans

Meanwhile, other operations took place through the European Investment Bank, namely loans to Portuguese banks to finance investments by Portuguese enterprises. In these cases, the Portuguese banks acted as financial intermediaries, because the final destination of the funding was normally small and medium-sized enterprise projects. In this context, it is important to highlight the importance of the European Investment Bank's action in a scenario of difficult access to credit. For instance, in order to finance small and medium-sized enterprises, the Banco de Fomento Nacional and the Caixa Geral de Depósitos obtained loans from the European Investment Bank. Thus, under the pre-accession aid agreement between the Portuguese Government and the European Economic Community of December 1980, the European Investment Bank granted to the Banco de

Fomento Nacional a loan of 30 million European units of account to finance small and medium-scale ventures in the industrial and tourism sectors.[89] The Portuguese Government guaranteed this European Investment Bank loan.[90] In addition, it assured the Banco de Fomento Nacional of exchange rate risk coverage.[91] Thereafter, the European Investment Bank also granted the *Caixa Geral de Depósitos* a loan of 20 ECUs to finance small and medium-sized investment projects in the industrial and tourism sectors.[92] The Portuguese Government also guaranteed this European Investment Bank loan.[93] In addition, it assured the *Caixa Geral de Depósitos* of exchange rate risk coverage.[94] Besides these loans granted to Portuguese banks to finance small and medium-sized enterprises, the European Investment Bank also granted direct loans to large Portuguese firms. For instance, under the pre-accession aid agreement, the European Investment Bank granted *EDP – Eletricidade de Portugal, E. P.* (at that time, a Portuguese electricity public corporation), a loan of up to 35 million ECUs, with a loan term of 17 years, to finance the construction of the Sines thermal power station.[95] The Portuguese Government guaranteed this European Investment Bank loan.[96] Thereafter, the European Investment Bank granted *ANA – Aeroportos e Navegação Aérea, E.P.* (at that time, a Portuguese public corporation in the field of airports) a loan of up to 35 million ECUs, with a loan term of 20 years, for financing projects to develop airports in Porto and Faro, in the north and south of Portugal respectively.[97]

5.3 The extension of pre-accession financial aid

On 21 September 1982, the Portuguese Government requested an extension of pre-accession aid, namely through the European Investment Bank's funding operations.[98] In effect, according to Portuguese authorities, until September 1982, almost 60 percent of the credits granted under the pre-accession financial aid had been allocated, nevertheless it was essential for Portugal's development to maintain the investment schedule and to implement new projects during 1983.[99] This request was very well received by the European Commission that considered, in general terms, the Community's response would be favourable, emphasizing that "the Community should continue to play an important role in Portugal's development".[100] Consequently the European Commission proposed that the Council of the European Communities agreed to the "principle of extending financial cooperation with Portugal" and, in this context, requested the European Investment Bank to make available to Portugal for 1983 loans from its own resources.[101] Based on the recommendation from the Council of the European Communities, the

European Investment Banks' Governors decided to authorise an extension of pre-accession financial aid for Portugal.[102]

Subsequently, the European Investment Bank granted several loans not only to the Portuguese Government[103] but also to large Portuguese firms and to Portuguese banks in order to finance small and medium sized enterprises. For instance, the European Investment Bank granted the *Caixa Geral de Depósitos* another loan of 20 000 000 ECU, with a loan term of 12 years, aimed at financing the initiatives of small and medium-sized industrial and tourism enterprises.[104] The Portuguese Government guaranteed this European Investment Bank loan.[105] In addition, it assured the *Caixa Geral de Depósitos* of exchange rate risk coverage.[106] The financing of 10 million ECU granted by the European Investment Bank to the *Sociedade Portuguesa de Investimentos* was another example.[107] The Portuguese Government guaranteed this European Investment Bank loan.[108] In addition, it assured the *Sociedade Portuguesa de Investimentos* of exchange rate risk coverage.[109]

Before this, a loan of 5 000 000 000 ECU had already been negotiated between the *Sociedade Portuguesa de Investimentos* and the European Investment Bank for the financing of projects in the industrial and tourism sectors to be carried out by small and medium-sized enterprises, with the Portuguese Government guaranteeing exchange rate risk coverage.[110] A loan of 5 000 000 ECU was also granted by the European Investment Bank to LOCAPOR (a leasing firm of *Caixa Geral de Depósitos* financial group) to finance small and medium-sized initiatives in the industrial sector that could contribute to increasing the productivity of the Portuguese economy or reducing energy consumption.[111] This loan was guaranteed by *Caixa Geral de Depósitos*, with the exchange rate risk being assured by the Portuguese Government.[112] The Autonomous Region of the Azores was also authorised to contract a loan from the European Investment Bank for a sum of 15 million ECU.[113] In addition, one basis of the extension of the pre-accession, the European Investment Bank granted *EDP – Eletricidade de Portugal, E. P.*,[114] another loan of 25 000 000 ECU, with a loan term of 20 years, to finance the Sines thermal power station.[115]

6 Specific financial aid for improving agricultural and fisheries structures

Other specific aid was designed for the period before Portugal joined the European Communities. As a matter of fact, it was found that improvements were needed in its agricultural and fisheries structures. Despite its low productivity, agriculture employed more than 30 percent of the Portuguese active population and the trade balance of the agricultural products sector was in deficit.[116] The situation in the fisheries sector was also worrying. There was a need to modernize the fishing fleet and the processing industries and to improve market organization.[117]

Following a proposal from the European Commission, on 13 March 1984 the Council of the European Communities decided to grant specific financial aid to Portugal to improve its agricultural and fisheries structures. The main goal was to facilitate the application of the common agricultural and fisheries policies.[118] On 13 April 1984 the delegations of both Parties met in Brussels, where they agreed on the terms and detailed arrangements for implementing this financial aid.[119] In June 1984 the European Commission submitted to the Council of the European Communities an Agreement proposal in the form of an exchange of letters between the European Economic Community and the Portuguese Republic, concerning the implementation of specific financial aid for improving agricultural and fisheries structures in Portugal.[120]

The text of the Agreement concerning the implementation of specific financial aid for improving agricultural and fisheries structures was attached to Council Regulation (EEC) No. 3598/84 of 18-12-1984.[121] In the same way, for the Portuguese legal order, the text was attached to Decree No. 87/84, of 31-12-1984.[122] Subsequently, other legislative acts were adopted by both Parties.

7 Specific agriculture and fisheries regime

The total amount of this specific financial aid for improving agricultural and fisheries structures was 50 million ECU, but the aid to the fisheries sector could not exceed the sum of 500 000 ECU.[123] This specific aid covered the following operations: advisory services, infrastructures, veterinary work and means of operation in that field, statistical organization, development of a spirit of association among agricultural producers and others for the purposes of marketing agricultural products, the establishment of production organizations in the fisheries sector, research, and the training of administrative staff.[124] The beneficiaries of this specific aid were the Portuguese Government and, with the government's agreement, public or private undertakings with a registered place of business or a place of business in Portugal, as well as individuals within the framework of cooperation projects or programmes and technical assistance operations.[125]

The beneficiaries were to submit their requests for aid to the Commission of the European Communities. Furthermore, the examination of project eligibility, programmes or operations, was to be carried out by the Community with a view to preparing Portugal for accession taking into consideration both Parties' interests and with due account being taken in the selection of the projects, and the objectives of coherence within an enlarged Community.[126] The execution, management and maintenance of schemes which were the subject of financing under this Agreement had to be the responsibility of Portugal or of the other beneficiaries.[127]

Once again, a special status was given to the "Joint Committee" referring to the Agreement between the European Economic Committee and the Portuguese Republic signed on 22 July 1972.[128] In fact, the implementation of the pre-accession aid could be examined by this "Joint Committee".[129] This financial aid covered the period from 1 January 1985 until the date when the Treaty governing Portugal's accession came into force. In this regard, it was also specified that no financial commitment should be made after the date of accession.[130] As in the pre-accession Agreement, this specific Agreement for improving agricultural and fisheries structures also emphasised the characteristic of it being pre-accession aid, but in reality there were projects which were not implemented until after the date of Portugal's accession to the Communities, *i.e.* January 1986.[131] Lastly, in similarity with the aid provided for in the pre-accession agreement of December 1980, the aid provided for in the December 1984 agreement was also managed by the Portugal-EEC Pre-Accession Actions Financing Fund.[132]

8 Overview assessment of the implementation of the pre-accession aid plan (1980 and 1984 Agreements)

It seems important to emphasize that European funding for Portugal started even before accession (Cunha, 2017). In order to prepare the Portuguese economy for the impact of accession, the Portuguese authorities sought to make the best use of pre-accession aid and its extension, namely to finance the modernisation and restructuring of SMIE, to improve vocational training, to develop the communications infrastructure network, and to reduce the costs of energy dependency.

According to the 1993 activity report of the Portuguese Financing Fund,[133] with respect to the first pre-accession agreement, *i.e.* the 1980 agreement, the European Economic Community contribution was thus applied to various sectors of the Portuguese economy, namely: ECU 18.35 million in the agricultural sector with a view to improving agricultural production conditions in the country; ECU 0.82 million in the fisheries sector, with the aim of better exploitation of natural resources; 10 MECU in a support programme for small and medium-sized industrial enterprises; 15.38 MECU for infrastructure projects at the regional level, including the autonomous regions; 15.15 MECU for the establishment of 10 vocational training centres, spread throughout the country; ECU 5.05 million for the construction of 8 secondary schools, in various parts of the country; ECU 4.67 million for an industrial estates project; ECU 30 million for road construction; ECU 0.06 million for a project to establish a laboratory for chemical and biochemical analysis; ECU 0.4 million for a technical assistance programme for the introduction of VAT in Portugal; and ECU 0.22 million for a low-income housing project.[134]

And, under the second pre-accession agreement *i.e.* the 1984 agreement, the Community contribution was mainly applied towards the agricultural sector (ECU 49.5 million), the aim being to improve, develop and modernize production structures in a number of loss-making sectors, including: ECU 17.1, in meat production; ECU 6.4 million, in wine production; ECU 7.2 million in vegetable, fruit and forestry production; ECU 7.2 million for the production of agri-food products, particularly milk and milk products; ECU 1.0 million for rice production; ECU 4.2 million for the development of research; ECU 3.8 million in the field of statistical organization; ECU 2.6 million for the extension and modernisation of Supply Markets. Finally, ECU 0.5 million was allocated to the fisheries sector in order to set up production organizations in the fisheries sector.[135]

According to the aforementioned 1993 Portuguese Financing Fund report, pre-accession aid under the two agreements (1981 and 1984) was spread throughout the country, including the Autonomous Regions. Thus, the Autonomous Region of Madeira was allocated a total of ECU 4.4 million for investments in the region and the Autonomous Region of the Azores was allocated a total of ECU 4.4 million also for investments in the region.[136] A total of 74 financing agreements were signed and supplementary credits granted. More precisely, 29 conventions with regard to the first agreement (1981) and 45 conventions regarding the second agreement (1984).[137]

Although the funding was pre-accession, the fact was that there were several delays, both in the approval and the implementation of the projects. Therefore, in the first half of the 1990s, there were still projects underway. In any event, the Administrative Board of the

Portugal-EEC Pre-Accession Actions Financing Fund expected to complete virtually all programmes/projects during 1994, with the exception of a few.[138] Finally, the Fund was abolished in 1994 and its attributions and competences were transferred to the Directorate General of the Treasury, until the remaining residual situations were effectively extinguished.[139]

Finally, the successive loans granted by the European Investment Bank under the pre-accession aid scheme made it possible to finance businesses, particularly SMIE, and projects of importance to Portugal's economic development.[140]

9 Final remarks

The principle that special aid should be granted to facilitate Portugal's entry into the Community had already been recognised.[141] However, pre-accession financial aid was not prepared and designed all at once. For instance, special aid for SMIEs was sought but then it was realised that a more comprehensive financial aid programme was needed and so the overall pre-accession aid programme was born. However, even this was not enough. An extension of pre-accession aid had to be proposed, as well as the creation of specific financial aid for the agricultural and fisheries sectors. Even admitting that it was not the financial aid that Portugal needed at the time, what is certain is that it was an important step towards financing the country's reconversion and modernisation. At the same time, officials from the Portuguese and Community public administrations exchanged experiences and improved the implementation of pre-accession aid. It was therefore the result of a process in which both parties – Portugal and the Communities – created new measures and improved existing instruments. After all, it was a dynamic and ongoing process.

Despite criticisms, particularly with regard to delays in the presentation, approval and implementation of projects, what is certain is that pre-accession aid proved to be a valuable element for both Portugal and the Communities. For the former, because it allowed the financing of important projects for economic and social development (e.g. infrastructures, equipment, companies, professional training), as well as the restructuring of public administration for the management of European funds. For the Communities (nowadays the European Union), because, firstly, it allowed them to successfully expand to countries with different experiences and economic and social structures and, furthermore, it certainly provided them with an experience that would be useful to them at the time of the major accession of the

Eastern and Mediterranean countries. Ultimately, it is the success of integration that matters.

Notes

1   Letter on behalf of the Council of the European Communities to the Portuguese Government (OJ L 349 of 23-12-1980).
2   Article 1 Annex 1 Council Regulation (EEC) No. 3323 of 18 December 1980 (OJ L 349 of 23-12-1980).
3   European Parliament Working Documents (Doc. 1-706/79, of 11-02-1980).
4   OJ L 302 of 15-11-1985.
5   Resolution of the National Assembly, Government Diary No. 96, Series I of 25-04-1960.
6   Commission of the European Communities, Information Directorate-General, Relations between the European Community and Portugal, Information No. 133/76.
7   OJ L 73 of 20-03-1972.
8   Commission of the European Communities, Information Directorate-General, Relations between the European Community and Portugal, Information No. 133/76.
9   *Ibid.*
10 *Ibid.*
11 OJ L 301 of 31-12-1972.
12 Article 32 of the Agreement between the European Economic Community and the Portuguese Republic (OJ L 301 of 31-12-1972).
13 See below.
14 Commission of the European Communities, Information Directorate-General, Relations between the European Community and Portugal, Information No. 133/76.
15 Bull. EC 6-1975, point 2338.
16 Bull. EC 10-1975, point 2333.
17 The EIB, 1958–2008, European Investment Bank, 2008, pp. 175-195.
18 COM (76) 349 final.
19 OJ L 274 of 29-09-1978.
20 Articles 1 and 2 of the Finance Protocol.
21 Article 2 of the Finance Protocol.
22 COM (78) 120 final.
23 COM (78) 220.
24 *Ibid.*
25 COM (78) 120 final.
26 COM (78) 489 final.
27 COM (79) 442 final.
28 European Parliament Working Documents (Doc. 1-706/79, of 11-02-1980).
29 *Ibid.*

30   COM (79) 442 final.
31   See above.
32   OJ C 257 of 11-10-1979.
33   OJ C of 24-03-1980.
34   *Ibid.*
35   European Parliament, Working Documents 1979–1980, Document I-706/79, of 11-02-1980.
36   OJ C of 08-04-1980.
37   *Ibid.*
38   COM (80) 278 final.
39   European Parliament, Working Documents 1980–1981, Document I-683/80, of 15-12-1980.
40   *Ibid.*
41   OJ C 319 of 06-12-1980.
42   *Ibid.*
43   COM (80) 776 final.
44   Council Regulation (EEC) No. 3323/80 of 18-12-1980.
45   Decree-law No. 143-A/80, of 26-12-1980.
46   OJ C 346 of 31.12.1980.
47   OJ L 367 of 31.12.1980.
48   OJ L 349 of 23.12.1980.
49   Republic Diary No. 297/1980, Series I of 26-12-1980.
50   Article 1 of the Agreement for pre-accession aid.
51   The value of the European unit of account was determined in Annex II to Council Regulation (EEC) No. 3323/80 of 18-12-1980.
52   Article 2 of the Agreement for pre-accession aid.
53   Articles 2 and 4 of the Agreement for pre-accession aid.
54   The EIB, 1958–2008, European Investment Bank, 2008, pp. 175–195.
55   Article 3 of the Agreement for pre-accession aid.
56   Protocol on the Statute of the European Investment Bank.
57   Article 3 of the Agreement for pre-accession aid.
58   See above.
59   Article 4 of the Agreement of pre-accession aid.
60   Articles 5 and 7 of the Agreement for pre-accession aid.
61   Articles 3, 4, 5, 6 and 7 of the Agreement for pre-accession aid.
62   Article 8 of the Agreement for pre-accession aid.
63   Articles 10 and 11 of the Agreement for pre-accession aid.
64   Article 11 of the Agreement for pre-accession.
65   Articles 10 and 12 of the Agreement for pre-accession aid.
66   Article 16 of the Agreement for pre-accession aid.
67   Article 18 of the Agreement for pre-accession aid.
68   Articles 14 and 15 of the Agreement for pre-accession aid.
69   Article 17 of the Agreement for pre-accession aid.
70   See above.
71   Article 19 of the Agreement for pre-accession aid.
72   Article 2 of the Agreement for pre-accession aid.

73 See below.
74 Secretariado para a Integração Europeia, Plano de Ajuda de Pré-Adesão, Ponto de situação, 09-1982.
75 *E.g.* Law No. 11/81, of 21-07-1981.
76 Decree-law No. 491/82, of 31-12-1981.
77 *Ibid.*
78 Commission of the European Communities, Press-release, of 16-12-1981.
79 Secretariado para a Integração Europeia, Plano de Ajuda de Pré-Adesão, Ponto de situação, 09-1982.
80 Decree-law No. 72/81, of 07-04-1981.
81 *Ibid.*
82 *Ibid.*
83 *Ibid.*
84 *Ibid.*
85 Portuguese Order No. 18/82, of 12-03-1982 (Official Gazette No. 76/1982, Series II of 01-04-1982).
86 Administrative Board of the Portugal-EEC Pre-Accession Actions Financing Fund, activity report 1982–1983.
87 *Ibid.*
88 *Ibid.*
89 Resolution of the Council of Ministers No. 256/81, of 15-12-1981.
90 *Ibid.*
91 Decree-law No. 338/82, of 20-08-1982.
92 Resolution of the Council of Ministers No. 126/82, of 06-08-1982.
93 *Ibid.*
94 Decree-law No. 413/82, of 10-07-1982.
95 Resolution of the Council of Ministers No. 106/1982, of 01-07-1982.
96 *Ibid.*
97 Resolution of the Council of Ministers of 08-11-1983(Official Gazette No. 266/1983, Series II of 18-11-1983).
98 COM (82) 845.
99 *Ibid.*
100 *Ibid.*
101 *Ibid.*
102 European Investment Bank, annual report 1983, of 05-1984.
103 Law No. 35/84, of 21-12-1984.
104 Resolution of the Council of Ministers of 09-12-1983 (Official Gazette No. 286/1983, Series II of 14-12-1983).
105 *Ibid.*
106 Decree-law No. 206/84, of 25-06-1984.
107 Resolution of the Council of Ministers No. 25/84, of 14-04-1984.
108 *Ibid.*
109 Decree-law No. 155/84, of 16-05-1984.
110 Decree-law No. 72/83, of 07-02-1983.

111 Resolution of the Council of Ministers of 31-05-1984 (Official Gazette No. 135/1984, Series II of 11-06-1984).
112 Decree-law No. 249/84, of 23-07-1984.
113 Law No. 24/84, of 28-06-1984.
114 See above.
115 Resolution of the Council of Ministers of 09-12-1983 (Official Gazette No. 286/1983, Series II of 14-12-1983).
116 European Parliament, Working Documents 1984–1985, Document 2-805/84, of 26-10-1984.
117 *Ibid.*
118 COM (84) 297 final.
119 *Ibid.*
120 *Ibid.*
121 OJ L 333 of 21-12-1980.
122 Official Gazette No. 301/1984, Series I of 31-12-1984.
123 Articles 1 and 2 of the Agreement for the specific aid.
124 Article 3 of the Agreement for the specific aid.
125 Article 8 of the Agreement for the specific aid.
126 Article 9 of the Agreement for the specific aid.
127 Article 9 of the Agreement for the specific aid.
128 See above.
129 Article 14 of the Agreement for the specific aid.
130 Article 2 of the Agreement for the specific aid.
131 See below.
132 Decree-law No. 72/81, of 07-04-1981.
133 Administrative Board of the Portugal-EEC Pre-Accession Actions Financing Fund, activity report 1993.
134 *Ibid.*
135 *Ibid.*
136 *Ibid.*
137 *Ibid.*
138 *Ibid.*
139 Decree-law No. 30/94, of 05-02-1994.
140 See above.
141 See above.

References

Amaral, J. F. 2006: *O impacto económico da integração de Portugal na Europa*. Nação e Defesa, 115(3), 113–128.
Chaves, M. M. 2012: *As negociações de adesão de Portugal à Comunidade Económica Europeia – C.E.E. – 1977/1985*. Lisboa: Universidade Católica Portuguesa.
Cunha, A. 2012: *O alargamento Ibérico da Comunidade Económica Europeia: A experiência Portuguesa*. Lisboa: Faculdade de Ciências Sociais e Humanas – Universidade Nova de Lisboa.

Cunha, A. 2017: Nota introdutória. A face visível da Europa. Os fundos euro-peus em Portugal. *Relações Internacionais*, 53, 5–9.

Cunha, A. 2019: A welcome incentive: Pre-accession aid to Portugal within the context of the Iberian enlargement. *Journal of European Integration History*, 25(2), 207–223.

Dauderstädt, M. 1986: The EC's Pre-accession aid to Portugal: A critical look. *Intereconomics*, 21(2), 94–100.

Dauderstädt, M. 1987: The EC's Pre-accession aid to Portugal. A First appraisal. *Estudos da Economia*, 4, 397–417.

Magone, J. M. 2017: A governança dos Fundos Estruturais em Portugal. Um caso de europeização superficial. Relações Internacionais, 53, 55–69.

Rollo, M. F. 2015: *Diplomacia europeia: desígnios e meios da integração europeia de Portugal (1945–1986).* Esboços: Histórias em contextos globais 21, 65.

Royo, S. and Manuel, P. C. 2003: Some Lessons from the Fifteenth Anniversary of the Accession of Portugal and Spain to the European Union. *South European Society and Politics*, 8 (1–2), 1–30.

Vayssière, B. 2009: L'élargissement de 2004 au regard des précédents espagnol et portugais: un jeu de miroirs?. *Revue européenne d'histoire*, 2009, 16(4), 477–497.

5

The IMF in Portugal, 2011–2014: An Economic and Political Analysis

Joaquim Ramos Silva

Since the re-democratisation of Portugal in 1974, there have been three assistance programmes supervised by the International Monetary Fund (IMF). As usually expressed, in all cases, the country was on the verge of bankruptcy, and substantial foreign lending, through the support of the international institution that protects world financial stability, was necessary to come in and provide such a rescue. Thereby, the three IMF interventions are often placed together, in a relatively undifferentiated manner, however, in a number of aspects their dissimilarities are far from negligible, particularly between the two first programmes (begun respectively in 1977–78 and 1983), and the third one that lasted from May 2011 to May 2014. This chapter will focus on the last one.

However, before proceeding, it is necessary to consider the Portuguese economy on the threshold of the IMF third intervention, as this is indispensable to fully understanding the core subject of this analysis. In the middle of the twentieth century, it was crystal clear that Portugal, in relation to most other Western European countries, had lagged behind in key areas of its economic and social structure. Only immediately after World War II and up to the early 1970s had Portugal carried out an effective and broad industrialisation process, from heavy industries to light electronics, but its roots remained fragile in many sectors, and the pace of their upgrading was slow. Moreover, during this period, despite significant improvements, Portugal maintained a comparative low level of education and professional training, and consequently, its economy was also characterised by low productivity and incomes. At the same time, although relatively developed, the Portuguese banking system was very much cartelised and protected (Ribeiro et al., 1987), and did not have true international experience; in addition, it had been profoundly weakened by the wave of nationalisations of 1975.

In the period of higher economic growth, 1960–73, in spite of a large deficit in the trade of goods, the current account was in balance (even with surpluses), but mainly due to emigrant remittances and rising revenues from tourism. Any researcher knows that in case of a global shock, these flows can be seriously affected, and put the country's economic path in doubt. From this point of view, the basic problem was that Portugal had not built a strong, competitive and flexible exporting sector able to respond to changes in international demand (Silva, 2019b). A small country in the European context, Portugal preserved many features of a closed economy for several decades in the post-war period, and the beginning of a timid and reluctant strategy of openness only became visible in 1960s and, even so, with ups and downs until the twentieth first century (Silva, 1990; 1999; 2013; 2019b).

After the mid-1970s, a new problem was added to the vulnerabilities just described from the perspective of macroeconomic management. Indeed, the public sector gained considerable weight in this period and a deficit arose in its accounts, and this would be maintained at various levels for decades to come (only in 2019 would a small surplus be noted). It was not only an increase in traditional public spending (such as the salaries of employees, social transfers, interests), but the state also had considerable responsibilities in many firms at various levels: ownership, partnerships, subsidies, etc. Some privatisations carried out, especially after the second half of the 1980s, which reduced the scope of state intervention in the economy, but far from making it irrelevant. Furthermore, up to the new century, public debt remained within acceptable limits,[1] but in the 2000s, it started to rise, first gradually and then with the financial crisis of 2008 it jumped in subsequent years. The ratio of public debt (in gross terms) to GDP reached 111 per cent in 2011 (from 83.6 per cent in 2009), and more than 130 per cent in 2014, one of the highest ratios in the Eurozone.[2]

Of course, during all this time, the Portuguese economy in many aspects had evolved positively, particularly since its European Community membership in 1986; for example, regarding infrastructures (roads, social amenities and others) and the educational system, where historical backwardness had been clearly visible, were substantially improved. However, to complete the macroeconomic picture relevant to our subject, it is important to bear in mind that after half a dozen years of high growth rates just following its membership, the Portuguese economy fell into a declining path throughout most of the 1990s and 2000s (Silva, 2019a: 63), in spite of a spurt at the end of 1990s, and that in the decade before 2011, growth was clearly characterised as being very sluggish. In this last period, and considering the launch of the euro in 1999, there is a vast literature seeking to explain the causality of the quasi-stagnation of the Portuguese economy that sometimes intertwines both subjects (Blanchard, 2007; Andrade and Duarte, 2011; Reis, 2013; Blanchard and Portugal, 2017).

One more point must be added. The main theme of this chapter, the 2011–14 IMF assistance programme in Portugal, as well as other similar programmes in the early 2010s, particularly within the European Union framework, have since that time led to many discussions and controversies among politicians and economists (the case "for" or "against" austerity is probably the best example), both in Portugal and externally, that persisted much later. In 2020–21, the plans to fight the consequences of the Covid-19 pandemic in the EU perhaps gave even more emphasis to that debate (despite the very different contexts and peculiarities). It must be stated bluntly: we do not deny that these issues are important, but in no way do we intend to give a full account of all of them here or even contribute to their discussion. Based on the Portuguese experience of those years, however, an attempt will be made to call attention to certain less explored, or even underestimated, facts and pointers in the literature.

Therefore, before analysing the IMF intervention in 2011–14 in detail, it is necessary to take into account the previous stylised facts about the structure and performance of the Portuguese economy in recent decades. Given this, the present chapter is divided into several sections. In Section 1, I provide a brief overview of the relationship of Portugal with the IMF, from its membership in 1961 up to 2011. In Section 2, I will consider the Memorandum of Understanding (April/May 2011) and the specificities of its programme, without forgetting the economic and political environment in which it arose. In Section 3, I will focus on the implementation and monitoring of the policy guidelines incorporated in the memorandum as well as highlighting certain representative results of its programme and discuss them. Finally, in Section 4, I will take a look at the legacy of this IMF programme from the perspective of the end of the 2010-decade, and stress the need for further research.

1 An overview of the relationship between Portugal and the IMF prior to 2011

Just after its accession to the European Free Trade Association (EFTA), in 1960, Portugal became a member of the IMF in 1961 (29 March). During the rest of the 1960s and in the early 1970s, the country was a regular member fulfilling its quota, and exchange rates were kept stable (differently from close trading partners such as the UK or France, for example, that devalued their currencies in the 1960s). However, major changes occurred after the first oil crisis at the end of 1973 (the price of oil tripled), followed by the Democratic Revolution of 25 of April 1974. These two shocks contributed to a radical shift in the conditions that had prevailed in the first twelve years of IMF membership. Of course, it was not only these two shocks but the whole economic and political environment which was changing, both internationally, as demonstrated by the collapse of the Bretton Woods System in 1971, as well as the fact that, after democratisation, the door became open for Portugal to be an integral part of the European process. Consequently, the Portuguese government would apply to be a member of European Economic Community in 1977.

In the meantime, imported inflation as well as domestic inflation became quite high in relation to the main trading partners of Portugal, and the escudo began to devalue. Due to unrealistic welfare expectations raised by the revolution, the general rise in prices were not considered as a mounting crisis, even less so that there was a need for effective domestic adjustment to it in time, but that turnaround gradually became clear in the years that followed 1974, in particular with the Portuguese accumulated foreign exchange reserves being depleted by the end of 1975 (Lopes, 1996: 242). However, Portugal had, at the time, an important volume of gold reserves, but for obvious reasons it was politically difficult to take a decision on their extensive use to compensate the external deficit, and, even if that had been the case it would not have been enough to respond to the increase in demand for hard currency to pay foreign goods and services generated in the years 1974–76, particularly fuelled by consumption.

Thus, that evolution led to the Portuguese government increasingly considering recourse to the IMF, i.e., beyond the use of unconditional tranches of its quota. Compared to previous decades, and to deal with the new problems (for example, generalised exchange rates instability), it must also be pointed out that the role of IMF had to be "reinvented" in the 1970s (Davies and Woodward, 2014: 295–96), to respond to these cases. As regards the negotiations of the IMF with Portugal over the 1975–85 period, the recent release of internal documents sheds light on this bilateral process (Zorrinho, 2018). After more informal contacts, the first round of relevant negotiations for the first programme began in 1977 and was concluded with a stand-by agreement in May 1978. The main objectives of the programme, particularly as far as the current account was concerned, were reached in 1979. However, with the impact of the so-called "second oil shock" in 1979–80 (the oil price doubled at the end of 1979), the basic macroeconomic situation once again seriously deteriorated, first slowly, but worsened in the following years. Before this, a second round of negotiations with the IMF had become necessary, and in 1983, a new programme was set up. In the immediate aftermath, the second scenario was not very different from that of the first programme: by the end of 1985, the current account was again in balance. In both cases, objectives regarding the level of public accounts were much less successful, and a more balanced budget was far away from being attained.[3]

From the economic policy point of view, it is important to emphasise that the first programme, as well as the second, followed the dominant IMF approach of that period as regards similar cases, i.e., beyond currency devaluation (particularly large in the 1983 programme) and plans to cut public spending, and among other measures, interest rates were increased and credit restrictions imposed, leading to a fall in real wages, an escalation in unemployment, and a rise in prices (Lopes, 1996: 242–43).

After showing the institutional features of Portugal's membership of the IMF, and some data and approaches of the two initial programmes, it is also necessary to undertake an economic interpretation of their results. In short, perhaps among the most significant aspects was the rapid success in stabilising external accounts through currency devaluation although the fundamental macroeconomic disequilibria remained relatively high and unstable. Indeed, even in the external accounts, success did not last, and they soon deteriorated again, with international factors surely needing to be taken into account, but domestic macroeconomic mismanagement, particularly the late awareness of the seriousness of the situation at this level, was decisive in the setting of both programmes (Zorrinho, 2018). Perhaps, more important still in characterising the profile of the Portuguese economy, from 1975 until the late 1980s, it was the only modern period where Portugal's share in the world exports of goods grew significantly (Silva, 2008: 9), which also proves that its competitiveness was essentially based on price rather than on the quality of goods. In addition, it must be pointed out that, despite European Community membership in 1986, the currency devaluation process resulting from the two previous programmes was essentially maintained up to the end of the 1980s.

Be that as may, just after 1986, mainly due to the process of European integration that led to an increase in the inflow of structural funds, foreign direct investment (Silva, 1990), and to major changes in the world oil market (leading to less dependency on the price of this commodity), these had a positive impact on the balance of payments, and a new path in the Portuguese economy became clear, as already underlined above. As regards the size of these changes, and as a conclusion for the period 1975–85, we can cite the words of José da Silva Lopes, certainly the person who, as the Governor of the Bank of Portugal from 1975 to 1980, most closely participated in these programmes (Cardoso, 2018), particularly in the first:

> "While the deterioration of the terms of trade, associated with the first and second oil shocks, caused the loss of around 8 per cent of the purchasing power of the national product, the changes in the opposite direction, caused by the fall in oil and the dollar in 1984–86, brought a gain of about 6 per cent in the same purchasing power."
> (Lopes, 1996: 244)

2 The 2011 Memorandum and its specificities: The Troika (IMF, EC, ECB) and the political context

The third assistance programme of the IMF in Portugal came much later, about 28 years after the beginning of the second, which I have just described in very general terms. The new programme cannot be separated from the European sovereign debt crisis that broke out at the end of 2009, initially very focussed on the Greek case, but gradually affecting other Southern European countries in the Eurozone, and Ireland. Compared to other member states, in the fall of 2010, despite the rapid increase in public debt, Portugal was not yet in a dramatic position given its main macroeconomic indicators,[4] but contagion progressed in the same way. It must be pointed out that, in the first years of the sovereign debt crisis, the EU had no instruments to deal with such a crisis or even a strategy to face the problems related to it. For example, the necessary balance between debtor and creditor countries, an important relationship within the Eurozone as a whole, was not taken into due account, although its necessity was a lesson from previous debt crises (Bayne, 2012). Only in the summer of 2012 an intervention of the European Central Bank to "save the Euro" was clearly decided, and, among other consequences, sovereign bond yields of the most affected member states began to decline (Tooze, 2018). Moreover, seeking for an appropriate solution, the participation of the IMF was considered critical due to its experience in the field of the financial management of major macroeconomic disequilibria, huge debts, and other special needs for international lending in more favourable conditions than those offered by the financial market in the short run.

Therefore, after negotiations in the first months of 2011, the programme took form and was based on a Memorandum of Understanding agreed with the Portuguese government in April and signed in May, to be applied in the subsequent three years (i.e., up to May 2014). Through the agreement Portugal had access to loans up to 78,000 million euros. Differently from the previous cases, in the coordination of this programme, the European Commission (EC) and the European Central Bank (ECB) now accompanied the IMF in what became known as the "Troika". In spite of its importance for funding and to monitor the implementation of the programme, details about the European participation will not be considered, for example as regards the European Financial Stabilisation Mechanism (EFSM, EU) and the European Financial Stability Facility (EFSF, Eurozone). Each member of Troika had to finance one third of the total loan to Portugal.

Once more, the traditional domestic causes were at the origin of the programme (high and systematic public and current account deficits) but also the general context of the Global Financial Crisis that broke out in 2007–08 and developed in the following years, including a deep world recession in 2009. As a consequence of closer integration with Europe and the world economy, the Portuguese economy had become more exposed to external shocks than in the past, which was particularly evident in the case of its integration into the Eurozone. Moreover, from the point of view of the programmes, this last feature made a very large difference from the previous crises of the 1970s and 1980s (where the exchange rate played a pivotal role as referred to above) and new solutions had to be found as means to find a way out of the 2011 crisis.

Before proceeding to the content of the memorandum and its follow-up, the troubled political environment of the period must also be emphasised. In the national elections that occurred in the fall of 2009, the incumbent Socialist Party was the most voted party but lost its majority in parliament, but even so formed the new government, hoping to survive through occasional alliances, i.e., it was in a weak political and institutional position. Furthermore, the Presidency of the Portuguese Republic was not in harmony with the government in office. Before the agreement, as happened with other affected Eurozone countries, there was a discussion as to whether the Portuguese lack of funds could have a solution mainly within the context of the EU resources (under the so-called Programmes of Stability and Growth, PEC in Portuguese). Prior to April 2011 there had been several attempts in that direction by the Portuguese government, and PECs introduced the first adjustment measures such as cutting salaries for public administration employees. However, the situation quickly precipitated, the downgrading of the Portuguese state by credit rating agencies playing an important role in that (Rato, 2020: 5–6; Alexandre et al., 2019: 130–31), and so, at the beginning of April 2011, there was no other choice, except for the aforementioned Troika solution, and the government officially asked for assistance under those terms. At the same time, new elections were scheduled for June, when the Social-Democratic Party (PSD) and the Centre Democratic and Social Party (CDS), both on the Right, won the majority of seats in the parliament, and so formed the new government that, from the Portuguese side, would manage the programme designed by the memorandum. Moreover, both parties had participated, directly or indirectly, in the negotiations that led to the memorandum, and just like the Socialist Party in government, had essentially approved its content.[5]

The memorandum (Portuguese Government, 2011) established a set of measures to be implemented in the following three years involving seven areas: fiscal policy, regulation and supervision of the financial sector; structural budgetary measures; labour market and education; market for goods and services; housing market; framework conditions. Clearly, it is not an objective of this work to provide a detailed analysis of the document and its parts. Due to the interest in understanding the entire process established by the programme and its results, it will focus on the two first areas, as policy priorities. In terms of content, the memorandum was clearly inspired on what became known as the Washington Consensus: fiscal discipline, structural reforms in the main markets (products, labour, housing) in order to promote efficiency and competition, privatisations, more rigorous evaluation and transparency of public policies, flexibility instead of rigid controls, etc. In the case of public policies related to the budget, including structural budgetary measures, the document was more detailed.

3 The implementation of the memorandum:
Results and discussion

The memorandum programme began to be implemented immediately after being signed (17 May 2011), and for its monitoring and evaluation, twelve regular reviews were established between September 2011 and April 2014 (i.e., quarterly) on which the disbursement of the loans was dependent. In general, the media tried to explore the content of each review, but their terms were too generic, and allowed for different interpretations. "The programme is on track, but challenges remain . . . Looking ahead, the Portuguese economy will continue to face headwinds . . . The fiscal deficit target for 2012 remains within reach . . . Further progress on protecting the banking system and ensuring orderly deleveraging has been made . . . Nevertheless, more efforts are needed to clear Portugal's structural reform backlog in the network and sheltered services sectors . . . In sum, Portugal is making good progress toward adjusting its economic imbalances".[6] In any event, the reviews led to some adjustments in the programme, generally small (for details, see Alexandre et al., 2019), but the government proved to be efficient in following many of the memorandum's recommendations (including privatisations that were previously unsuccessful, as it was the case of TAP – the national air transportation company, traditionally in debt) and attaining important objectives, particularly as far as fiscal policy was concerned, such as putting public deficit on a sustained path of reduction, as described below. Moreover, there were no problems with the disbursement of loans.

As stressed before, due to their significance as choices for economic policy, and taking into account the specificity of the Portuguese situation, the two most interesting parts of the programme to analyse here concern fiscal policy (budget, public deficit and debt), and the kind of treatment given or not to the financial and banking system. However, before doing this, it is necessary to raise an initial point on the sequencing of the programme. Indeed, in the face of the largest recession (an accumulated fall in production of around minus 8 per cent of GDP in 2011–13) before the pandemic Covid-19, and a very high unemployment rate (16.2 per cent in 2013, also a historical record in recent decades), among other major consequences, it can be discussed if a more gradualist approach would have produced better and not so costly results.[7] The radical option of the government had perhaps more of a symbolic than effective value, increasing the dramatic side of the political situation (for example, such as the elimination of certain public and religious holidays or announced purposes hard to achieve such as "to go beyond the Troika!"). On the other hand, this facilitated the campaign of its critics and enlarged the leeway of future governments.

Firstly, as regards fiscal policy and particularly the objective of a significant reduction in public deficit, public spending was essentially maintained at a high level and taxation was substantially increased.[8] Indeed, if we consider the year 2010, as a basis, and look at the participation of these indicators in the GDP, public spending went from 51.8 to 51.7 in 2014, and public receipts from 40.6 to 44.6 in 2014 (in considering these numerical values, we must bear in mind that there was a fall in production in the initial years of the programme, and that they do not necessarily correspond to an increase in monetary terms). According to Alexandre et al (2019: 148–9), these trends were however not explicit in the memorandum, which on the contrary created expectations of a budgetary consolidation based more on a reduction in public spending rather than on an increase in taxation. But, the programme cannot only be analysed during the precise period of its implementation, and much of its results could be seen in the following years, as explained below. For example, it must be recognised that, in 2015, the last year of the PSD/CDS government, both spending and taxation were reduced, in relation to the previous year, and the public deficit fell to -4.3 per cent of the GDP (from minus 11.2 per cent in 2010), and this general trend continued up to the end of the decade.

In addition, from the point of view of fiscal policy, as an example of cuts in public spending, the case of investment must be highlighted because it had been important for growth since the 1980s up to 2010, but it substantially shrunk in 2011–14 (as an annual average for the years 2000–9, public investment was 6,401 million euros, and reached 9,478 million in 2010, but fell to only 3,446 million in 2014, and until the end of the 2010s, it maintained values of this latter order, i.e., much less than at the beginning of the twentieth first century). As domestic demand diminished at various levels, this led many firms, particularly small and medium sized ones, to look more at internationalisation and the production of traded goods and services (Brás-dos-Santos and Silva, 2020), instead of the sheltered sectors (where the previous weight of public investment is a good example), as had happened before, and one of the trends that had most contributed to the vulnerability of the Portuguese economy (Silva, 2013).

These points concerning fiscal policy must be emphasised here insofar as the programme essentially put the macroeconomic management of Portugal on a right track, i.e., it was sustained and lasted a relatively long period in very important aspects, and particularly in the reduction of the public deficit. This is particularly obvious if we compare the 2011–14 programme with the stabilisation processes of the 1970s and the 1980s.

Secondly, as regards the point "regulation and supervision of the financial sector", in the first years of the Great Financial Crisis, despite some problems, including bankruptcy (the case of the nationalisation of the Banco Português de Negócios in 2008), there was a benign narrative concerning this sector. However, throughout the 2010s, it proved to be a very unrealistic view, which was also reflected in the IMF 2011–14 programme. Indeed, according to Mateus (2020), Portugal "had one of the largest banking crises among developed countries. The IMF systemic crisis database shows that the 2008–15 banking crisis caused a loss of GDP and a fiscal cost that was only surpassed by Greece in the crisis that started in 2008 and Finland in 1991". Let us see this issue in more in detail.

To begin with, I will refer to a recent study on the Portuguese banking system that involves a survey of risk management professionals regarding the culture of risk in the sector, which concludes concerning its unpreparedness in the following terms:

"The interviews suggest that banking in Portugal was not prepared for the 'regime change' that constituted privatisation, the single currency, and financial liberalisation. Much less were they prepared for the shock after the great financial crisis and the subsequent programme of financial adjustment and intervention of the so-called 'Troika'. Benefiting from a few decades of generous liquidity and easy profits (derived from the amount of credit granted), and accustomed to very little intrusive supervision, Portuguese bankers nurtured a corporate culture that came from the distant ('*Estado Novo*'[9]) and recent (nationalised banks) past, where concerns about risk were absent, and personal (and political) influences predominated, with an authoritarian management style, without tolerating internal disputes." (Braga de Macedo et al., 2020: 261)

Taking into account this characterisation of the banking and financial sector in Portugal in facing the challenges of recent decades, it is now necessary to analyse the question in the light of the 2011–14 IMF programme. It would seem, in a study for the Bruegel Institute, Véron (2016: 18–20) clearly lays out the main points:

"The IMF lack of an assertive approach to the Portuguese financial sector may have resulted from a combination of ideological, political and practical factors. First, the IMF team appears to have displayed an inherent bias linked to the perception of the Portuguese crisis as 'mostly fiscal' and not directly linked to financial sector weakness . . . The reasons for the IMF's reluctance to be assertive during the programme's implementation were similar to those described above with respect to programme design. The IMF staff's attention focused on the public sector, while the role of the banking system as an enabler of public-sector excesses were downplayed . . . As a consequence, *at the time of Portugal's exit from the programme in May 2014, the banking sector remained fragile . . .*" (my italics, JRS)

Indeed, despite its second place in the list of policy measures of the memorandum, and considering the historical proximity of the Great Financial Crisis, in practice, the programme for Portugal was much less focussed on the banking and financial sector. Although the problems were not comparable in their nature and relative size with those of Ireland that had a programme centred on banking and finance (and quickly emerged from the crisis!), the sector in Portugal had serious flaws in its own foundations, and the crisis led to an accumulation of losses and bad loans in the banking system, exacerbating the situation. As such, there were many serious problems to be overcome in the Portuguese banking and financial sector, and some of them appeared during the implementation of the programme. Not only were small banks such as BPN, Banco Privado Português (BPP), liquidated in 2010, and Banco Internacional do Funchal (BANIF) which received an intervention in 2013 allowed by the Troika, and which was later sold to Santander in 2015, affected, but also the larger entities within the system such as: Caixa Geral de Depósitos (CGD), a public bank, Banco Português de Investimento (BPI), and Banco Comercial Português (BCP).

Indeed, the most illustrative case of the Portuguese banking crisis, also the one with the most far-reaching consequences, was without doubt that of the Banco Espírito Santo (BES), or better, the BES group, that significantly collapsed in July 2014, i.e., two months after the "clean" exit of the country from the Troika programme (although BES had been ailing at least in the months beforehand). BES, the origins of which dated back to 1869, was the only existing private bank being restored as such after the wave of nationalisations of 1975, and was a leading bank with close ties to much of the Portuguese economy (Esteves and Jesus, 2018). After the "debacle", BES became Novo Banco and its resolution is still a "hot issue" in Portugal, almost seven years since the initial dismantling decision.

CGD, BCP and BPI were also in trouble, for example they had very risky and disastrous international exposure, particularly in Angola (like BES), but their case was not comparable in size or potential to

BES, and they had to be restructured or downgraded through the cleaning of their balance sheets essentially under the supervision of the ECB. Of course, only a small idea of this entire banking crisis (for details, see Braga de Macedo et al., 2020) can be provided here, which in some cases is far from being concluded at the time of writing (at the beginning of 2021).

Of course, although essential from the economic point of view, including for a sustained recovery from the crisis, in the circumstances just described, it would not be easy to solve the problems of the banking and financial sector in Portugal through an approach within the context of the 2011–14 programme, or even to start it to a considerable extent. According to Véron: "IMF staff interviewees acknowledged that senior private-sector bankers had very high social status in Portugal, and that IMF questioning of the soundness of their institutions would not elicit domestic support. Even ostensibly independent Portuguese individuals, whose opinions the IMF thought reliable, provided views of these banks' situation that with hindsight were overly optimistic." (2016: 19) However, as shown by the Irish and Spanish cases, whose programmes to overcome the crisis were much more focussed on the banking and financial sector, they had much better results, earlier and at lesser costs. Moreover, since the Great Depression (1929–1933), it is well known that the stabilisation of the banking system is a first premise for a sound recovery.

The comparison of these two major policy objectives of the programme, as regards the fiscal policy and the regulation and supervision of the financial sector, shows well the achievements and also the dilemmas of its implementation. In the first case, we may conclude that the period under analysis opened the way to an improvement in fiscal policy, particularly in the following years, which was also reflected in other areas, perhaps first of all in external accounts and to a much lesser degree in economic growth (Silva, 2019a). This is undoubtedly important and must be underlined, after decades of carefree unbalanced budgets, sometimes at a very high level. As far as the financial sector was concerned, in practice, the programme was much more timid and success was not reached in time, although we have to recognise the complexity of the task, and even the lack of awareness of its necessity for a large number of actors in the process, particularly those located in Portugal.

4 Conclusion: The legacy of the programme and further research

The period of the intervention in the early 2010s, bringing together the IMF and EU frameworks, was a new step in the historical relations between Portugal and the IMF. Moreover, it has been very instructive for economic policy purposes, and fruitful lessons can be extracted. A little more than a year after the official end of the programme, following the October national elections of 2015, a new government took office by the end of the year, this time led by the Socialist Party (insofar this party did not have the majority of the seats, such a political solution was made possible through the support of the Communist Party and the Left Bloc in parliament), which lasted four years. From an economic perspective in quantitative terms, this experience has been analysed in Silva (2019a). We may conclude that during 2016–19, following the previous improvements, the main short-term problems that lay at the origin of the 2011 crisis gradually evolved in the right direction, most notably regarding public and external deficits. As mentioned in the introduction, in 2019, the public sector for the first time in more than four decades generated a slight surplus. In addition, the huge public debt decreased slightly up to 2019. Moreover, from the point of view of stability and length, the current account in this period had a much more positive evolution (Silva, 2019a), if compared with what had happened in the preceding decades during which it was one of the weakest links in the Portuguese economy.

This does not mean that in 2016–19 the evolution and state of the Portuguese economy was satisfactory in other critical domains, for example, although the rate of growth became positive and higher than before the crisis, it was still low (and too dependent on the performance of the tourism segment), and the country was far from having been placed on the way towards steady real convergence with more advanced EU partners, a central objective for Portugal since membership. After 2015, public expenses as a per cent of GDP were in a more pronounced decline than current revenues (Silva, 2019a: 67), but as before the reduction of the public deficit was only possible through taxation, particularly indirect taxation. In this period, it would probably have been possible to make a different mix of fiscal policy (on both sides, spending and revenues). For example, due to lower interest rates, and to other factors, such as the reduction in the benefits to the unemployed and similar expenses (there was a large creation of jobs in 2016–19), the level of public investment could have been increased, particularly in the health sector, which in Portugal is mainly public, and where the Covid-19 pandemic revealed large and urgent necessities. It is however true that the reversal of certain expense measures applied during the programme and mainly aimed at the public administration were strongly protested by the parties of the Left, putting political restrictions on such a solution; given this, there was no other alternative, since more public investment would mean more deficit, or at least, making it more difficult to obtain a balance in the public accounts. Therefore, the facts also demonstrate the fragility of the adjustment process, subsequent to the 2011 memorandum: macro-equilibrium was approached in crucial areas, but a short-term perspective prevailed over long-term considerations (surely, requiring structural reforms that have costs but also leading to higher productivity and competitiveness, the true bases of better social conditions). In 2020–21, the Covid-19 pandemic, introduced many uncertainties regarding the future economic path of Portugal, as in other countries, but in any case the third IMF programme and its results remain as a significant experience to be considered.

To sum up, the period under analysis represents a major step in the evolution of the Portuguese economy. As regards the fundamentals of macroeconomic management, the experience demonstrated the importance of looking for a balance between its major determinants, which was far from being the case in most of the preceding decades, including the period after entering into the European Monetary Union in 1999. The practical experience of 1975–85, and later that of the new century, showed that the retreat from this logic of fundamentals has had a price, translated into low or unbalanced growth and macroeconomic instability that tends to be chronic or at least lasting. Benefiting from the shift introduced by the 2011–14 programme, notwithstanding certain flaws in its design and application, the better results of the years 2016–19 show the reverse as they sought to proceed along the same fundamental line in critical respects (Silva, 2019a).

Furthermore, the analysis of the subsequent period corroborates that cultural and political forces are now operating in the right direction, among other key objectives, effectively concerned with the maintenance of public and current deficits within manageable limits, and in reducing the public debt. However, there is still a gap between the significance of this positive evolution based on sound policies, and the degree of their understanding and recognition by the main recipients (in the first place, Portuguese policymakers). As such, it is perhaps too early to share the view of Rato (2020: 124–25): "the importance of good market performance became consensual in Portugal in most political circles. Two different governments, with different bases of support, but both seem to court market performance and investor participation". Indeed, the policy followed in most of the 2010s would enable growth in better conditions as well as dealing with crises (financial or pandemic) in less costly and more effective terms, but it is not sure that these teachings were fully understood and are here to stay. Thus, in order to anchor the foundations of these new beliefs in Portuguese economic policy (in practice and not only in words), we must continue to discuss the experience of 2011–14 in all its aspects, and specifically in those issues that are not yet clearly settled.

Notes

1   In 1997, the year when candidate member states had to meet the criteria of nominal convergence for the European Monetary Union, the only criterion Portugal did not meet was public debt with 62 per cent of GDP (the limit was 60 per cent); however, all the other candidates had, on average, a higher level with 72.1 per cent; Silva, 2002: 92.

2   Figures taken from the IMF (2018: 63); between 2009 and 2011, the same ratio in the Euro Zone went from 79.2 per cent of GDP to 86.6 per cent (the Portuguese net public debt, in per cent, went from 76 per cent in 2009 to 104.8 per cent in 2012, i.e., an increase of 37.9 per cent). Moreover, it must be pointed out that, as far as debt was concerned, public debt was not the only problem, and private debt was also quite high in Portugal. As much of the literature on the period has underlined, between the inception of the euro and the financial crisis of 2007–8, countries like Portugal benefited from low interest rates, in relation to those they had had before, leading to a rise in the level of national debt (data provided by the Bank of Portugal shows that, by the end of 2009, the total national debt, including all sectors, was over 300 per cent of GDP, and continued to increase in the following years). In addition, Portugal was particularly exposed to foreign lenders.

3   The reader interested in the annual changes of rates in Portugal during the 1976–86 period as regards the effective exchange rate, exports and imports of goods and services, and the balance of the current account (in monetary terms and per cent of GDP), can consult Silva, 1992: 227. While the current account balance became slightly negative in 1979, i.e., almost in balance, and positive in 1985, the public accounts deficit in the same years remained quite high (over 5 per cent of GDP in both cases), with only a marginal reduction in relation to previous years; see Mateus, 2006: 116.

4   According to Ali (2012: 426) based on Eurostat, if Portugal "seems similar to Greece, its indebtedness and deficit are minimum . . . at the end of 2010, Portugal had a public debt of 93 per cent less than Greece 142.8 per cent, Italy 119 per cent and Ireland 96 per cent". Furthermore, at the end of 2010, 10-year bond yields of the Portuguese government were close to those of Spain and Italy (around 5–6 per cent), and only in the first months of 2011 did they depart from their Spanish and Italian equi-

valents reaching almost 15 per cent in late 2011. It is however true that between 2009 and 2011, Portugal increased its level of public spending and degree of indebtedness at a higher pace than the Euro Zone average, which was dangerous and risky for a country in long-term quasi-stagnation and characterised by low productivity.

5   This does not mean that there was a broad social consensus on the programme, for example including the trade unions, as had happened in Ireland in the context of incomes policy (Andrade, 2014).

6   I selected these leading passages from the Third Review Mission as being representative EC/ECB/IMF (28 February 2012).

7   For a critique of the shock therapy as an IMF/World Bank approach to reforms, not from the perspective of economic stabilisation but from that of economic development, see Lin, 2009: 52–6.

8   In this point, the data is taken from Silva, 2019a: 67; IMF, 2018; and PORDATA.

9   The self-called name of the dictatorial regime that ruled Portugal from 1926 to 1974, which was used during most of the period.

References

Alexandre, F., Aguiar-Conraria, L. and Bação, P. 2019: *Crise e Castigo e o Dia Seguinte*. Lisbon: Fundação Francisco Manuel dos Santos.

Ali, T. M. 2012: The impact of sovereign debt crisis on the Eurozone countries. *Procedia – Social and Behavioral Sciences* 62, 424–430.

Andrade, J. S. 2014: *A Crise Portuguesa é Anterior à Crise Internacional*. Coimbra: Estudos do GEMF (Grupo de Estudos Monetários e Financeiros), nº 2, Faculty of Economics of the University of Coimbra.

Andrade, J. S. and Duarte, A. 2011: The Fundamentals of the Portuguese Crisis. *Panœconomicus* 2, 195–218.

Bayne, N. 2012: The economic diplomacy of sovereign debt crises: Latin America and the euro-zone compared. *International Journal of Diplomacy and Economy*. 1 (1), 4–18.

Blanchard, O. 2007: Adjustment within the euro, the difficult case of Portugal. *Portuguese Economic Journal*, 6, 1–21.

Blanchard, O. and Portugal, P. 2017: Boom, slump, sudden stops, recovery, and policy options. Portugal and the Euro. *Portuguese Economic Journal*, 16 (3), 149–68.

Braga de Macedo, J., Cassola, N. and Lopes, S. R. 2020: *Por onde vai a Banca em Portugal?* Lisbon: Fundação Francisco Manuel dos Santos.

Brás-dos-Santos, A. and Silva, J. R. 2020: The importance of Latin American Space in the internationalization of Portuguese SMEs. *JANUS NET, e-journal of international relations*, 11 (1), 77–97.

Cardoso, T. 2018: Ensaio sobre o próprio Professor José da Silva Lopes. In A. Mendonça, J. R. Silva, J. M. Brandão de Brito, M. M. Godinho and M. St. Aubyn, (Coord.), *Estudos de Homenagem a José Silva Lopes*. Coimbra: II Série, nº 29, Colecção Económicas, Ed. Almedina, 15–18.

Davies, M. and Woodward, R. 2014: *International Organizations, A Companion.* Cheltenham, UK / Northampton, MA, USA: Edward Elgar.

Esteves, J. P. and Jesus, A. 2018: *Caso BES: O Impacto da Resolução na Economia Portuguesa.* Lisbon: Clube do Autor.

IMF 2018: Managing Public Wealth. *Fiscal Monitor.* Washington: October, IMF.

Lin, J. Y. 2009: *Economic Development and Transition: Thought, Strategy, and Viability.* Cambridge (UK): Cambridge University Press.

Lopes, J. S. 1996: A Economia Portuguesa desde 1960. In A. Barreto (Org.), *A Situação Social em Portugal, 1960–1995.* Lisbon: Vol. 1, Instituto de Ciências Sociais, University of Lisbon, 233–364.

Mateus, A. 2006: *Economia Portuguesa.* Lisbon: 3rd Edition, Editorial Verbo.

Mateus, A. 2020: Conseguirá Portugal escapar à cauda da União Europeia? *Observador.* Last accessed on 10 December: https://observador.pt/especiais/conseguira-portugal-escapar-a-cauda-da-uniao-europeia/

Portuguese Government 2011: *Memorando de Entendimento sobre as Condicionalidades de Política Económica.* Lisbon: Portuguese Government, Portuguese version, 17 May.

Rato, J. M. 2020: *The European Debt Crisis: How Portugal Navigated the post-2008 Financial Crisis.* Cham (Switzerland): Palgrave/Macmillan published by Springer Nature.

Reis, R. 2013: *The Portuguese Slump and Crash and the Euro Crisis.* Cambridge (MA/USA): NBER Working Paper Series, no. 19288.

Ribeiro, J. F., Fernandes, L. G. and Ramos, M. M. C. 1987: Grande indústria, banca e grupos financeiros, 1953–1973. *Análise Social,* XXIII (99), 5, 945–1018.

Silva, J. R. 1990: Luso-American Economic Relations and Portuguese Membership of the European Community. *Portugal: An Atlantic Paradox, Portuguese/US Relations after the EC Enlargement* (Authors of other parts of the book: J. C. de Magalhães and Á. de Vasconcelos), Lisbon: Ed. Institute for Strategic and International Studies, 77–139.

Silva, J. R. 1992: *Política de Preços.* Lisbon: Coleção Estratégia de Exportação, CEDIN/ISEG-PEDIP. Available at (Last accessed 06.12.2020): https://www.researchgate.net/publication/263846291_Politica_de_Precos

Silva, J. R. 1999: The Portuguese economy in the light of Irish experience: A comparison of the 1990s decade. In *Issues on the European Economics,* Lisbon: Proceedings of the 3rd International Workshop on the European Economy, 10–11 December 1999, Lisbon, CEDIN – ISEG/UTL, 221–42. Available at (Accessed 21.11.2020): https://www.researchgate.net/publication/263274752_The_Portuguese_economy_in_the_light_of_Irish_experience_A_comparison_of_the_1990_decade

Silva, J. R. 2002: *Portugal/Brasil: Uma década de expansão das relações económicas, 1992–2002.* Lisbon: Editora Terramar.

Silva, J. R. 2008: *Internationalization Strategies in Iberoamerica: The case of Portuguese trade.* Santiago de Chile: Economic Commission for Latin

America and the Caribbean (ECLAC) – Project Documents collection, United Nations Publication.

Silva, J. R. 2013: A integração mundial da pequena economia e o caso português. In J. C. Lopes, J. Santos, M. St. Aubyn and S. Santos (Eds), *Estudos de Homenagem a João Ferreira do Amaral,* Coimbra: Coleção Económicas, Edições Almedina, 623–59.

Silva, J. R. 2019a: Economia portuguesa após 2015: O triunfo incerto do modelo improvável. In A. C. Q. Barbosa and Cristina Parente (Orgs.), *Gestão, Sociologia e Economia: Diálogos transversais entre Brasil e Portugal,* Curitiba: Editora CRV, 59–81.

Silva, J. R. 2019b: Etapas e Desafios da Estratégia Comercial Portuguesa, 1945–2018. In I. Veiga, C. Rodrigues and A. Cunha (Orgs.), *Economia e História: Estudos em Homenagem ao Professor José Maria Brandão de Brito,* Lisbon: Edições Colibri, 105–117.

Tooze, A. 2018: *Crashed: How a Decade of Financial Crises Changed the World.* New York: Viking.

Véron, N. 2016: *The International Monetary Fund's role in the euro-area crisis: financial sector aspects.* Bruegel: Policy Contribution no. 13.

Zorrinho, J. 2018: *O Processo de Intervenção do FMI em Portugal entre 1975 e 1985.* Lisbon: Master's Dissertation in Political Science and International Relations, Faculty of Social Sciences and Humanities, NOVA University of Lisbon.

6

The Impact of the 2011 Troika Intervention in Portugal on the National Legal Framework

NUNO CUNHA RODRIGUES[1]

The 2008 economic and financial crisis plunged many of the EU Member States into a deep recession, threatening the stability of the Union and the irreversibility of the Eurozone.

This chapter aims to analyse the Troika's intervention in Portugal and how the measures that were implemented due to the MoU signed between the Portuguese Government and the International Monetary Fund, the European Central Bank and the European Commission, changed the Portuguese legal framework.

1 A moment of crisis providing an openness for policy change?

The financial crisis of 2007–2008 derived, to a large extent, from a failure of governments in North America and Europe to appropriately supervise and provide an answer to systemic financial risk, through a lack of more prudent credit policies and practices. The consequent vicious cycle relating sovereign debts and national banking credit conditions revealed not only a crisis of the periphery of the Eurozone but also a failure of the Eurozone as a whole, in particular of its centre and its main actors and mechanisms, to act, promptly and adequately.[2]

The fail of Lehman Brothers and the subprime crisis in the United States were the tipping point to an unprecedented economic recession that affected some of the EU Member States (in particular those who were ironically called PIIGS).[3]

In 2010, following the request from Greece for financial assistance, Portugal observed a significant increase in its interest rates, that were at their highest level since Portugal's entry in the European Union in 1986. At that time, the Portuguese government had minority support in the national parliament which made it difficult to obtain political support from the opposition to pass the parliament budgetary measures that were considered to be necessary.

Accordingly, in March 2010, the opposition parties ended up rejecting the Portuguese Government's package to overcome the crises, which led to the demand for international financial help from the ECB, the EC and the IMF – the so-called *Troika*.

Knowing how a moment of crisis can be perceived as a turning point,[4] one can ask if the 2008 crisis represented – and resulted in – an opportunity for economic, political and social change in Portugal.[5] It will be concluded that the *Troika* intervention led to some reforms, namely in the national legal framework, but the price that the Portuguese economy had to pay for this was too high.

2 The reform policies of the MoU – A brief analysis

The Memorandum of Understanding (MoU) was signed in March 2011 by the meanwhile elected new right-wing Portuguese government. It aimed to achieve three different goals: (i) budgetary consolidation; (ii) financial stabilization and (iii) to implement structural reforms. As such, it established several conditionalities that were to be implemented by the Portuguese Government according to a pre-defined timeline.[6]

These conditionalities were similar to others, considered in former IMF economic interventions in countries worldwide. Those were designed in the late 1980s, based on a simple set of ten recommendations identified by the economist John Williamson and designated as the "Washington consensus".[7]

The Washington consensus advocates free trade, floating exchange rates, free markets and macroeconomic stability. The pursuit of these policies was criticized by many, including Nobel Award Winners like Joseph Stiglitz and Paul Krugman who underlined the fact that these IMF policies would lead to recession and contribute towards the deepening of the crisis.[8] The Washington consensus stood for deeply liberal policies, from an economic point of view, based on the neoclassical economic belief in the market's invisible hand that motivated the so-called austerity measures in several countries worldwide – from Africa to Latin America and Asia – where IMF bailouts took place. The IMF exercised conditionality in indebted countries' decisions to push through macroeconomic stabilisation reforms and structural adjustment programmes based on the idea "one size fits all".

Usually, there were two major stages of intervention: the first focused on macroeconomic stability and structural adjustment programmes[9], and the second included objectives so as to improve institutions, reducing corruption or dealing with infrastructure inefficiency.

Following the "Washington consensus" ideas and the typical IMF role in countries receiving interventions, the emergency loan provided by the MoU to Portugal – forming a total of 78 billion over three years – was tied to conditionalities often referred as structural adjustment policies.

As such, the MoU defined seven major objectives related to (1) Fiscal policy; (2) Financial sector regulation and supervision; (3) Fiscal-structural measures; (4) Labour market and education; (5) Goods and services markets; (6) Housing market and (7) Framework conditions, including the judicial system.

The majority of the measures defined in the MoU (out of a total of 222) represented typical examples of conditionality imposed by the IMF following the "Washington consensus" ideas.

However, new measures were added to the Portuguese MoU, namely related to reforms in local administration[10] which led many to consider that the government – and the Troika – had gone beyond their mandate by imposing so-called structural reforms on the country, which severely reduced the welfare state and citizens' social rights.[11] In fact, similarly to what happened in other countries[12], this was an opportunity for the government to pursue reforms that would have otherwise received tremendous opposition.[13]

The following three major areas can be considered to have been more significant in the context of the reform measures established and the impact they produced on the Portuguese legal framework:

(i) Enhancement of firms' competitiveness based on labour measures such as limiting the increase in the national minimum wage;[14]

(ii) Liberalisation of protected sectors such as electricity and gas markets,[15] railways and telecommunications through the elimination of market-entry barriers;[16]

(iii) Improvement of the judicial system in order to increase the procedural speed of the resolution of cases brought to courts.[17]

The implementation of these measures will be detailed in the following sections.

3 The labour market

The 2008 European crisis caused substantial social problems across the Union, particularly in the southern member States – 12 percent of the European labour force without a job and youth unemployment (relating to 16–24 year olds) reaching unprecedented levels (24.4 percent or 3.58 million individuals under 25 years of age were unemployed across the EU, over 50 percent in Greece and Spain).

Departing from these numbers, the MoU defined several objectives for the Portuguese labour market, once more based on liberal economic ideas coming from the IMF.

As is recognised by the IMF, labour market institutions can affect inequality through different channels that include the wage bargaining system (comprising the coverage of collective agreements, the strength of unions, the level at which bargaining takes place, and the degree of coordination); the effects on unemployment; and the influence on the determination of redistributive policies.[18]

In fact, IMF interventions are known for developing various labour market reforms.[19]

One of the most discussed measures established in the Portuguese MoU referred to the need to change the rules for the dismissal of workers, thereby enabling the firing of employees without cause. Although changes were made in the Portuguese Law – following the publication of Law 23/2012, of 25 April – these did not include some of the measures established in the MoU[20] as they opted for discriminatory criteria for dismissal[21] and, accordingly, were considered to establish procedures that breached the principle of a prohibition on unfair dismissal[22] established in the Portuguese Labour Code. Instead five hierarchical criteria for dismissal were alternatively proposed by the Portuguese Government, that were later included in the Portuguese Labour Code (see article 368 of Law 7/2009, of 12 December).

Nonetheless, the Portuguese Government complied with several other measures proposed by the MoU for the labour market. These measures allowed individual dismissal due to unsuitability, even if new technologies or other changes in the work place had not been introduced; the establishment of a minimum wage freeze; the introduction of new rules that limited the extension of the effects of collective agreements to most workers, among others measures.[23] In this sense, some say that the implementation of the MoU, although partial, affected the

Portuguese labour paradigm – until then based on prohibiting dismissals -, without providing for an adequate time for Portuguese society to understand the need for this.[24]

Additionally, one can say that the labour market reforms implemented by the MoU were unnecessary knowing that the market already had some degree of flexibility, including a high rate of temporary work contracts.[25] In fact, the increased use of this hiring mechanism was followed by a decrease in job protection for permanent workers, without this resulting in a change in the proportion of temporary workers in relation to the total number of workers. It is known that the mitigation of the segmentation existing between a protected sector of employees and a growing sector of unemployed, in particular those looking for their first job, was recurrent in IMF programmes and, in the short term, could not mitigate the economic recession.[26]

Accordingly, one can conclude that the adjustment reforms in labor markets brought less protection to workers and did not produce any of the benefits expected.[27] Moreover, the implementation of labour changes was not well perceived particularly because the evolution of the salaries among European countries that had had similar interventions from the Troika was significantly low as a decrease in salaries was seen as an objective with which to achieve competitiveness.[28]

Furthermore, between 2010 and 2013, the weight of the budget deficit on GDP decreased by six percentage points and the unemployment rate grew by five percentage points.[29] Even so, the IMF argued that the labour reforms implemented improved the business environment and helped to lower Portugal's unemployment rate from more than 16 percent in 2013 to 7 percent by 2018.[30]

4 Liberalisation of protected markets

As was briefly explained above, liberalisation of various sectors, such as the electricity and gas markets[31], railways and telecommunications, was considered essential in order to increase competition in those markets.

Accordingly, the MoU established that market-entry barriers should be eliminated or lowered in those markets.[32]

In the case of the energy sector, extra costs related to electricity production, which came to be known as *excessive rents* and the tariff deficit, were the Troika's first two major targets.

Additionally, it was demanded that the so-called Third EU Energy Package should be transposed[33] in order to ensure the independence of the National Regulatory Authority, known today as the *Entidade Reguladora dos Serviços Energéticos* (ERSE).

Measures implemented included an assessment report in order to understand the lack of diversification in gas sources in the market.[34] For that purpose, ERSE launched an audit in order to evaluate the existence of restrictive competition practices and to identify information asymmetry issues, caused by the dominant undertaking at the time, in the gas sector, that could cause difficulties in the process of the liberalisation of the market.

At the same time, actions were taken in the telecommunications sector in order to provide for the entry of new competitors. Furthermore, the National Regulatory Authority (ICP-ANACOM) launched a new tender to choose the company in charge of the telecommunications universal service and achieve a reduction in mobile termination fees. Here, one can say that the main developments in the Portuguese process of liberalisation of the telecommunications sector had little to do with the implementation of the MoU measures as those had already been pursued by the EU since the beginning of the year 2000.[35]

5 Reform of the judicial system

The judicial system was also one of the sectors targeted by the MoU, following typical IMF conditionality measures that looked at judicial reform and control of corruption as key structural reform priorities.

The objective defined was clear: to eliminate pending cases in the Portuguese courts, thus helping to speed up judicial decisions. The ambiguity of the measures package was because it was wide-ranging in nature, since delaying judgments was not only a financial issue but also a social one and it was clear courts would always have pending cases.

Nevertheless, by the end of 2013, a reduction of 10 percent of the cases pending in the courts of first instance was achieved[36] although this was somehow due to the fact that a significant amount of debt collection actions were filed as it was not possible to identify assets or funds that could settle the existing debt.

The Portuguese Government also implemented several changes to civil procedural legislation, including the approval of an Arbitration Law[37], the revision of the Civil Procedural Code[38] and an optimisation of the mediation procedure (*Julgados de Paz – Justice for Peace*).[39]

These measures were considered essential to alleviate the complexity of civil actions, particularly by ending unnecessary formalities.[40] Furthermore, a restructuring of the Portuguese court order was made through the creation of new specialised courts in the field of intellectual property rights and competition law.[41]

The output of the implemented reforms is still unclear. Even after the conclusion of the MoU, in 2015, the IMF recognized that it was "too early to fully assess the broader economic impact of the reforms" implemented in the judicial system, although there were positive indicators such as the reduction in backlogs, a decrease in processing time, and greater recovery efficiency through the bank garnishment process.[42]

6 Income cuts: Pensions and public salary reductions

The legal framework of public finance underwent a major change as one of the main objectives of the MoU was also to restructure revenue administration and the social security system.

The Portuguese social security system fits within the Mediterranean model of social protection that includes not only Portugal, but also countries like Greece and Spain.

Its framework demonstrates a level of duality, since it appears to privilege certain professional sectors which benefit from a satisfactory and complete social protection system, while the most deprived social sectors still obtain very rudimentary levels of social security.[43] These structural weaknesses became more evident through the Troika's intervention, since the origin of this is strictly associated with the own country's debilities.[44]

Similar to what was previously mentioned, the Portuguese Government partially complied with the measures established in the MoU related to the social security sector. One of the most significant changes determined by the financial crises and, afterwards, by the MoU related to public expenditure with salaries of civil servants that, at that time, were reduced.[45] This measure was put in motion from 1 January 2011, when a reduction of of public salaries, above 1500 euros, of between 3.5 percent to 10 percent, was recorded.

Income cuts implemented by the MoU operated in two different ways: by restricting access conditions or limiting the amount or duration of those conditions.[46] Either way, the consequences of the adopted measures were felt by Portuguese society and severely criticized.

Later, the Portuguese Constitutional Court issued a unanimous decision[47] declaring the unconstitutionality of the Decree that established a 10 percent cut in retirement pensions[48] as it violated the principle of protection of trust established in article 2 of the

Constitution according to which every legislative measure that is subject to an excessive burden and that frustrates the legitimate expectations of their holders, in the continuity of the regimes where the constitution of these rights and interests are protected, should be censured.[49]

The Court's decision clearly mentioned there were expectations in question being violated as the measures concerned pensions already being paid.

7 Reform of private debt restructuring procedures

The MoU aimed to set a new group of rules for company and individual debt procedures including the legal framework in force for company insolvency.[50]

The requests established in the MoU resulted in the creation of *Sireve*[51] – a company recovery system functioning through extrajudicial means. However, the system was hardly taken up by national firms, since the functioning of the financial restructure plan imposed by this system, had to be accepted by two thirds of the participating creditors (with these, in many cases, located abroad), and required only non-judicial means, such as the mediation carried out by the public institute IAPMEI.

At that time the PER[52] legal framework was also created that changed the insolvency legal framework by implementing a special company revitalization procedure. This measure allowed firms that were in a difficult financial or imminent insolvency situation, to initiate judicial proceedings to submit a liability restructuring proposal to courts in order to extend deadlines for debt payments; implement debt interest reduction; benefit from a partial pardon of the debt; conversion of credits into equity interests; or presentation of a new business model, amongst other possibilities. Nonetheless, these changes were criticised.[53]

8 Local administrative reform

Following one of the measures established in the MoU, the financial and budgetary regime for local authorities and intermunicipal entities (RFALEI) was approved.

Here, one can say that the MoU went beyond typical IMF measures as IMF interventions do not usually impact on the national model of administration. By defining those measures in the MoU, the opportunity to start a reform of the local administration many times delayed due to a lack of political consensus was created.

Accordingly, the RFALEI defined a new budgetary framework for local municipalities, achieving, at the same time, one of the objectives of the MoU for expenditure restraint and creating mechanisms that controlled municipality indebtedness.

This regime was followed by the approval of others specially targeted to limiting the public expenditure of local administration.[54]

This was the case for:

(a) The legal regime defining rules related to the assumption of commitments and delayed payments by public entities;[55]
(b) The local business activity and local participation legal regime;[56]
(c) The municipalities and local associativism legal regime;[57]
(d) Changes to the national and local budgetary legal framework;[58]
(e) The legal regime that created a support fund to rescue and bailout municipalities.[59]

The second one – local business activity and local participation legal regime – is particularly interesting, since it made the restrictions of the municipality-owned companies' financial capacity clearer, particularly in regard to their indebtedness ratio, in order to comply with the budgetary and long-term sustainability of local finance budgetary principles.

Furthermore, legal action required by the MoU ended up resulting in a local administrative reorganisation that implied the merger of various parishes.[60]

This was motivated by the acknowledgement that the administrative design of the Portuguese territory was marked by the existence of circumscriptions that were increasingly moving away from the optimal circumscription model which, according to the traditional normative proposals of the theory of fiscal federalism, should correspond to circumscriptions of optimal dimension and population, that is to say, of intermediate population.[61] However, although the local administration reform was based on microeconomic efficiency criteria one can say that it did not have any real impact on expenditure efficiency.[62]

9 Conclusions

The implementation of the MoU in Portugal stands as an example of consolidation of the Washington consensus policies by the European

Union.[63] Differently from the IMF adjustment programmes that took place in 1978 and 1983 in Portugal,[64] the 2011 MoU had very few measures to stimulate the economy and was essentially aimed at achieving financial goals, for which it did not take care to establish an economic growth strategy that would make these feasible.

This orthodox approach to the economic crisis assumed in the MoU was well synthetized and criticized as it did not consider "(a) the negative impacts of the asymmetric process of European integration on peripheral countries; (b) the weaknesses of the institutional architecture or the Monetary Union and (c) the structural imbalances of the economic growth model in Portugal, associated with an increasingly dependent and fragile insertion in the Eurozone".[65]

It is now clear for many that the effects of fiscal consolidation caused by the economic and financial adjustment programme were recessive as there was an increase in unemployment rates, tax revenues decreased, transfers increased and there was a deterioration of the budgetary balance and an increase in public debt.[66] However, the Troika intervention left a legacy of several changes in the national legal framework that have remained until the present day.

Nowadays, the EU is more prepared to face economic crises similar to the 2008 one. The creation of the European Stability Mechanism (ESM), that replaced the provisional European Financial Stability Facility (EFSF), established in 2010, allowed the EU to equip itself with an institution that can provide financial assistance to Euro Area countries experiencing or threatened by severe financing problems, if it is proven necessary to safeguard the financial stability of the Euro Area as a whole as well as that of ESM Members.

Although ESM loans are conditional upon the implementation of macroeconomic reform programmes prepared by the EC, we can now refer to the existence of a new "Brussels consensus" different from the Washington one. As such, one can say that the approval of the MoU in Portugal represented the sunset of the Washington consensus policies, at least within the European Union.

Knowing this, one can hope that, in the future, the "Washington consensus" will be replaced by what some call a post-Washington consensus based on aligning national accounting systems to intangible values, including the incorporation of externalities and the introduction of innovative indicators, guaranteeing basic income, rationalizing intermediation financial systems, redesigning tax systems, adopting budgets that aim at improving the redistribution of resources according to economic, social and environmental results, and taxing and registering speculative transactions.[67]

Notes

1

Co-funded by the
Erasmus+ Programme
of the European Union

The European Commission support for the production of this publication does not constitute an endorsement of the contents which reflects the views only of the authors, and the Commission cannot be held responsible for any use which may be made of the information contained therein.

The preparation of this work counted on the support of Mrs. Carolina Ramalho dos Santos, to whom I am grateful for the support provided.

2   Some authors, such as Nicolas Véron, have discussed whether the policy errors of the Commission were or are less damaging than the absence of decisions. See *Challenges of Europe's fourfold Union*, a hearing before U. S. Senate on "The future of the Eurozone: Outlook and lessons" (August 1, 2012), available at https://www.bruegel.org/2012/08/the-challenges-of-europes-fourfold-union/.

3   The acronym is composed by the initial letter of each country (Portugal, Ireland, Italy, Greece and Spain).

4   See Moury, C. and Freire, A. 2013: Austerity Policies and Politics: The Case of Portugal. *Pôle Sud*, 2(39), p. 37; Clifton, J., Diaz-Fuentes, D. and Gómez, A. L. 2018: The crisis as opportunity? On the role of the Troika in constructing the European consolidation state. *Cambridge Journal of Regions, Economy and Society*, 11, pp. 587–608; and Cunha Rodrigues, N. and Gonçalves, J. R. 2017: The European Banking Union and the Economic and Monetary Union: The Puzzle Is Yet to Be Completed. In N. Cunha Rodrigues, J. R. Gonçalves and N. Costa Cabral (eds.), *The Euro and the Crisis – Perspectives for the Eurozone as a Monetary and Budgetary Union, Financial and Monetary Policy Studies*, London: Springer, Volume 43, 271–288.

5   For an outlook of the Portuguese economy in 2011 see European Commission 2011: The Economic Adjustment Programme for Portugal, Occasional Papers 79, available at https://ec.europa.eu/economy_finance/publications/occasional_paper/2011/pdf/ocp79_en.pdf

6   The MoU and additional information provided by the Portuguese Government and the institutions involved is available at https://www.imf.org/external/np/loi/2011/prt/051711.pdf.

7   The list of ten recommendations is the following: 1) fiscal discipline; 2) redirecting public expenditure; 3) tax reform; 4) financial liberalization; 5) adoption of a single, competitive exchange rate; 6) trade liberalization; 7) elimination of barriers to foreign direct investment; 8) privatization of state owned enterprises; 9) deregulation of market entry and competition; and 10) secure property rights.

8   See Lopes, C. 2012: Economic Growth and Inequality: The New Post-Washington Consensus. RCCS Annual Review [Online], 4; and Magalhães Prates, D. and Maryse Farhi, M. 2015: From IMF to the Troika: new analytical framework, same conditionalities. Économie et institutions [Online] 23, p. 2. See also Fitoussi, J. P. and Saraceno, F. 2013: European economic governance: the Berlin–Washington Consensus. *Cambridge Journal of Economics*, 37, p. 483: "The IMF proposed a development model based on essentially three elements: first, a reduced role for stabilisation policy (macroeconomic policy should be limited to fighting inflation and keeping public finances under control); second, an increased role for market mechanisms (privatisation, deregulation and other structural reforms); and, third, full integration into the global economy (which means openness to trade and free financial flows). The model did not prove as successful as its proponents had hoped and is today increasingly challenged".

9   See Ferreira Amaral, J. and Lopes, J. C. 2017: Forecasting errors by the Troika in the economic adjustment programme for Portugal. *Cambridge Journal of Economics*, 41, p. 1022, explaining that, "from a macroeconomic point of view, the philosophy (...) translates into very harsh fiscal austerity measures (increased revenues and reduced public expenditure) and the erosion of labour rights and the purchasing power of workers and pensioners (falling wages, pensions, unemployment benefits and other social benefits, flexibility of redundancies and collective bargaining, etc.)".

10 See Cunha Rodrigues, N. 2014: Apreciação geral do memorandum de entendimento. *Revista de Finanças Públicas e Direito Fiscal*, ano IV, n.º 2(06), 11, pp. 15–18.

11 See Moury, C. and Freire, A. 2013: Austerity Policies and Politics: The Case of Portugal. *Pôle Sud*, 2(39), p. 36.

12 See Drazen, A. 2002: Conditionality and ownership in IMF lending: A political economy approach. CEPR Discussion Papers 3562, C.E.P.R. Discussion Papers.

13 See the proposed measures by the Portuguese government established in the Memorandum of economic and financial policies available at https://www.imf.org/external/np/loi/2011/prt/051711.pdf.

14 See point 4.7. of the Memorandum of Understanding: "The Government will promote wage developments consistent with the objectives of fostering job creation and improving firms' competitiveness with a view to correct macroeconomic imbalances. To that purpose, the Government will: (i) commit that, over the programme period, any increase in the minimum wage will take place only if justified by economic and labour market developments and agreed in the framework of the programme review;", and point 4.8.: "The Government will promote wage adjustments in line with productivity at the firm level. To that purpose, it will: (iii) present a proposal to reduce the firm size threshold for works councils to conclude agreements below 250 employees (...)". The

Memorandum of Understanding is available at: https://ec.europa.eu/economy_finance/eu_borrower/mou/2011-05-18-mou-portugal_en.pdf.

15 See point 5.1 of the Memorandum of Understanding: "Regulated electricity tariffs will be phased out by January 1, 2013 at the latest. Present a roadmap for the phasing out following a stepwise approach by end-July 2011. The provisions will specify: (...) (iii) The definition of vulnerable consumers and the mechanism to protect them." and point 5.2: "Transpose the Third EU Energy Package by the end of June 2011. This will ensure the National Regulator Authority's independence and all powers foreseen in the package.

16 See point 5.17 of the MoU: "Facilitate market-entry by auctioning 'new' radio frequencies (i.e. auction of spectrum) for broadband wireless access and lowering mobile termination rates.", and point 5.18: "Ensure that the provision on universal service designation and the incumbent's concession contract are non-discriminatory: re-negotiate the concession contract with the undertaking currently providing the universal service and launch a new tender for designation of universal service providers".

17 See point 7.2. of the MoU: "Based on the audit, better target existing measures and assess the need for additional measures to expedite the resolution of the backlog. Additional measures to be considered include, among others: (i) establishing separate Chambers or Teams (solely) directed toward resolving the backlog. (...) (vii) assigning special court managers to manage the court agenda/hearings allowing judges to focus on the cases".

18 See IMF working paper WP/20/29 by Stepanyan, A. and Salas, J. 2020: Distributional Implications of Labor Market Reforms: Learning from Spain's Experience, p. 5.

19 Describing a database of major labour and product market reforms covering 26 advanced economies over the period 1970–2013, see: IMF working paper, WP/18/19, A Narrative Database of Major Labor and Product Market Reforms in Advanced Economies, 2019.

20 See, particularly, subparagraphs (ii) and (iii), of point 4.5 of the MoU.

21 See point 4.5 of the MoU: "Individual dismissals linked to the extinction of work positions should not necessarily follow a pre-defined seniority order if more than one worker is assigned to identical functions (article 368 of the Portuguese Labour Code). The predefined seniority order is not necessary provided that the employer establishes a relevant and non-discriminatory alternative criteria (in line with what already happens in the case of collective dismissals)."

22 See article 338 of Law no. 93/2009, of 12 February.

23 See article 340 of the Portuguese Labour Code.

24 See Leite, J. 2013: *A Reforma Laboral em Portugal*. Revista da Faculdade de Direito da Universidade da Lusófona do Porto, 3(3), 4–6.

25 See World Labor Organization, *Trabalho Digno em Portugal 2008–18: Da crise à recuperação*, 2018, p. 3, available at

https://www.ilo.org/wcmsp5/groups/public/—-dgreports/—-dcomm/—-publ/documents/publication/wcms_647524.pdf.

26   See dos Santos, E. 2013: Dois anos de memorando: um balanço. In E. Paz Ferreira (org.), *Troika, ano II*, Lisboa: Edições 70, p. 182.

27   On the opposite side, see IMF working paper WP/20/29 by Stepanyan, A. and Salas, J. 2020: Distributional Implications of Labor Market Reforms: Learning from Spain's Experience. According to the conclusion of this study "there is strong evidence that the 2012 labor market reforms increased wage flexibility, which helped the Spanish economy to regain competitiveness and create jobs".

28   See Castro Caldas, J. 2015: Desvalorização do trabalho: do Memorando à prática. Cadernos do Observatório, p. 5, available at https://eg.uc.pt/bitstream/10316/36659/1/Desvalorização%20do%20trabalho_do%20Memorando%20à%20prática.pdf

29   See Coelho, J. C. 2020: Self-defeating austerity in Portugal during the Troika's economic and financial adjustment programme. REM Working Paper 0124-2020, available at https://www.repository.utl.pt/bitstream/10400.5/20026/1/REM_WP_0124_2020.pdf, p. 2: "In 2013, and compared to 2010, the programme resulted in a severe recession (GDP at constant 2011 prices decreased by 6.8%), in a colossal destruction of jobs (less 469000 employees), in a high growth of the unemployment rate (with an increase of 5.4 percentage points, having reached 17.5% in the first quarter of 2013), and, in particular, an increase of the youth unemployment rate, which reached the maximum value in 2013, 38.1%, and which are values much higher than those foreseen in the programme adjustment, and in massive emigration (350504 people, 149742 permanent emigrants). The weight of public debt on GDP increased, between 2010 and 2013, more than thirty percentage points, from 100.2% to 131.4%".

30   See IMF post "Political Consensus at the Heart of Portuguese Recovery", May 2019, available at https://www.imf.org/en/Countries/PRT/portugal-lending-case-study.

31   See point 5.1 of the MoU: "Regulated electricity tariffs will be phased out by January 1, 2013 at the latest. Present a roadmap for the phasing out following a stepwise approach by end-July 2011. The provisions will specify: (…) (iii) The definition of vulnerable consumers and the mechanism to protect them." and point 5.2.: "Transpose the Third EU Energy Package by the end of June 2011. This will ensure the National Regulator Authority's independence and all powers foreseen in the package".

32   See point 5.17 of the MoU: "Facilitate market-entry by auctioning 'new' radio frequencies (i.e. auction of spectrum) for broadband wireless access and lowering mobile termination rates", and point 5.18: "Ensure that the provision on universal service designation and the incumbent's concession contract are non-discriminatory: re-negotiate the concession contract with the undertaking currently providing the universal service and launch a new tender for designation of universal service providers".

33 In some EU Member States this sector (energy and gas) was controlled by state-owned vertically-integrated companies who benefited from nationwide or regional monopolies, in order to ensure the fundamental pillars on which the European energy policy rests: security of supply and public service provision, which led to some difficulties in the process of the liberalization of this market. See Hancher, L. 1997: Slow and Not So Sure: Europe's Long March to Electricity Market Liberalization. *The Electricity Journal*, p. 93. See the ECJ's decision Commission v. Belgium, 4th of July, 2002, paragraph 46, I – 4833, ECLI:EU:C:2002:328, considering the definition of legitimate public interest in a specific case regarding the safeguarding of energy supply in the event of a crisis.

34 See point 5.5 of the MoU: "Review in a report the reasons for lack of entry in the gas market, despite the availability of spare capacity, and the reasons for the lack of diversification of gas sources. The report will also propose possible measures to address the identified problems".

35 In this sense, see Directive 2002/01/EC, 7th March 2002; Directive 2002/19/EC, 7 March 2002; Directive 2002/21/EC, 7th March 2002 and Directive 2009/136/CE, 25 November 2009.

36 See Correia, P. M. A. R., Videira, S. A., Oliveira Mendes, I., The Troika's Portuguese Ministry of Justice Experiment: Dissipation of Doubts about Success, Continuation and Confirmation of Positive Results, available at http://www.enajus.org.br/2018/assets/sessoes/021_EnAjus.pdf, point 5.

37 See Law no. 63/2011, 14 December. See Máximo dos Santos, L. 2014: Sistema Judicial. *Revista de Finanças Públicas e Direito Fiscal*, ano IV, n.º 2(06), 11, pp. 55–57.

38 See point 7.13 of the MoU: "The Government will review the Code of Civil Procedure and prepare a proposal by end-2011 addressing the key areas for refinement, including: (i) consolidating legislation for all enforcement cases before the court, (ii) giving judges the power to expedite cases, (iii) reducing administrative burdens on judges, and (iv) enforcing statutory deadlines for court processes and in particular injunction procedures and debt enforcement and insolvency cases".

39 See point 7.7 of the MoU: "Optimize the regime for Justices for the Peace to increase its capacity to handle small claim cases".

40 See Correia, P and S. Videira, S. 2015: Troika's Portuguese Ministry of Justice Experiment: An Empirical Study on the Success Story of the Civil Enforcement Actions. *International Journal for Court Administration*, 7 (1), 37–50.

41 See point 7.11 of the MoU: "Make specialized courts on Competition and on Intellectual Property Rights fully operational". See Law no. 46/2011, 24 June.

42 See IMF working paper WP/15/279, Reforming the Legal and Institutional Framework for the Enforcement of Civil and Commercial Claims in Portugal, 2015.

43 See Cunha Rodrigues, N. and Costa Cabral, N. 2020: *Finanças dos*

Subsetores – Segurança Social, Sectores Regional e Local, 2nd edition, Coimbra: Almedina.

44 See Adão e Silva, P. 2000: O Estado de Providência português num contexto europeu – elementos para uma reflexão. *Revista Sociedade e Trabalho*, no. 8/9, p. 49.

45 See point 1.9., subparagraph (ii): "Freeze wages in the government sector in nominal terms in 2012 and 2013 and constrain promotions".

46 See Cunha Rodrigues, N. and Costa Cabral, N. 2020: *Finanças dos Subsetores – Segurança Social, Sectores Regional e Local*, 2nd edition, Coimbra: Almedina, p. 134.

47 The Portuguese Constitutional Court's decision is available at https://dre.pt/application/conteudo/606350.

48 See point 1.11 of the MoU: "Reduce pensions above EUR 1,500 according to the progressive rates applied to the wages of the public sector as of January 2011, with the aim of yielding savings of at least EUR 445 million", and point 1.12: "Suspend application of pension indexation rules and freeze pensions, except for the lowest pensions, in 2012".

49 Translation of article 2 of the Portuguese Constitution.

50 See point 2.17 of the MoU: "To better facilitate effective rescue of viable firms, the Insolvency Law will be amended by end-November 2011 with technical assistance from the IMF, to, inter alia, introduce fast track court approval procedures for restructuring plans"; point 2.18: "General principles on voluntary out of court restructuring in line with international best practices will be issued by end-September 2011" and point 2.19: "The authorities will also take the necessary actions to authorise the tax and social security administrations to use a wider range of restructuring tools based on clearly defined criteria in cases where other creditors also agree to restructure their claims, and review the tax law with a view to removing impediments to voluntary debt restructuring".

51 See Decree-Law no. 178/2012, 3 August. This measure was later revoked by Law no. 8/2018, 2 March 2018.

52 See Law no. 16/2012, 20 April.

53 See Salazar Casanova, N. 2018: *Os Efeitos Processuais do PER e do PEAP nas Ações Declarativas de Condenação*. Actualidade Jurídica Uría Menendez, 5–10, available at https://www.uria.com/documentos/publicaciones/5890/documento/art005.pdf?id=8342.

54 Referring to the measures related to the public administration and considering them as "the institutionalization of a list of individual measures that aimed, first of all, for an immediate cut in the costs of public expenditure" see Madureira, C. 2015: A reforma da Administração Pública Central no Portugal democrático: do período pós-revolucionário à intervenção da troika. *Revista de Administração Pública – Rio de Janeiro* 49 (3), p. 558.

55 See Law no. 8/2012, 21 February.

56 See Law no. 50/2012, 31 August.

57   See Law no. 75/2013, 12 September.

58   See Law no. 37/2013, 14 June. See also Law no. 41/2014, 10 July.

59   See Law no. 53/2014, 25 August.

60   See point 3.44 of the MoU: "Reorganize local government administration. There are currently 308 municipalities and 4,259 parishes. By July 2012, the government will develop a consolidation plan to reorganise and significantly reduce the number of such entities. The Government will implement these plans based on the agreement with EC and IMF staff. These changes, which will come into effect by the beginning of the next local election cycle, will enhance service delivery, improve efficiency, and reduce costs".

61   See Costa Cabral, N. 2014: Administração Fiscal e segurança social: administração pública. *Revista de Finanças Públicas e Direito Fiscal*, ano IV, n.° 2 (06), 11, pp. 25–36.

62   See Afonso, A. and Venâncio, A. 2019: Local Territorial reform and regional spending efficiency. Local Government Studies, p. 19, available at https://www.repository.utl.pt/bitstream/10400.5/17366/1/REM_WP_071_2019.pdf: "From a policy perspective, it is then less obvious that such reform, which implied a reduction of the number of parishes, has enhanced the efficiency of government spending across the board for the municipalities".

63   Considering that the EU has gone very far in the internalisation of the original Washington Consensus prescriptions see Fitoussi, J. P. and Saraceno, F. 2013: European economic governance: The Berlin–Washington Consensus. *Cambridge Journal of Economics*, 37, 479–496.

64   The adjustment programmes signed between Portugal and the IMF in 1978 and 1983 had the instrument of exchange rate policy to enable, in the short term, to make the economy grow through a cycle sustained by exporting. In 2011, Portugal did not have that instrument of exchange rate policy to face the crisis. See dos Santos, E. 2013: Dois anos de memorando: um balanço. In E. Paz Ferreira (org.), *Troika, ano II*, Lisboa: Edições 70, p. 182.

65   See Rocha, F. and Stoleroff, A. 2014: The Challenges of the Crisis and the External Intervention in Portugal. In *The New Economic Governance and its Impact in National Collective Bargaining Systems*, Madrid: Fundacíon 1.° de Mayo, pp. 153–155.

66   See Coelho, J. C. 2020: Self-defeating austerity in Portugal during the Troika's economic and financial adjustment programme, REM Working Paper 0124-2020, available at https://www.repository.utl.pt/bitstream/10400.5/20026/1/REM_WP_0124_2020.pdf, p. 3. See also Perez, S. A. and Matsaganis, M. 2018: The Political Economy of Austerity in Southern Europe, *New Political Economy*, 23(2), 192–207, showing that in Italy, Greece and Spain, even when austerity measures were designed to reduce inequality by compressing incomes downward, their second-order macro-economic effects ultimately increased inequality (except in Portugal); and Ferreira Amaral, J. and Lopes, J. C. 2017: Forecasting

errors by the Troika in the economic adjustment programme for Portugal. *Cambridge Journal of Economics*, 41, 1021–1041, explaining the technical flaw of the adjustment programme and the huge economic and social costs it unnecessarily caused. Considering positive effects caused by the MoU in the economy, see Viegas, M. and Ribeiro, A. P. 2014: The Economic Adjustment Program for Portugal: Assessing welfare impact in a heterogeneous-agent framework. *Portuguese Economic Journal*, 13, 53–70: the study "(...) strongly supports the motivation for the adoption of the Economic Adjustment Program which considers the large external indebtedness of Portugal as a central issue in the economic diagnosis".

67 See Lopes, C. 2012: Economic Growth and Inequality: The New Post-Washington Consensus. *RCCS Annual Review* [Online], 4, p. 82.

References

Adão e Silva, P. 2000: O Estado de Providência português num contexto europeu – elementos para uma reflexão. *Revista Sociedade e Trabalho*, no. 8/9, 49–62.

Afonso, A. and Venâncio, A. 2019: Local Territorial reform and regional spending efficiency. *Local Government Studies*, Vol. 46 (6), 888–910.

Castro Caldas, J. 2015: *Desvalorização do trabalho: do Memorando à prática*. Cadernos do Observatório, 6.

Clifton, J., Diaz-Fuentes, D. and Gómez, A. L. 2018: The crisis as opportunity? On the role of the Troika in constructing the European consolidation state. *Cambridge Journal of Regions, Economy and Society*, 11, 587–608.

Coelho, J. C. 2020: Self-defeating austerity in Portugal during the Troika's economic and financial adjustment programme. REM Working Paper 0124-2020.

Correia, P and S. Videira, S. 2015: Troika's Portuguese Ministry of Justice Experiment: An Empirical Study on the Success Story of the Civil Enforcement Actions. *International Journal for Court Administration*, 7 (1), 37–50.

Correia, P. M. A. R., Videira, S. A., Oliveira Mendes, I., The Troika's Portuguese Ministry of Justice Experiment: Dissipation of Doubts about Success, Continuation and Confirmation of Positive Results. Available at http://www.enajus.org.br/2018/assets/sessoes/021_EnAjus.pdf.

Costa Cabral, N. 2014: Administração Fiscal e segurança social: administração pública. Revista de Finanças Públicas e Direito Fiscal, ano IV, n.º 2(06), 11, 25–36.

Cunha Rodrigues, N. 2014: Apreciação geral do memorandum de entendimento. *Revista de Finanças Públicas e Direito Fiscal*, ano IV, n.º 2(06), 11, 15–18.

Cunha Rodrigues, N. and Costa Cabral, N. 2020: *Finanças dos Subsetores – Segurança Social, Sectores Regional e Local*, 2nd edition, Coimbra: Almedina.

Cunha Rodrigues, N. and Gonçalves, J. R. 2017: The European Banking Union and the Economic and Monetary Union: The Puzzle Is Yet to Be

Completed. In N. Cunha Rodrigues, J. R. Gonçalves and N. Costa Cabral (eds.), *The Euro and the Crisis – Perspectives for the Eurozone as a Monetary and Budgetary Union, Financial and Monetary Policy Studies*, London: Springer, Volume 43, 271–288.

dos Santos, E. 2013: Dois anos de memorando: um balanço. In E. Paz Ferreira (org.), *Troika, ano II*, Lisboa: Edições 70, 181–195.

Drazen, A. 2002: Conditionality and ownership in IMF lending: A political economy approach. CEPR Discussion Papers 3562, C.E.P.R. Discussion Papers.

European Commission 2011. The Economic Adjustment Programme for Portugal, Occasional Papers 79.

Ferreira Amaral, J. and Lopes, J. C. 2017: Forecasting errors by the Troika in the economic adjustment programme for Portugal. *Cambridge Journal of Economics*, 41, 1021–1041.

Fitoussi, J. P. and Saraceno, F. 2013: European economic governance: the Berlin–Washington Consensus. *Cambridge Journal of Economics*, 37, 479–496.

Hancher, L. 1997: Slow and Not So Sure: Europe's Long March to Electricity Market Liberalization. *The Electricity Journal*, Vol. 10 (9), 92–101.

IMF working paper WP/20/29 by Stepanyan, A. and Salas, J. 2020: Distributional Implications of Labor Market Reforms: Learning from Spain's Experience, available at https://www.imf.org/en/Publications/WP/Issues/2020/02/13/ Distributional-Implications-of-Labor-Market-Reforms-Learning-from-Spain-s-Experience-48962.

IMF working paper, WP/18/19. A Narrative Database of Major Labor and Product Market Reforms in Advanced Economies, 2019

IMF working paper WP/15/279, Reforming the Legal and Institutional Framework for the Enforcement of Civil and Commercial Claims in Portugal, 2015.

Leite, J. 2013: A Reforma Laboral em Portugal. *Revista da Faculdade de Direito da Universidade da Lusófona do Porto*, 3 (3), 4–6.

Lopes, C. 2012: Economic Growth and Inequality: The New Post-Washington Consensus. *RCCS Annual Review* [Online], 4.

Madureira, C. 2015: A reforma da Administração Pública Central no Portugal democrático: do período pós-revolucionário à intervenção da troika. Revista de Administração Pública – Rio de Janeiro 49 (3), 547–562.

Máximo dos Santos, L. 2014: Sistema Judicial. *Revista de Finanças Públicas e Direito Fiscal*, ano IV, n.º 2(06), 11, 55–57.

Moury, C. and Freire, A. 2013: Austerity Policies and Politics: The Case of Portugal. *Pôle Sud*, 2(39), 35–56.

Perez, S. A. and Matsaganis, M. 2018: The Political Economy of Austerity in Southern Europe, *New Political Economy*, 23(2), 192–207.

Magalhães Prates, D. and Maryse Farhi, M. 2015: From IMF to the Troika: new analytical framework, same conditionalities. *Économie et institutions* [Online] 23.

Rocha, F. and Stoleroff, A. 2014: The Challenges of the Crisis and the External Intervention in Portugal. In *The New Economic Governance and its Impact in National Collective Bargaining Systems*, Madrid: Fundacíon 1.º de Mayo, 150–174.

Véron, N. 2012: The Challenges of Europe's fourfold Union. Bruegel Policy Contribution, 2012 (13), available at https://www.bruegel.org/2012/08/the-challenges-of-europes-fourfold-union/.

Viegas, M. and Ribeiro, A. P. 2014: The Economic Adjustment Program for Portugal: assessing welfare impact in a heterogeneous-agent framework. *Portuguese Economic Journal*, 13, 53–70.

7

EU Funds and Taxation: Lessons from Portugal in Times of Covid

GUILHERME WALDEMAR D'OLIVEIRA MARTINS
AND JOANA GRAÇA MOURA

1 COVID-19 public integrated support: Budget and Taxation views

In the wake of the COVID-19 crisis, the pressure on public finances to provide protection – either social, economic or health – triggered the need for State action. This action may ultimately involve actual economic support, tax relief, re-organization of State resources, among others, and will thus require that a balance be made between budgetary and tax instruments.

From a budget perspective, countries that, similarly to Portugal, do not have any past tradition in the field of budgeting according to objectives, have heightened concerns and challenges. In these cases, it is paramount to ensure a smooth transition from the pre-existing conventional model (line-item classification) to the new model (classification by objectives), adapting the latter to the practical limitations and constraints that exist in the functioning of Public Administration. This path towards a budget management culture based on performance must be undertaken gradually and prudently. In fact, the implementation of this new budgetary system involves not only changes to the budgetary structure, but also progressive changes in administrative praxis, so as to better adapt it towards achieving the budgetary objectives and goals thus defined, and becoming less dependent on traditional management views. The change also implies mental and cultural changes, because, as we will see below, the performance-based system calls for greater management flexibility, less bureaucracy, a management model adapted to the market and, finally, the development of a culture of transparency and accountability.

In keeping with the truth, it must be said that the implementation of a performance-based system does not necessarily imply the eradication of conventional forms of budgeting typically based on the budget line item. In particular, preservation of functional and economic classifications is recommended, given their benefits in terms of budgetary control, and requires both that:

> a single budget statement, covering public revenue and expenditure be approved; the segregation of the respective current and capital expenses in the structuring of the programme.

What is intended, even from this point of view, is to guarantee the necessary balance between two autonomous and not easily aligned objectives: on the one hand, guaranteeing that the budget has an adequate level of detail and disaggregation and thus provides for the control of expenditure; and on the other hand, av oiding excessive detail, which prevents the budgetary flexibility that is key to a performance-based system, and which may ultimately prove to be rather counterproductive. As may easily be perceived, excessive detail in in the budgetary breakdown hinders (i) the clear cognizance of the objectives underlying those lines of expenditure, (ii) the differentiation between the essential and the accessory, and (iii) management based on the allocation of costs to objectives. Striving to achieve this balance will ensure that budget programmes are compatible with the 'line-item' classification whilst keeping to a classification by objective. This alignment between both classifications is therefore not impossible insofar as both classification systems translate into two distinct manners of portraying the same reality: the reality of public revenue and expenditure.

From a fiscal perspective, tax benefits[1] are the result of a system of tax monopolization by the State[2] as they "are situations of tax advantage characterized by excessive favoring of certain tax subjects in violation of the principle of equality".[3] The starting point of this concept resides in the notion of "ability to pay", which is a logical and conceptual condition of all principles that justify and simultaneously impose limits on the duty of contribution.[4] The ability to pay is generally seen as[5]:

(a) One of the criteria on which a given taxation policy should be drawn upon – though not the only one – and one that expresses the idea of tax justice (since it is a part of a wider principle which is tax equality);

(b) The basis of "the normative system of taxation" [6] – for where a given tax does not consider the taxpayer's ability to pay it can be deemed as confiscatory;

(c) A sort of moral justification for the duty to pay taxes;

(d) An underlying component of all public policy decisions, thus leading public decision makers to bear in mind the social and economic status of all taxpayers throughout the decision-making process;

(e) Having an elastic content that has to be determined on a case-by-case basis, notwithstanding the need to establish its basic core;

(f) The foundation and expression of the contributory principle that can be applied in other kinds of public charges.

In light of the foregoing, the concept of tax benefit can in fact be considered as a derogation of the principle of the ability to pay, which is one of the representations of the notion of tax equality, since it disregards the social and economic position of the taxpayer.

Actually, the origin of the tax benefit concept is associated with the doctrine of limitations to instruments of political power, which began in the medieval period,[7] making a case that the limitations to political power reside in the private sphere – with the legitimacy of a tax benefit beginning where the legitimacy to tax ends. The underlying idea is that citizens should only contribute to the satisfaction of public needs in view of their economic and social benefit. This means that the moment in which the State imposes a tax that has no relationship whatsoever with the taxpayer's ability to pay is the moment in which the State enters the private sphere in an illegitimate way, which should be safe from public intervention. Ultimately, this is a matter of the social responsibility of the State.[8]

Thus, tax benefits as such are outside the traditional unavailability of taxation regulation and inside the field of availability that resides outside that regulation's core.[9]

It should, however, be noted that not all tax reliefs show the existence of a tax benefit, since the latter implies a certain positioning of taxpayers as to the satisfaction of their needs, in a public-private duality. Furthermore, the derogation implied by a tax benefit results from a decision-making process that is focused on encouraging certain economic, social or cultural behaviour from taxpayers. Consequently, the tax relief given by the State in the context of the COVID-19 response may take on different forms and levels, depending on the objectives pursued by each State and the policies guiding their action, as can easily be inferred from the disparity in tax measures and programmes adopted worldwide and further reviewed below.

The integrated response from the State will necessarily involve a multi-layered approach involving changes to both taxation and budgetary frameworks. In short, Budget programmes should become more flexible, more transparent and be adjusted to the objectives of each State function as a whole. Taxation should help provide relief where no financial support can be granted directly, whilst also keeping with the levels of State revenues necessary to finance State action. Across the world, States have dabbled at achieving these objectives in different ways.

2 Fiscal system and tax benefits

2.1 Tax benefits and tax equality

2.1.1 Tax benefits as a derogation to the principle of tax equality

A rule that creates a tax benefit derogates the principle of tax equality, despite being legitimized or even required by a particular constitutional requirement. From this perspective, it is of utmost importance to focus both on the concept and on the extension of tax equality to understand the tax benefits being granted in the context of the COVID-19 response.

Whether in an alternative or cumulative fashion, the State can only tax and spend:

    (a) According to the so-called benefit logic (which we would call *quid pro quo* logic), by taking into account what taxpayers receive, that is, the public services of which they can enjoy;

or

    (b) According to the so-called "ability to pay logic" (following the ideas presented by Guicciardini in the 16th century, who advocated the ideal of progressive taxation on the ability to pay, or even the thought of Bodin, who argued for the idea of a contributive faculty as a basis for taxation under the rule of proportionality), the State can only tax within certain limits which are defined with reference to degrees of wealth, income or expenditure.

According to the principle of benefit, taxation should be defined in terms of consideration and tax justice should be understood under a logic of reciprocity. Accordingly, taxes should be regarded as prices for the protection and coordination of functions attributed to the State, whenever they are needed or requested by the individual. Under this logic, there is obviously no space to tax individuals who do not benefit from public services.

However, the principle subsides when one takes into account certain public goods or services which cannot be waived by citizens (although under the logic of the Social State this ability to waive public services should not be mistaken for the non-enjoyment of public goods or services – this would leads us to a discussion of the notion of pure public goods which is outside the scope of this work).[10] The principle of benefit or equivalence is, thus, overridden by the fact that there are functions pursued by the State which may not be voluntarily waived by the taxpayer.

On the other hand, the unilateral nature of the tax concept,[11] which distinguishes it from other kinds of public charges, is a stranger to the idea of consideration implied in the principle of benefit, allowing us to put forward the following assertion: all tax benefits, because they are located in the field of taxes, constitute a derogation to the ability to pay and not to the principle of benefit.

According to the ability to pay principle, taxation should be designed to meet every taxpayer's personal situation. In fact, the fair tax[12] is one that ensures substantive equality in the distribution of tax burdens, *i.e.*, that ensures that those who have the same ability to pay are charged with the same tax (horizontal equity) and that those who have different abilities to pay are charged differently (vertical equity).

Furthermore, the ability to pay principle does not require autonomous constitutional support since it stems from the general principle of equality in association "with the constitutional rules and principles relating to taxes or even to fundamental rights".[13]

2.1.2 The essential core of a tax, tax benefits and the derogation to the ability to pay principle   The starting point of this analysis is, in our view, the rehabilitation of the doctrinal principle of the ability to pay (or of economic capacity).[14] Recently, the importance of the ability to pay as a measure of taxation and even as a criterion for the allocation of certain public benefits has become a focal point in the debate on taxes and measures of taxation. In fact, the importance of that principle has enabled the creation of a new fundamental right to "an adequate contribution", one that certainly binds the legislator namely by forcing him/her to balance that principle with others that, in a given situation, point in a different direction.[15]

The general principle of equality argues, according to Leibholz, for a particular set of individual rights, which are directed at omissions, *i.e.*, "omissions or arbitrary disruptions of the *de jure* equality".[16] From this perspective, we can identify three different types of rights: definitive and abstract equality rights, definitive and concrete equality rights and *prima facie* abstract equality rights. All abstract rights lead to a set of concrete and very different rights that are usually called "defence rights". It is this dialogic relationship that explains the failure of the State, which, in turn, can lead to a demand for factual protection whether of a positive status (requiring public action) or of a negative one (not requiring public action).[17]

2.1.3 Indirect goals for taxation and the ability to pay principle

According to Maffezzoni,[18] the legislator is entitled with a significant degree of freedom to shape the content of the ability to pay principle, *i.e.*, in defining the most suitable way to finance public expenditure through various normative schemes that define the amount of revenue necessary to afford the proper mix of public services.[19]

However, the discretion assigned to the legislator "cannot be used arbitrarily and should be used in a way that allows for the achievement of the public purposes that have been previously defined"[20] such as "the expansion or contraction of investment and consumption, redistribution, etc". Thus, it is the previously established set of goals that defines the content and extension of the ability to pay principle.

Let us not forget, however, that the ability to pay is an instrument of taxation as a way of raising revenue to finance direct public expenditure and not public expenditure related to other indirect goals. From this perspective, the sharing of public revenue would not be possible except for some kind of modelling of the content of the ability to pay principle, whether according to the benefit deriving from public expenditure or indicators of the taxpayer's ability to pay, could be applied.

At this point, it should be noted that the ability to pay principle cannot be disregarded as it stands as a basic principle in defining the concrete measure of taxation that can be imposed. That does not mean, however, that it should not be modelled after other goals indicated by the Constitution and concretely singled out by the legislator from the *ensemble* of public services and goods to be provided, as well as in line with the economic capacity of the taxpayers.[21] So, as long as there are other indirect goals for taxation demanding the compression of the ability to pay principle in a proportional way, there is no reason why that cannot be admitted, namely by the Constitutional Court.[22]

2.2 Tax benefits as tax policy instruments to overcome a global crisis: the case of the COVID-19 pandemic

Being an economic, social or cultural incentive, the tax benefit represents all the advantages granted to taxpayers with a view to obtaining a particular behaviour, which would otherwise be achieved on a smaller scale. As an incentive, the tax benefit is somehow dynamic in nature and should always be regarded in a prospective way instead of a static one, along with the tax preferences that it creates (except for those situations in which the reliefs apply to past situations, whether for political, social, defence, diplomatic or other reasons because in that case the incentive becomes award).[23]

The material content of the incentive is variable[24] but ultimately related to the right to development,[25] which is internationally recognized, not only generally in Article 28 of the Universal Declaration of Human Rights[26] but mainly in Article 1 of the United Nations Covenants on Civil and Political Rights and on Economic, Social and Cultural Rights[27], expressly providing for a right of peoples to freely pursue economic, social and cultural development. This right entails that peoples may not under any circumstances be deprived of their own means of subsistence.

In this context, the COVID-19 pandemic has brought about severe concerns relating to the subsistence of taxpayers and thus jeopardizing this right to development. As a major public-health concern that has spread across the world, the COVID-19 pandemic has led to a disruption of global supply chains, paralyzed economic activity resulting therefrom, particularly in the tourism and services industries, and resulted in the fall of financial markets. Stemming from this framework is the expected setback of GDP Growth in 2020 which will probably be non-existent or even reach negative values.

The main challenge lies in the shift of the economic balance underlying the ability to pay principle which has been endangered in the case of several taxpayers. both natural and legal persons: By the (i) severe loss of income, (ii) need for significant investments on the taxpayers' part to create the necessary biosecurity conditions to prevent the propagation of the virus, and (iii) lack of liquidity for firms.

In response to this shift, most countries have sought to implement targeted emergency-response measures intended to counter the economic pressure incumbent upon economic markets. Most of these measures – which have been sanctioned on a European level by the European Union – do not qualify as tax incentives *per se* (since they do not imply a waiver of tax revenues). This is the case with tax-payment and reporting deferrals, accelerated refunds, suspension of tax inspections, direct financial support, among others, which have been put in place with a special focus on industries most affected by the spread of the virus across global markets.

The actual tax incentives approved which are characterized by the three principal elements of a tax incentive (i.e. chargeability, economic advantage, and financing) can generally be organized around five main areas of concern: (i) securing and stimulating employment, (ii) facilitating acquisition of materials and goods to counter the outbreak of the virus, (iii) economic subsistence of corporate bodies, (iv) mitigation of additional expenditure connected to the prevention of the virus., and (v) financing of investments and expenses made by State, regional or local bodies as well non-profit organizations in the management of the COVID-19 emergency-response. These five vectors compose the public policy option adopted by Governments in pursuance of the legal mandate granted by the people under a principle of "no taxation without representation".[28]

This having been said, one would do well to note that, in line with what has been detailed above, these options are modelled both by the ability to pay principle and the Constitutional framework imposing economic, social and cultural rights. The similitude of these objectives should therefore come as no surprise in spite of the differences in tax systems across the world and more specifically across Europe. Accordingly, the nature of the adopted measures and the manner in which they propose to mould taxpayer behaviour and prevent adverse economic consequences through the granting of economic advantages is in itself also quite similar.

Specifically on the securing employment front, actions put into effect or announced by governments are mainly linked to reducing the costs borne by companies with employees. This is achieved, on the one hand, by a supply of financial support in relation to a part or the entirety of employee remuneration (which does not constitute a tax incentive in itself) and, on the other hand, with total or partial relief in the payment of social security contributions due by employers. Inherent to both sets of actions described is the financing by the State of the preservation of employment contracts during the period of the duration of the suspension of corporate activities in connection with the virus. Whereas in the first instance this financing is represented by an actual transfer of money, in the latter only by a virtual one, as represented by the waiver of public revenue (qualifying as a public expense), which is in line with the very nature of the tax incentive.

On a European level for instance, Hungary has sought to temporarily modify social security rules for the period between March and June 2020 in certain key sectors affected by the virus outbreak (e.g. tourism, events, entertainment). These modified rules provide for an exemption from social security contributions due by employers on wages paid during that period and corresponding lower social security contributions for employees during that period. An exemption to employers has also been granted in Spain for social security contributions due under employment contracts which have been temporarily suspended or subject to reduced working hours on the condition that the relevant contracts are maintained for a period of six months subsequent to activity being resumed. Similarly, in Croatia, an exemption may apply to employers who have received subsidies intended to provide relief to the payment of salaries in the portion of salaries that is borne by them.

In relation to the acquisition of materials and goods to counter the outbreak of the virus, the bulk of the adopted initiatives may be subsumed under an exemption from VAT or customs duties due on imports of medical, sanitary and protective equipment, which is the case with France and Croatia. This is in line with the European Commission decision to temporarily waive VAT and customs duties on the importation of vital medical equipment from third countries. Adding to the above, the Greek government has approved a reduced VAT rate on products, the purpose of which is to prevent COVID-19 propagation (e.g. masks, gloves, soap, antiseptic products, alcohol) with this applying until 31 December 2020.

The economic subsistence of corporate bodies is one of the main priorities of government actions in view of the former's role in the driving of the economy thus justifying a number of financing mechanisms and grants put in place to tackle COVID-19 effects. The liquidity concern resulting from a halt in revenues carries a significant effect on the ability to pay principle. By way of example, whilst income received in 2019 could justify – under such a principle – a given level of tax charges, such a level in the context of the losses incurred in 2020 could no longer be compatible with this principle to the extent that the tax charges pertaining to 2019 would only be effectively borne in 2020 (as is typical in most tax systems despite advance payments being put in place). Enforcing the ability to pay the standard as determined in 2019 could therefore lead to significant imbalances in taxpayer accounts to the detriment of their economic survival.

With this in mind, some governments have sought to approve systems enabling the carry-back of losses. In particular, the Czech Republic, Poland and the Netherlands have approved schemes permitting the total or partial offsetting of losses incurred in 2020 against profits obtained in 2019. Other schemes implemented by European governments include the reduction of the Corporate Income Tax taxable base (notably by excluding subsidies obtained to mitigate COVID-19 effects) or the granting of tax rebates to companies facing severe difficulties as a result of the COVID-19 pandemic.

Also on the topic of economic subsistence, the mitigation of additional expenditure deriving from the virus takes on a vital role in view of the important amount of investments and additional costs incurred. To this end, Spain has granted a Stamp Duty exemption on the novation of mortgage for taxpayers' permanent homes. Italy, on the other hand, has provided for a tax credit with sanitization costs including costs for equipment and materials necessary for the protection of employee health.

Lastly, on the financing of investments and expenses made by State, regional or local bodies as well non-profit organizations in the management of the COVID-19 emergency-response, measures have included exemption from VAT on donations of goods and services (Croatia, Portugal, Greece) and the deduction for corporate income tax purposes or personal income tax purposes of such donations (Poland, Italy).

Other tax benefits have also been implemented in various countries as a way to promote economic recovery. This policy choice has mostly been directed at helping those sectors of activity which have been the most affected by the COVID-19 pandemic, notably, restaurants, catering, tourism, and the cultural sector. Austria has implemented a reduced VAT rate of 5 percent for the catering, tourism and cultural sector, applying from 1 July 2020 to 31 December 2020. Similar measures have been adopted by Belgium which has also sought to approve a reduced rate of 6 percent VAT for restaurant and catering services (with some exceptions in the case of beverages). Germany has also sought to apply a reduced VAT rate to restaurants. The Czech Republic for its part has chosen to lower VAT rates on accommodation, wellness and cultural activities. In different ways, Belgium has ensured the full deductibility of restaurant expenses as business expenses for PIT or CIT and Italy has created touristic vouchers in the form of tax credits.

Tax incentives to R&D in the form of tax credits have also been approved for countries such as Denmark or Italy. Germany has also chosen to improve the maximum threshold of R&D tax support. Tax incentives have thus assumed a crucial role in the legislative package approved by Governments in response to the social, health and economic crisis resulting from the COVID-19 pandemic. This role is two-fold. Firstly, it intends to adapt taxpayer behaviour, notably by mobilizing private resources towards a concerted emergency response intending to promote healthcare and social responsibility actions, as well as securing employment conditions. Secondly, it seeks to adjust the tax charges incumbent upon taxpayers to their actual ability to pay in view of increasing liquidity needs. The cornerstone of these policies is the core of economic, social or cultural rights which are incumbent upon the State to protect.

3 Finding New Sources of Revenues

As noted above, the tax policy adopted in the context of the COVID-19 response has focused on ensuring liquidity for businesses and families alike. Whilst most liquidity measures have not had an impact on State revenues as these related mostly to payment deferrals, some of the tax relief measures granted have signified a decrease in State revenue (indirect taxes and social security contribution cuts). This decrease has only been heightened by the fact that both consumption and income (and hence revenue deriving from taxation of these) have plummeted. On a budgetary level, however, expenditure has increased, with the need to mobilize a significant amount of State resources. This has driven States to find alternative sources of revenue both at the national and supra-national level. Such alternative sources of revenue may summarily be found in one of two places: (i) through funding, which will need to be repaid, or (ii) through a change in the fiscal policy.

3.1 Next Generation EU and the EU's long-term budget: A new national constraint policy?

In this context, the EU's long-term budget, coupled with Next Generation EU, the temporary instrument designed to boost recovery, will be the largest stimulus package ever financed through the EU budget. A total of 1.8 trillion will help rebuild a post-COVID-19 Europe. It will be a greener, more digital and more resilient Europe. The new long-term budget will increase flexibility mechanisms to guarantee it has the capacity to address unforeseen needs. It is a budget fit not only for today's realities but also for tomorrow's uncertainties. The last step of the adoption of the next long-term EU budget was reached on 17 December 2020.[29]

Recently,[30] the European Commission has set out its strategic guidance for the implementation of the Recovery and Resilience Facility in its 2021 Annual Sustainable Growth Strategy (ASGS). This Guidance states that: "The Facility is the key recovery instrument at the heart of Next Generation EU which will help the EU emerge stronger and more

Table 7.1 Multiannual Financial Framework 2021-2027

		Next Generation EU	*TOTAL*
1. Single market, innovation and digital	€ 132.8 billion	€ 10.6 billion	€ 143.4 billion
2. Cohesion, resilience and values	€ 377.8 billion	€ 721.9 billion	€ 1 099.7 billion
3. Natural resources and environment	€ 356.4 billion	€ 17.5 billion	€ 373.9 billion
4. Migration and border management	€ 22.7 billion	-	€ 22.7 billion
5. Security and defence	€ 13.2 billion	-	€ 13.2 billion
6. Neighbourhood and the world	€ 98.4 billion		€ 98.4 billion
7. European public administration	€ 73.1 billion	-	€ 73.1 billion
TOTAL MFF	**€ 1 074.3 billion**	**€ 750 billion**	**€ 1 824.3 billion**

All amounts in € billion, in constant 2018 prices.
Source: European Commission
* The amounts include the targeted reinforcement of ten programmes forming a total of €15 billion, compared to the agreement from 21 July 2020. The programmes are Horizon Europe, Erasmus+, EU4Health, Integrated Border Management Fund, Rights and Values, Creative Europe, InvestEU, European Border and Coast Guard Agency, Humanitarian Aid.

resilient from the current crisis. The Facility will provide an unprecedented 672.5 billion in loans and grants in frontloaded financial support for the crucial first years of the recovery.

The publication of the ASGS launches this year's European Semester cycle. In last year's ASGS the Commission launched a new growth strategy based on the European Green Deal and the concept of competitive sustainability. This year's ASGS is in full continuity with the previous one. The four dimensions of environmental sustainability, productivity, fairness and macroeconomic stability identified in last year's ASGS remain the guiding principles underpinning Member States' recovery and resilience plans and their national reforms and investments. These dimensions lie at the heart of the European Semester and ensure that the new growth agenda helps to build foundations for a green, digital and sustainable recovery.

In order to benefit from the Recovery and Resilience Facility, Member States should submit their draft recovery and resilience plans outlining national investment and reform agendas in line with the aforementioned EU policy criteria. Member States' recovery and resilience plans should address the economic policy challenges set out in the country-specific recommendations of recent years and in particular in the 2019 and 2020 cycles. The plans should also enable Member States to enhance their economic growth potential, job creation and economic and social resilience, and to meet green and digital transitions.

Based on their relevance across Member States, the very large investments required, and their potential to create jobs and growth and reap the benefits of green and digital transitions, the Commission strongly encourages Member States to include in their plans investment and reforms in the following flagship areas:

1. Power up – The frontloading of future-proof clean technologies and acceleration of the development and use of renewables;
2. Renovate – The improvement of energy efficiency of public and private buildings;
3. Recharge and Refuel – The promotion of future-proof clean technologies to accelerate the use of sustainable, accessible and smart transport, charging and refuelling stations and extension of public transport;
4. Connect – The fast rollout of rapid broadband services to all regions and households, including fibre and 5G networks;
5. Modernise – The digitalisation of public administration and services, including judicial and healthcare systems;
6. Scale-up – The increase in European industrial data cloud

capacities and the development of the most powerful, cutting edge, and sustainable processors;

7. Reskill and upskill – The adaptation of education systems to support digital skills and educational and vocational training for all ages.

The implementation of the Facility will be coordinated by the Commission's Recovery and Resilience Task Force in close cooperation with the Directorate-General for Economic and Financial Affairs and will have an influence on EU member state budgets".

To cater for the above financing and grants, the EU strategy also includes finding new sources of revenue. Whilst this has been on the EU agenda for quite some time, the long-term EU budget for 2021–2027 is envisaging moving forward with the implementation of:

(i) A carbon border adjustment mechanism taxing any product imported from a country outside of the EU that does not have a system to price carbon;

(ii) A digital levy on digital business activities, which are intrinsically dematerialized and profiting from mostly intangible assets;

(iii) A financial Transaction Tax;

(iv) A financial contribution linked to the corporate sector; or

(v) A new common corporate tax base.

It is unclear from the EU budget whether some of the aforementioned sources of revenue would follow the mechanics of previous proposals made by the EU (e.g. digital levy and new common corporate tax base) or would alternatively materialize in alternative schemes. In any case, the choice to revive/continue the discussion on these topics – which include environmental, financial and digital taxation – is undeniably marked by the economic rise in these sectors of activity in a post-Covid world, being for the most part aligned with either OECD studies and also reflected at the level of the revisions in tax policy underway in some countries.

3.2 Future outlook: Tax Policy as an Instrument to Increase State Revenues

The discussion on finding new sources of revenue through changes in the fiscal policy is not restricted to the European Union but also an individual concern of each State. This discussion, which has been underway since the 2009 crisis, particularly for poorer economies, has been transformed into a matter of priority by the increase in expenditure brought about by the COVID-19 pandemic and the decrease in tax revenues.

The choices to make are not easy ones. Because the State can only tax within certain limits which are defined with reference to degrees of wealth, income or expenditure, the key issues may therefore be summarized as follows:

(i) There has been an evident shift in the taxpayers' ability to pay: whereas some taxpayers have lost a significant portion of (if not their entire) income, some have maintained the same economic capacity and yet others have increased this capacity. Should the shift in taxpayer ability to pay be reflected in the level of income taxes, which are typically deemed as the champions for the ability to pay principle due to their application on income (reflecting the taxpayer's increase in wealth), their progressivity (with higher levels of taxation applying to higher income) and their ability to consider actual taxpayer's available wealth (as they take into account expenses borne by the taxpayer, charges, etc.), or would this shift rather need to be reflected in the level of other taxes with a less permeable tax base (e.g. consumption, wealth, environment), which are not in themselves necessarily marked by the ability to pay principle but could nevertheless be adapted accordingly?;

(ii) Should any modifications to the fiscal policy be temporary or permanent?;

(iii) Are there other avenues to explore to achieve the necessary funding for the COVID-19 expenditure?

3.2.1   The choice to impose higher taxes   In June 2020, an open letter from millionaires across the globe (mostly based in the US and UK) asked governments to increase their taxation so as to fund COVID-19 expenses.[31] Insofar as the Government needs to finance State activity it seems inevitable that the ability to pay principle will require those wealthier persons to contribute in a higher measure to the State pool of revenues. This is – as explained – a direct result of the ability to pay principle which requires States to ensure substantive equality in the distribution of tax burdens.

Pursuant to an over-simplistic approach to the ability to pay principle as a tool to apply in the distribution of the increased State budgetary needs, one would be forgiven in thinking that the simplest solution would be to increase income taxation for those who have retained their revenues. In fact, public discussion in many countries has circled this solution to a greater or lesser degree. Adopting such a solution would not theoretically be in breach of the ability to pay principle insofar as both the horizontal equity and the vertical equity components would be safeguarded. However, this approach would disregard detrimental implications both from a social or economic standpoint, particularly in poorer economies.

In such poorer economies, where the number and economic capacity of large taxpayers is reduced, the aforementioned solution would not be economically sustainable in the long run and would certainly not serve to foster economic growth. Such economies are usually sustained by a large number of middle-class taxpayers earning only income deriving from their labour. From a social equity stand-point, the fact that these taxpayers have retained their economic capacity (notably because they work in industries which have not been affected) does not necessarily equate to it being fair to require them to pay more taxes on their income (in addition to those they already pay) nor would such a choice be efficient. In truth, the rule of thumb for middle-class taxpayers is that where income taxation increases, economic power decreases, thus leading to lower consumption rates. This would necessarily imply loss of income throughout other economic players and lower consumption taxes being collected.

As noted by the OECD in its July 2018 report on Tax Policies for inclusive growth in a changing world, raising income taxes (particu-larly with an emphasis on employment income) may ultimately prove to be counterproductive and lead to a loss in revenue rather than its increase. The solution which has been argued for by the OECD is to seek to increase taxation of those fiscal bases that are not as perme-able, notably, consumption tax and wealth/assets taxes, as well as regarding environmental taxes as new sources of revenues.

Tax measures in European countries to ensure the economic recovery have been spearheaded by the Hungarian government which has created a special retail tax, applicable to retailers with annual revenue of over HUF 500 million (EUR 1.5 million) and a special tax on the financial sector on the amount of the adjusted balance sheet total exceeding HUF 50 billion (EUR 143 million). Whereas the foreign ownership of large retailers remains high, the financial sector has profited from very high performance over the course of previous years. Both taxes intend to capture windfall gains by either taxing very high revenues or assets.

In February this year, the French left-wing suggested that (i) the Solidarity Tax on Wealth be reinstated so as to fund COVID-19 and (ii) higher taxation be imposed on speculative income. In the UK, the Wealth Tax Commission said targeting the richest in society would be the fairest and most efficient way to raise taxes in response to the pandemic. Across the globe, this idea of imposing special taxes on wealth or windfall gains rather than employment income is gaining traction in countries such as Canada, the US and Argentina.

The discussion is still at an early stage and most solutions that are being formally proposed involve imposing higher or new taxes on wealth / other assets / passive income / inheritance. This raises the question as to whether these tax changes will actually signify a permanent change to the tax system and the manner of construing the ability to pay principle.

3.2.2 Temporary or Permanent Tax Policies? The problem is that construing a tax policy around excessive taxation of wealth and assets to support excessive expenditure may ultimately lead to structural imbalances in the system. Definitive changes to tax policies should be mindful of long-term sustainability concerns by fostering economic growth and development.

As has been more than amply depicted and described by economists over the past century, there is a taxation bliss-point. And while wealthier taxpayers may well understand the temporary concerns raised by COVID-19, in the long-run it is expected that these taxpayers will continue to adjust their behaviour depending on the level of taxation. By way of example, high-income earners tend to find ways to avoid taxes legally, through mobility (to say nothing of tax evasion). Moreover, high tax rates or charges also tend to discourage investment, entrepreneurship, and even employment. States thus considering these measures as permanent may well be on the way to putting a damper on their fiscal competitiveness.

To summarize, the tax system will and should undeniably be used as the main tool to support businesses and individuals with lower income and thus reduce inequalities. The danger is that temporary fixes to the management of public debt are used to model the tax system to the detriment of a national development strategy. Rather than resorting to these very specific fixes – which may briefly resolve the public debt issue –, States that have suffered significantly from this crisis should definitely consider undergoing comprehensive fiscal reforms ensuring a more just distribution of wealth between citizens, while also nurturing economic development. This requires a strategy covering both the tax and the budgetary side.

3.2.3 Paving the Way for Structural Reforms The problems brought to light by the COVID-19 pandemic require a structural approach both at the level of revenues and at the level of expenditure. While this has been done while supporting businesses and citizens in the context of an emergency response, the same cannot be said with respect to construing fiscal and budget reform policies. Discussion on these topics is still very incipient and the approval and effectiveness of a structured fiscal package that addresses these concerns is yet to be seen.

Relieving budgetary pressure may, in a first approach, be achieved through more efficient and smarter expenditure, which requires the adoption of more flexible budgetary models and a rethinking of expenditure as a whole. This could inclusively help shift the focus from wealth taxes, to other forms of taxation.

To give an idea, taxing wealth to the detriment of consumption seems to derive from a one-sided interpretation of the ability to pay principle and disregard the fact that the same should be analysed in the full context of the system. It is therefore possible to construct a system that takes into account ability to pay while also raising VAT rates, for example. This would be the case if the expenditure side is reformed so as to specifically allocate VAT revenues to support lower income taxpayers in pursuance of equity objectives.

Alternatively, imposing environmental taxes could also be construed as a viable avenue. The OECD has been encouraging countries to developing recovery packages based on green objectives, particularly with respect to carbon pricing, which could serve to increase tax revenues and, at the same time, incentivize low-carbon alternatives that would enable a more sustainable future. Again, this would require the rethinking of the tax system as a whole to implant an environmental component at its very core, rather than merely seeking to tax high-emissions.

States should therefore seek to consider tackling the issue from an integrated perspective rethinking expenditure, while reforming tax policies. Though it is expected that public discussion on these topics will continue to grow and evolve, governments should be promoting this type of solution as a matter of priority rather than delaying the inevitable and perpetuating unsustainable pressures on State budgets.

Notes

1 Tax benefit is a similar expression to tax subsidy, tax relief, tax concession, and, in German, *Indirekte Förderungen*. Each of these names identifies the positive part of the concept, that is, the advantage coming from the public will to waive certain public revenue. Nevertheless, each of them has a specific nature within the wider concept of tax expense (which all of them are). On the concept of tax benefit see, in Portuguese, Sá Gomes, N. 1993: *Manual de Direito Fiscal, Cadernos de Ciência*

Técnica e Fiscal. Lisbon: Centro de Estudos Fiscais, p. 323; Sá Gomes, N. 1991: *Teoria Geral dos Benefícios Fiscais*. Lisbon: CCTF, p. 12; Vaz Freire, M. P. 1995: *Nascimento, modificação e extinção dos benefícios fiscais*. Lisbon: Edição do Autor, *passim*; Xavier, A. 1974: *Manual de Direito Fiscal*, Lisbon: AAFDL, pp. 291–293; Sílvio da Costa, A. Paulo Rato Rainha, J. H. and Freitas Pereira, H. 1987: *Benefícios fiscais em Portugal*, Coimbra: Almedina, pp. 15–16; Fichera, F. 1973: *Imposizione ed extrafiscalità nel sistema costituzionale*. Naples: ESI, *passim*.

2 In the particular case of Portugal, that process of centralization was set in motion with the Portuguese tax reform of 1830, which began to dismantle the tax system of the old regime that was, in fact, a coexistence of three systems: the Church's tax system, the State's tax system and the manor' tax system. In fact, despite the fact that the Renaissance's taxation system had a national component, it was very distant from the characteristics of generality and equality that stand out in modern tax systems, which induced the development of the concept of "tax privilege".

3 Bacelar Gouveia, J. 1993: Os Incentivos Fiscais Contratuais ao Investimento Estrangeiro no Direito Fiscal Português – Regime Jurídico e Implicações Constitucionais. In Ministério Das Finanças – DGCI, XXX Aniversário do Centro de Estudos Fiscais – Colóquio sobre "A Internacionalização da Economia e a Fiscalidade. Lisbon: DGCI, p. 277.

4 In the draft bill of the "Tax Benefits Code", prepared by Xavier, A. and Sousa Franco, A. L. (Xavier, A. and Sousa Franco, A. L. 1969: Anteprojecto de Estatuto dos Benefícios Fiscais, Lisbon), we can find, in Article 1/1, that same idea that we hereby reproduce: "All people are obliged, under the law, to contribute, in accordance to their personal assets, to public costs."

5 See Martínez Lago, M. Á. and García de la Mora, L. 2005: *Lecciones de Derecho Financiero y Tributario* (2nd ed.), Madrid: Iustel, Portal Derecho, SA, pp. 73–75.

6 In an attempt to answer the question raised by De Freitas Pereira, M. H. 2005: *Fiscalidade*. Coimbra: Almedina, p. 355, note 518, as to the idea that the meaning of "normative system of a tax" is not quite established in the scientific community, we think that the analysis should concentrate firstly on what is the place occupied by norms that create tax benefits within the legal order and, afterwards, on setting out the limits of the aforementioned normative system. On this subject, see Tipke, K. and Lang, J. 2002: *Steuerrecht* (17th ed.), Cologne: Verlag Dr. Otto Schimdt, pp. 719–722, and Casalta Nabais, J. 1998: *O Dever Fundamental de Pagar Impostos*. Coimbra: Almedina, pp. 645–654. For further developments see Friauf, K. H. 1966: *Verfassungsrechtliche Grezen der Wirtschaftslenkung und Socialgestaltung*. Tübingen: Krainer Wernsmann, Vogel, K. 1999: Verfassungsrechtsprechung zum Steuerrecht. Schriftenreihe der Juristischen Gesellschaft zu Berlin, Heft 160, Wernsmann, R. 2000. *Das gleichheitswidrige Steuergesetz –*

Rechtsfolgen und Rechtsschutz. Berlin: Münsterische Beiträge zur Rechtswissenschaft.

7   On the doctrine of limitations to instruments of political power see, among others, the work of Hespanha, A. M. 1994: *As Vésperas do Leviathan – Instituições e Poder Político, Portugal, século XVII.* Coimbra: Almedina, pp. 472–487.

8   On the evolution and actual meaning of the idea of the Welfare State see, among others, Wilensky, H. L. 2002: *Rich Democracies – Political Economy, Public Policy and Performance.* London: University of California Press, pp. 430–493, and, more generally, Leisering, L. and Walker, R. (eds.) 1988: *The Dynamics of Modern Society.* Bristol: Policy Press, Alcock, P., Erskine, A. and May, M. (eds.) 2003: *The Student's Companion to Social Policy.* Oxford: Blackwell., Pierson, P. (ed.) 2001: *The New Politics of the Welfare State.* Oxford: Oxford University Press.

9   The Portuguese legislator, in a somewhat unclear manner, prefers to talk about "rule-taxation" or "normal-taxation" (see Article 12 of the Tax Benefits Code – EBF) without ever specifying what that is. However, we were able to put together a few clues, which allow us to highlight the following circumstance: the legislator wants to keep that concept because certain types of tax benefits contemplate partial reliefs, which could become problematic at the time of their revocation. Let us imagine a certain tax benefit that provided for a lower tax rate for certain entities (say 20% instead of 25%). If that benefit was revoked it would not be enough to establish that the revocation of such benefit would simply reinstate the application of that tax to those entities, since they were already taxed, only at a smaller rate. Therefore, what the legislator means by "rule-taxation" is that the reinstatement of the "rule-taxation" means the reinstatement of the taxation that is usually applicable to similar entities, if no discrimination is applied. This concept of "rule-taxation" does not match, however, the essential core of the tax that we hereby present, as the latter has an evaluative element that the former does not have as it refers to the mere disappearance of partial reliefs from the legal order.

10 Public goods are goods that are both non-excludable and non-rivalrous in that individuals cannot be effectively excluded from use and where use by one individual does not reduce availability to others. Pure public goods (or services) are *equally available* to all members of the relevant community. A single unit of the good, as produced, provides a multiplicity of consumption units, all of which are somehow identical. Impure public goods are goods that are neither purely private nor purely public. Impurity or imperfect publicness in this respect has been defined as any departure from the availability of "equal quantities of homogeneous-quality consumption units" to all customers.

11 On the concept of tax see, in Portugal, Soares Martinez, P. 1995: *Direito Fiscal.* Coimbra: Almedina, pp. 26–57, Casalta Nabais, J. 2006: *Direito Fiscal,* Coimbra, Almedina, pp. 10–66, Saldanha Sanches, J. L. 2002:

Manual de Direito Fiscal (2nd edition), Coimbra: Coimbra Editora, pp. 13–16.

12 On tax justice see Tipke, K. 1993: Die Steuerrechtsordnung, . . . , pp. 260–261 and, from the same author, Besteuerungsmoral und Steuermoral, Köln, Westdeutscher Verlag GmbH.

13 Casalta Nabais, J., *O Dever* . . . , *op. cit.*, p. 449.

14 We assume the conceptual identity of the two concepts. Although one could argue in favour of their distinction, there is no relevant normative reason to do so. On this subject, see Moschetti, F. 1993: *La capacità contributiva – Profili Generali*. In F. Moschetti et al., La Capacità Contributiva, Milan: CEDAM, pp. 25–26, to whom the evaluation of the ability to pay is a synthesis of the following elements: "a) article 53 [of the Italian Constitution] aims at establishing a justice criterion in taxation issues; b) the said criterion is different from the principle of equality and from formal standards like simple rationality and legislative coherence; c) the same criterion assumes, as a necessary but non-sufficient condition, the economic capacity of the taxpayer; d) the economic capacity should be above a minimum and should be considered as adequate considering the level of public expenses and given the values established in the Constitution; e) the aforementioned parity may therefore result in a conceptual difference between the ability to pay and economic capacity". From this perspective, the ability to pay refers only to a means of financing and can be composed of several levels according to the evidenced economic capacity.

15 On the rehabilitation of the ability to pay principle and its double standard as a measure of taxation and as a fundamental right see Herrera Molina, P. M. 1998: *Capacidad Económica y Sistema Fiscal – Análisis del ordenamiento español a la luz del Derecho alemán*. Madrid: Marcial Pons, pp. 23–80 and, more recently, Vasques, S. 2004: *Capacidade Contributiva, Rendimento e Patrimônio*. Fórum de Direito Tributário (Brasil), 11, pp. 32–40.

16 Cfr. Leibholz, G. 1959: *Die Gleichheit vor dem Gesetz. Eine Studie auf rechtsvergleichender und rechtsphilosophischer Grundlage* (2nd ed.), Munich/Berlin: Mohr Siebeck, p. 235. *Legal* equality is a product of a collision of principles and therefore is different from *factual* equality – hence the "equality-paradox" (since what is equal treatment according to one is unequal treatment according to the other, and vice versa, if both equalities are put together under a single principle of equality that principle would contain an equality-paradox) [Alexy, R. 2002: *Teoria de los Derechos Fundamentales* (trad. Ernesto Garzón Valdés). Madrid: Centro de Estudios Políticos y Constitucionales]. For example, until 2010, article 31/2 of the CIRS, which creates a simplified regime of taxation on professional income established that the determination of net income in the case of professional income depended on the application of the ratios provided for that legal rule as long as a minimum of taxable income was preserved. This minimum taxable income ensured legal equality for all taxpayers for

as long as their income was below that minimum they all had to pay the same amount of tax. However, it did not guarantee factual equality since many taxpayers had to pay that minimum despite the fact that they did not generate any income at all.

17 See Alexy, R., *Teoria* . . . , *op. cit.*, pp. 415–418. Next note to read.

18 Maffezoni F., *Il principio* . . . , *op. cit.*, pp. 325–326.

19 As an example, the author refers to the fact that progressive taxes may take on several forms: taxes on real income that include several kinds of income, progressive taxes on unitary and global income whether spread or not spread over several categories; singular income can be effective or presumed; corporate income can be determined through ordinary or accelerated depreciation, etc.

20 Maffezoni F., *Il principio* . . . , *op. cit.*, p. 326.

21 Consider the need to help a country's least developed areas or even the ones hit by natural disasters. In each of these situations, there are different "abilities to pay". Which allows us to argue, like Moschetti (Moschetti, F. 1993: La capacità . . . , *op. cit.*, pp. 42–47), that the ability to pay has several degrees according to each of its variables, the content of which is made more complex with reference to the constitutional system at stake. According to Moschetti (Moschetti, F. 1993: La capacità . . . , *op. cit.*, pp. 46–47), the scope of discretion granted to the Italian legislator as to the establishment of indirect goals for taxation should be guided by the following principles: (1) situations or facts that do not show any kind of economic capacity cannot be subject to taxation; (2) as a result of a systematic interpretation of article 53 of the Italian Constitution and of other constitutional norms, economic capacity should be considered as part of the ability to pay; (3) normative principles invoked by tax rules should be respected along with those rules; (4) the principle of coherence, which states that taxes should be used according to their nature and thus avoiding punitive goals should also be respected.

22 Maffezoni F., *Il principio* . . . , *op. cit.*, p. 329.

23 As argued by Bacelar Gouveia, J.: "Os Incentivos Fiscais Contratuais. . .", *op. cit.*, p. 278. Moreover, the author recognizes that "is it obvious that a certain frailty has to be attributed to the distinction (between dynamic and static tax benefits) which is not entirely safe in borderline situations in which it is difficult to establish a relationship with one of the two terms" (p. 278, note 30).

24 Because it depends on the degree of State intervention in that given system.

25 For further developments see Paz Ferreira, E. 2004: *Valores e Interesses – Desenvolvimento e Política Comunitária de Cooperação*. Coimbra: Almedina, pp. 198–200.

26 Signed in the UN on 10 December 1948 (A/RES/217).

27 Both adopted and opened for signature, ratification and adhesion by Resolution 2200-A (XXI) of the General Assembly of the UN, on 16 December 1966.

28 On this topic, see D.'Oliveira Martins, G. W. 2006: O princípio da auto-tributação: perspectivas e evoluções recentes. In AAVV, *Estudos em Homenagem ao Professor Doutor António Luciano de Sousa Franco*, Coimbra: Coimbra Editora, pp. 410–423.

29 According to
    https://ec.europa.eu/info/strategy/recovery-plan-europe_en,
    the Commission put forward its proposal for the EU's next long-term budget on 2 May 2018. The framework proposal was immediately followed by legislative proposals for the 37 sectoral programmes (e.g. cohesion, agriculture, Erasmus, Horizon Europe, etc). Between 2018 and the beginning of 2020, the Commission worked hand in hand with the rotating Presidencies of the Council, and in close collaboration with the European Parliament, to take the negotiations forward. On 27 May 2020, in response to the unprecedented crisis caused by the coronavirus, the European Commission proposed the temporary recovery instrument Next Generation EU of 750 billion, as well as targeted reinforcements to the long-term EU budget for 2021–2027. On 21 July 2020, EU heads of state or government reached a political agreement on the package. On 10 November 2020, the European Parliament and the Council reached an agreement on the package. On 10 December 2020, EU Member States in the European Council agreed to finalise the adoption of the MFF Regulation and the Own Resources Decision, at the level of the Council. On 17 December 2020, the Council decided to adopt the next long-term EU budget for the 2021–2027 period. This was the final step in the adoption process following the vote in the European Parliament on 16 December, which endorsed the MFF Regulation with a significant majority. On 18 December 2020, the European Parliament and the Council reached an agreement on the Recovery and Resilience Facility, the key instrument at the heart of Next Generation EU.

30 And in accordance with https://ec.europa.eu/commission/presscorner/detail/en/IP_20_1658.

31 https://www.millionairesforhumanity.com/.

References

Alcock, P., Erskine, A. and May, M. (eds.) 2003: *The student's companion to social policy*. Oxford: Blackwell.

Alexy, R. 2002: *Teoria de los Derechos Fundamentales* (trad. Ernesto Garzón Valdés). Madrid: Centro de Estudios Políticos y Constitucionales.

Bacelar Gouveia, J. 1993: Os Incentivos Fiscais Contratuais ao Investimento Estrangeiro no Direito Fiscal Português – Regime Jurídico e Implicações Constitucionais. In Ministério Das Finanças – DGCI, *XXX Aniversário do Centro de Estudos Fiscais – Colóquio sobre "A Internacionalização da Economia e a Fiscalidade*. Lisbon: DGCI.

Barbas Homem, A. P. 2006: *O Espírito das Instituições – Um estudo de História do Estado*. Coimbra: Almedina.

Bonney, R. and Ormrod, W. M. 1999: *Crisis, revolutions and self-sustained growth: Towards a conceptual model of change in Fiscal History*, Stanford: Paul Watkins Publishing.

Carvalho Fernandes, L. A. 1996: *Teoria Geral do Direito Civil*. Vol. II, Lisbon, Lex.

Casalta Nabais, J. 2006: *Direito Fiscal*. (4th ed.), Coimbra: Almedina.

Casalta Nabais, J. 1998: *O Dever Fundamental de Pagar Impostos*. Coimbra: Almedina.

D'Amati, N. 1980: Agevolazioni ed esenzioni tributarie. In *Novissimo Dig. It.*, Turin: Appendice.

D'Oliveira Martins, G. W. 2004: *A Despesa Fiscal e o Orçamento do Estado no ordenamento jurídico português*. Coimbra: Almedina.

D'Oliveira Martins, G. W. 2006: O princípio da autotributação: perspectivas e evoluções recentes. In AAVV, *Estudos em Homenagem ao Professor Doutor António Luciano de Sousa Franco*, Coimbra: Coimbra Editora, 410–423.

De Freitas Pereira, M. H. 2005: *Fiscalidade*. Coimbra: Almedina.

De Matos Antunes Varela, J. 1997: *Das Obrigações em Geral*. Vol. II (7th ed. – reprinted), Coimbra: Almedina.

Faveiro, V. 2002: *O Estatuto do Contribuinte – A Pessoa do Contribuinte no Estado Social de Direito*. Coimbra, Coimbra Editora.

Fichera, F. 1973: *Imposizione ed extrafiscalità nel sistema costituzionale*. Naples: ESI.

Freitas do Amaral, D. 2001: *Curso de Direito Administrativo*. Vol. II, Coimbra: Livraria Almedina.

Friauf, K. H. 1966: *Verfassungsrechtliche Grezen der Wirtschaftslenkung und Socialgestaltung*. Tübingen: Krainer Wernsmann.

Gomes Canotilho, J. J. 2002: *Direito Constitucional e Teoria da Constituição*. (6th ed.), Coimbra: Almedina.

Herrera Molina, P. M. 1998: *Capacidad Económica y Sistema Fiscal – Análisis del ordenamiento español a la luz del Derecho alemán*. Madrid: Marcial Pons.

Hespanha, A. M. 1994: *As Vésperas do Leviathan – Instituições e Poder Político, Portugal, século XVII*. Coimbra: Almedina.

Legrand, J., Propper, C. and Robinson, R. 1992: *The economics of social problems*. London: Macmillan.

Leibholz, G. 1959: Die Gleichheit vor dem Gesetz. Eine Studie auf rechtsvergleichender und rechtsphilosophischer Grundlage (2nd ed.), Munich/Berlin: Mohr Siebeck.

Leisering, L. and Walker, R. (eds.) 1988: *The dynamics of modern society*. Bristol: Policy Press.

Martínez Lago, M. Á. and García de la Mora, L. 2005: *Lecciones de Derecho Financiero y Tributario* (2nd ed.), Madrid: Iustel, Portal Derecho, SA.

Moschetti, F. 1993: La capacità contributiva – Profili Generali. In F. Moschetti *et al.*, *La Capacità Contributiva*, Milan: CEDAM.

OECD 2018: *OECD Report to G-20 Finance Ministers and Central Bank*

Governors: *Tax Policies for inclusive growth in a changing world*. Paris: OECD.

OECD 2020: *Tax and Fiscal Policy in Response to the Coronavirus Crisis: Strengthening Confidence and Resilience* in *Tackling Coronavirus (Covid-19): Contributing to a Global Effort*. Paris: OECD.

Paz Ferreira, E. 2004: *Valores e Interesses – Desenvolvimento e Política Comunitária de Cooperação*. Coimbra: Almedina.

Pereira Coelho, F. M. 1995: A renúncia abdicativa no Direito Civil (Algumas notas tendentes à definição do seu regime). Coimbra: Coimbra Editora.

Pierson, P. (ed.) 2001: *The New Politics of the Welfare State*. Oxford: Oxford University Press.

Sá Gomes, N. 1993: *Manual de Direito Fiscal, Cadernos de Ciência Técnica e Fiscal*. Lisbon: Centro de Estudos Fiscais.

Sá Gomes, N. 1991: *Teoria Geral dos Benefícios Fiscais*. Lisbon: CCTF.

Saldanha Sanches, J. L. 2002: Manual de Direito Fiscal (2nd edition), Coimbra: Coimbra Editora.

Saldanha Sanches, J. L. 2006: *Os limites do planeamento fiscal*. Coimbra: Coimbra Editora.

Sílvio da Costa, A. Paulo Rato Rainha, J. H. and Freitas Pereira, H. 1987: *Benefícios fiscais em Portugal*, Coimbra: Almedina.

Soares Martinez, P. 1995: *Direito Fiscal*. Coimbra: Almedina.

Tipke, K. and Lang, J. 2002: *Steuerrecht*. (17th ed.), Cologne: Verlag Dr. Otto Schimdt.

Vasques, S. 2004: Capacidade Contributiva, Rendimento e Patrimônio. *Fórum de Direito Tributário* (Brasil), 11, 32–40.

Vaz Freire, M. P. 1995: *Nascimento, modificação e extinção dos benefícios fiscais*. Lisbon: Edição de autor.

Vaz Serra, A. 1954: Remissão, reconhecimento negativo de dívida e contrato extintivo da relação obrigacional bilateral. *Boletim do Ministério da Justiça*, 43.

Vogel, K. 1999: Verfassungsrechtsprechung zum Steuerrecht. *Schriftenreihe der Juristischen Gesellschaft zu Berlin*, Heft 160.

Xavier, A. 1972: *Conceito e Natureza do Acto Tributário*. Coimbra: Almedina.

Xavier, A. 1974: *Manual de Direito Fiscal*, AAFDL: Lisbon.

Xavier, A. and Sousa Franco, A. L. 1969: Anteprojecto de Estatuto dos Benefícios Fiscais, Lisbon.

Wernsmann, R. 2000. *Das gleichheitswidrige Steuergesetz – Rechtsfolgen und Rechtsschutz*. Berlin: Münsterische Beiträge zur Rechtswissenschaft.

Wernsmann, R. 2000. *Das gleichheitswidrige Steuergesetz – Rechtsfolgen und Rechtsschutz*. Berlin: Münsterische Beiträge zur Rechtswissenschaft.

Wilensky, H. L. 2002: *Rich Democracies – Political Economy, Public Policy and Performance*. London: University of California Press.

8

The International Monetary and Financial System and the Right to Assistance from the International Monetary Fund

JOSÉ RENATO GONÇALVES

1 The International Monetary and Financial System and its functions

The Articles of Agreement of the International Monetary Fund (IMF) refer successively to the International Monetary System without defining it, while proclaiming that its essential purpose is to provide a framework to facilitate the international exchanges (of goods, services and capital) and to promote sound and sustainable economic growth (see Article IV – section I).

The designation is somewhat ambiguous, as it can lead to misunderstandings if understood in its strict sense, referring to the monetary aspect, precisely because it is difficult to distinguish between the monetary and financial components, despite the close and perhaps inevitable interconnection between the two in the present day.

Therefore, the most diverse national and international bodies, including the Bank for International Settlements, have recognised and emphasised that the world's financial markets have become so integrated in recent decades as never before since the gold standard period – which predominated in the years before the outbreak of the First World War in 1914. Growing financial interdependence on a practically universal scale has to some extent thrown into crisis the usual distinctions between bank lending and securities financing, between domestic and international securities, between spot and derivative instruments, as well as the very different categories of these latter instruments.

In view of all these and other difficulties, and in order to better understand the complex contemporary international financial and monetary reality, it would certainly be preferable to speak of the public and private International Monetary and Financial System, as various authors have already understood so, the former referring to predominantly interstate or intergovernmental (i.e. public) monetary and financial relations, and the latter referring to predominantly private (monetary and financial) relations, i.e., relations between private and public entities, but, in the case of the latter, when they are deprived of their special and privileged status, therefore acting as if they were relations between private subjects.[1]

The distinction is essentially based on the quality or position, public or private, in which the subjects participate in legal relations, not in their personal legal position or nature, respecting the field of the financing of economies, which includes both the financing of private entities and the financing of public entities, but, in the latter case, only the part of the financing that public entities resort to under the same conditions as the other, non-public entities, without the special and privileged position exclusively reserved to public entities.[2]

Thus, the public or interstate system comprises the set of international provisions, institutions, mechanisms and understandings established and accepted by the States, as well as by international organisations established by them, for the purpose of preventing and helping to resolve monetary and financial crises of the greatest impact and seriousness, particularly cross-border ones, in cooperation with the representatives and leaders of national authorities.

As is well known, the official launch of the International Monetary System took place before the end of the Second World War, in July 1944, at the Bretton Woods conference, which gave rise to the International Monetary Fund (IMF) and the World Bank or International Bank for Reconstruction and Development, the two major international economic institutions "of Bretton Woods".

The rules established at that time, particularly those contained in the IMF Statutes, in no way exhaust the international monetary and financial framework, with a universal or 'global' vocation, which came into force and to which all the countries of the world agreed to be subject, sooner or later, with greater or lesser resistance, until the present day.[3] Among other sources of law, the most important are those of unilateral origin, including the numerous decisions of the IMF itself (estimated to number between one and two tens of thousands), which form a legal bloc that is substantially more significant than the Articles of Agreement themselves, even though they are based on and inspired by them. However, the unilateral acts of States are also important, as they concretise and develop their conventional provisions and close loopholes.

Legal theory also adds a set of customary norms, few in number, such as that stipulating that a State's currency must not be used without its assent by another State or an international organisation. However, in this regard, the practice followed by the United States of America should be noted, which is very tolerant of the use of its currency by various States of the world, even in cases where they have gone so far as to declare the US dollar legal tender in their territory.[4]

The IMF is the international organisation that was entrusted by the founding member States (and later by States that have become members) to manage the new International Monetary System – interstate and public in nature, having been created by and for States, as it only applies to them, in principle at least in the first instance.

This does not mean that the IMF does not also constrain the activities of private entities – indeed, it does, and very decisively so. The transactions constantly carried out by various operators, both public and private, are subject to and must conform to international monetary rules in force, to the extent that these have become applicable in the various countries of the world. In principle, the rules that make up the interstate International Monetary System do not have direct or immediate effect on the domestic legal orders of IMF member States. However, they strongly condition them.

As in other areas of International Law, the International Monetary System is characterised by strong institutionalisation. And, almost paradoxically, also by a marked informalism, always in order to respond satisfactorily to the purposes and specific aspects of the system. The informal approach referred to is reflected in the many unsigned accords (*gentlemen's agreements*) and in the simple practices of States and their central banks.

The International Monetary System, which is managed by the IMF, and the regional monetary and financial subsystems set up on the various continents, carry out monetary and financial organisation and supervision through the exercise of the powers conventionally conferred on them by States – including powers in the area of sanctions, although these are rarely applied – and through recourse to the means and mechanisms provided for and in operation.[5]

Both the universal monetary system and the regional subsystems have two essential, complementary and closely interconnected but distinct tasks: firstly, *(i)* to prevent monetary and financial crises and, where it has not been possible to prevent them, secondly, *(ii)* to contain and resolve crises that have arisen and broken out.

Crisis prevention requires first and foremost that the system should include legal obligations that are sufficiently clear and binding on those who are part of it or who are members, so that they are enforceable and complied with.

Moreover, an international monetary system must also include appropriate assistance and cooperation mechanisms to aid member States in the event of serious difficulties, typically reflected in serious imbalances ("deficits") in their balance of payments (i.e. in their economic relations with the outside world), beyond the level of sustainability (which is relative and therefore dynamic, as this constantly fluctuates depending on the conditions existing and required at any given moment in the markets and by the financial institutions from which financing is sought, according to the individual risk assessment carried out).

A monetary system consists precisely of a code of good conduct or practice in the monetary field applicable to the participating States, which involves the acceptance of and compliance with a set of obligations that restrict the scope for public action in monetary matters, which corresponds to declaring a reduction of some of the sovereign powers of States.[6]

States are willing to comply with this monetary code of good conduct or practice in expectation of the benefits they expect to gain as members or participants in the system, including the stability of the applicable rules (in this case in the monetary, financial and exchange fields), in addition to the right to assistance in the event of serious (monetary or financial) difficulties, usually linked to a country's "excessive" exposure to external indebtedness (among many other examples, the crises in Mexico in 1995, in several Southeast Asian countries in 1997, in Argentina in 2002, in Greece, Ireland and Portugal in 2010–11, with the so-called Eurozone sovereign debt crisis . . .).

2 The complementarity of the private International Monetary and Financial System

By opting to form part of the International Monetary and Financial System, States accepted (and continue to accept) certain restrictions on their sovereign powers in the monetary field, through acceptance of and compliance with the established code of good conduct or practice, because they know and/or believe that the advantages arising from the application of the agreed rules will allow them to obtain benefits, particularly economic and social benefits, for their citizens, including a real increase in income and well-being conditions, over the medium and long term, which would otherwise (outside the system) be (much) more difficult to achieve, in addition to the right to technical and (above all) financial assistance, in the event of need (i.e. the occurrence of crises), as explained.[7]

The interstate International Monetary System, the management of which has been entrusted by its member States to the IMF, is still in the present day the essential pillar for international monetary and financial reality, but it has long ceased to cover this in its entirety, especially since the late 1960s and early 1970s, when the so-called "euro-markets" emerged and gradually gave way to a true international monetary and financial system of a private nature, which is interconnected with it but substantially autonomous.[8]

The private international financial system is clearly distinct from the public system in terms of its foundations, its aims and its formats, and the quality of the institutions operating within it is also distinct, both on the supply and on the demand side of financing.

Firstly, the deposit and loan transactions carried out in the "Euromarkets" are of a contractual nature, so that the clauses agreed upon depend on the free will of the parties and market conditions, and often comply with the law of the State of New York or English law and their respective jurisdictions.

These contracts are not standardised in the sense that they include general contractual clauses or are necessarily subscribed to through joining, but they do contain standard clauses generally intended to allow the parties to resort to the usual mechanisms to resolve any possible conflicts or disputes and are therefore particularly permeable to the so-called *lex mercatoria*.

In the beginning, the "Euromarkets" were designed for and became widely used by private economic operators, especially "multinational" companies, to obtain large amounts of financial resources more easily and at lower cost. Following the first oil crisis in 1973–1974, these markets engaged more widely and effectively in the so-called "petrodollar recycling" (desired by the oil-exporting countries, thanks to the consecutive accumulation of income in US currency, as a result of the sudden and very sharp rise in the price of this commodity on the markets).

Subsequently, the States themselves, or rather some companies and other public institutions instead of them, started to resort to the "euro-markets" with increasing frequency in order to finance themselves, either because of the scarcity or unavailability of resources from public international bodies (especially the IMF and the World Bank) to meet their needs, which were constantly increasing for various reasons (including the oil crises, for importing countries and those most dependent on this energy source), or because of the less demanding and less costly conditions offered by the new financial markets, which contributed to boosting and strongly strengthening '"eurocurrency" transactions.

It should be noted that the purpose of these "Euromarkets" is more restricted than that of the public interstate financial system, insofar as it only concerns supply and demand for financing and refinancing between the participating institutions, both banking and non-banking, of a private nature or acting as such, according to the rules of the market, without distinction of their position in the case of public or sovereign entities and, similarly, without normative pretensions, in the sense of the creation and unilateral and coercive imposition of norms — which are present and central to the public (interstate) international monetary and financial system.

Finally, the criteria for access to these markets are of an exclusively commercial and financial nature, and therefore depend on the individual risk assessment and financial capacity of each institution or operator that presents itself, its "signature", therefore regardless of its status, public or private, or its nationality, which, therefore, does not interfere in determining the conditions and the law applicable to the financing contracts signed, nor the competent jurisdiction or the mechanisms chosen for the resolution of any conflicts over the interpretation and fulfilment of these.

It is therefore important to ascertain the relations between the two international monetary and financial systems identified: the intergovernmental and those of a private nature (regardless of whether public entities also operate within them in search of financing, but in this case subject to the same provisions applied to private operators). Understandably, for some time, relations between the two, intergovernmental and private, international financing systems, were competitive.[9]

The inadequacy of IMF resources in the face of the growing financing needs of States meant that, as early as the 1970s and early 1980s, the "euro-markets" and the "euro-banks" almost overshadowed the lending function of the IMF and the interstate International Monetary System. In 1981, the funding offered by the "euro-markets" to States and other public bodies was already five times greater (some USD 100 billion) than the amount provided by public international institutions (some USD 20 billion).

The difference between the global amounts of resources offered by the two complementary international financial systems has generally not failed to increase significantly, albeit non-linearly, in line with fluctuations in needs or demand, as well as the availability or supply of financing, strongly dependent on the more or less expansive or recessive trends of the various economies and their respective severity, often linked to the degree of economic dependence with the outside world, with possible acknowledgements of inability to meet obligations assumed, both by private operators and by various States (as happened with Mexico in 1982 and again in 1994, with great international impact).[10]

Since then, and to sum up, the public international financial system and the private international financial system have worked in close harmony, as evidenced by the various sovereign debt "rescheduling" or "restructuring" operations in various countries throughout history. This is an informal cooperation relationship, without institutional basis, but close and effective. Hence the talk of "genuine co-management of the global international monetary system", involving, on the one hand, national monetary and financial authorities and specialised international intergovernmental organisations and, on the other hand, the "Eurobanks".[11] The International Monetary and Financial System is therefore composed, firstly, of *(i)* a set of monetary and financial obligations, whether universal or only regional in scope, or "codes of (good) conduct" which States formally accept and promise to respect in their reciprocal monetary and financial relations, and, secondly, *(ii)* a set of mechanisms of transnational monetary and financial cooperation aimed at financing international exchanges, including institutionalised techniques of interstate cooperation and financing techniques carried out by the private international banking system, which govern the operation of "euromarkets".

3 The International Monetary Fund (IMF) and its main objectives

The International Monetary System outlined at Bretton Woods in 1944 with the intention of becoming universal and involving all countries – regardless of their level of economic and social development and even of the economic system and regime adopted – had at its centre a specialised organisation created on that occasion to administer it, namely the International Monetary Fund.

It is one of the most important international economic organisations, working closely with other similar global or quasi-global organisations, including the World Bank – which was set up at the same time, essentially to provide international community aid for the economic recovery of the countries devastated by the war, an enormous and urgent task at that time, and, above all, to launch an even more ambitious medium and long-term programme of development assistance for the less prosperous countries of the world – and the World Trade Organisation (WTO), which succeeded the GATT (General Agreement on Tariffs and Trade) in 1995.[12]

Close cooperation among the main international economic organisations of universal or near-universal scope and between them and similar organisations of a more geographically restricted (regional) scope, in addition to the indispensable connection with the States that decided to create them and which are part of them as members, is a condition for the efficient and harmonious functioning of the set of systems of which they form part, as well as for the pursuit of the functions and objectives that have been and are assigned to them.

As regards organisations with universal or quasi-universal scope, such as those just listed, including the International Monetary Fund, the requirements of institutional cooperation and material consistency derive in particular from their placement within the United Nations Organisation (UNO), in addition to that which is specifically provided for in their respective statutes, and the same could be said of regional bodies with similar or overlapping nature and objectives (such as the international development banks – Inter-American Development Bank, African Development Bank. . . – inspired by the World Bank and often in partnership with various UN programmes).

Despite the global ambition of the Bretton Woods agreements, the countries that formed the socialist bloc at the time, led by the Soviet Union (Union of Soviet Socialist Republics – USSR), above all but not only "from the East" of the European continent, with strong influence and coverage in particular on the Asian and African continents, generally failed to ratify them, by determination of the Soviet Union, which also failed to ratify them, or by choice to abandon them (or by imposition of the Fund, as in the case of Czechoslovakia in 1954, due to non-compliance with the obligation to provide information, as foreseen in Article VIII-5, which was contested by that member).

However, until almost the implosion of the socialist political and economic system in the late 1980s and early 1990s, following the fall of the Berlin Wall in 1989, the participation of countries with centrally directed or socialist economies in the IMF tended to be lower than their participation in the GATT. For entirely different reasons, Switzerland also only became a member of the IMF in May 1992 (three days before Russia, on 1 June of the same year). As for the less developed countries, on the other hand, they accepted to become members of the IMF from the very beginning, in 1945, even when they understood that being bound to the GATT would not be justified.[13]

In addition to the listing and identification of the members of the Fund, which reflects the extent and nature of its action as manager of the public International Monetary and Financial System in force since the end of World War II, it is obviously important to consider the relative weight and influence of each of the members in the decision-making processes of the institution, as well as its organic structure – with its own organs, with a specific division of powers between them, with rules for the appointment of their respective holders and with their own articles of association – and another absolutely decisive aspect, the availability of a vast pool of monetary resources, on which the capacity for overall financial assistance to the members will largely depend, under the terms and conditions established in the statutes.

The relevance of all these aspects is obvious, but we will simply list the IMF's objectives below, which can be divided into domestic (or national) and international ones. In the first case, the Fund's mission is to "contribute to the promotion and maintenance of high levels of employment and real income and to the development of the productive resources of all member States", as stated in Article I-ii of its Articles of Association. At the international level, the Fund "shall facilitate the expansion and balanced growth of international trade" (*ibid*. Article I-ii).

In short, the IMF must therefore help to achieve and substantially improve people's prosperity and economic and social well-being, both at home and internationally. This means, inter alia, robust economic growth with high levels of employment and real income for 'everyone', but certainly sustainable and balanced or harmonious, without undesirable contradictions. As such, all programmes or actions and mechanisms of the Fund should be aimed at and focused on the pursuit of the general objectives proclaimed in its Articles of Association.

With a view to achieving these general objectives – the harmonious expansion and development of international trade and high levels of employment and real income and the development of the productive resources of all countries – the members of the IMF undertake to comply with a set of obligations that form a code of good conduct or practice designed to prevent the occurrence of monetary and financial crises, which usually entail major economic, financial and social costs.

In addition to the general objectives mentioned above, there are specific objectives, also stated in the Articles of Association. Firstly, the Fund must promote "exchange stability, to maintain orderly exchange arrangements among member States, and to avoid competitive exchange depreciation" (Article I-iii). Secondly, it must "assist in the establishment of a multilateral system of payments in respect of current transactions between member States and [contribute] in the elimination of foreign exchange restrictions which hamper the growth of world trade" (Article I-iv).

These specific aims constitute the so-called common law of the IMF and are very ambitious. However, the Articles of Association provide for a number of exceptional mechanisms to enable member States to gradually comply with their obligations and to cope with difficulties that have arisen and prevented or hindered that compliance for some time. All these schemes, more or less defined, are administered by the IMF.

4 The IMF code of good conduct

The monetary and financial discipline imposed by the IMF on its members and accepted by them or, in other words, the discipline conventionally self-imposed by the member States, which they undertake to observe, consists of a code of good conduct or practice, the essential aim of which is to prevent national and international crises and conflicts of an economic and financial nature, in a context of growing interdependence between the world's various national economies.

The IMF Articles of Association do not follow a methodology based on the affirmation of broad general principles, as would happen with the World Trade Organisation Agreements half a century later. Instead, at Bretton Woods, the various obligations required of the member States of the System in the monetary, financial and exchange rate fields were specified with great precision.

Before any other specific obligation, the Fund's Articles of Agreement were, from the outset, and as they still are, aimed at committing all member States to the convertibility of their currency against all the currencies of the other members, as was (and still is) provided for in Articles I-iv and VIII, section 2a), for current payments and transfers.

The basis for this commitment and its effective compliance is obvious, especially in terms of international economic relations, as has already been briefly pointed out: without international monetary convertibility, all international exchanges are not regularly and normally viable, otherwise they are completely dependent on case-by-case authorisations, inevitably discriminatory and, therefore, economically inefficient, with huge opportunity costs and, consequently, also welfare costs that are difficult to accept in modern societies open to the exterior.[14]

Secondly, the International Monetary System as provided for in the IMF Articles of Association had the objective (and still has, although in different terms, as we shall see below) of ensuring exchange rate stability, i.e., an ordering of the exchange rates of the currencies of the participating States so that the variation in value between the currencies participating in the system remains stable within fixed limits, a task very difficult to achieve because of the implications for the different countries.

This was certainly one of the most striking original rules of the monetary regime created at Bretton Woods in that, for the first time in human history, States agreed to restrict their powers in the field of foreign exchange by undertaking to comply with the following three obligations: firstly, *(i)* not to have recourse to competitive currency devaluations, secondly, *(ii)* to maintain a stable exchange rate and, thirdly, *(iii)* to apply a single exchange rate for the national currency in relation to the currencies of other countries (instead of multiple rates depending on the currency).

The ban on competitive devaluations *(i)* is provided for in Articles I-iii and IV, section 4-a of the Fund's Articles of Agreement, and reflects the unanimous condemnation of undesirable exchange rate manipulations as a weapon of protection and trade confrontation by any member State in relation to its partners. In this context, IMF members can no longer resort to devaluations of their currency in order to improve the competitive position of their exports in international markets.

However, while the general and abstract commitment to forego the use of competitive devaluations did not give rise to major reservations on the part of the founding States of the IMF, the same could not be said of the indicators, proportion and pace of devaluation movements undertaken, issues that have taken on new relevance and which have been no less controversial in recent years, particularly with the worsening of external deficits and surpluses in the accounts of the world's leading economic powers (the United States, China and the European Union), with immediate repercussions at the level of trade (particularly in the context of the WTO) and at the global political level (discussed at bilateral summits of the heads of State and government of these countries, as well as in international political forums such as the "G-7" and "G-20").[15]

As for the obligation to keep exchange rates stable *(ii)*, a distinction must be made between the initial regime, which lasted until 1978, and the new exchange provisions, with a different meaning, which have been in force since that year, when general fluctuations in the value of the currencies participating in the system were legalised.

After the Bretton Woods Agreements were approved and the IMF Articles of Association were first drawn up, stable but adjustable exchange parities were in force, based on the "gold parity" system, whereby each State had to declare to the Fund a given parity of its currency in relation to the "anchor currency" of the International Monetary System – the US dollar – which would be commonly used in international transactions.

Within this international monetary framework established at Bretton Woods, exchange rates were supposed to remain stable in principle, but not immutable, and therefore a procedure for notifying exchange rate parities, subject to IMF supervision, had been foreseen.

As is well known, in the gold parity system, the value of each member's currency is expressed directly in terms of a weight of that precious metal (gold), or else indirectly, by reference to an "anchor currency", the unit value of which corresponded to a given weight in gold. In the case of the International Monetary System created at Bretton Woods, on 1 July 1944, one US Dollar was legally equivalent to 0.888 grams of fine gold. Gold at that time then indirectly became the "common denominator" or "standard" of the participating currencies.[16]

While the exchange rate regime operated smoothly for some time, the continual growth in international trade and, as a result, the demand for foreign exchange reserves, especially Dollars, led to a continuous increase in the US trade deficit, which was essential to create the liquidity needed to carry out world trade. As Robert Triffin warned at the time, the system was facing a credibility problem, because the more Dollars were issued, the less Fort Knox would be able to convert them into gold, at the fixed value, whenever Dollars were presented to the Federal Reserve for that purpose.[17]

In this context, the unilateral declaration by the United States of the total inconvertibility of the Dollar into gold on 15 August 1971 cannot be considered surprising. The official parity of the currency was altered to 38 Dollars per ounce with the Smithsonian Agreement of 18 December of that year, which implied a devaluation of the Dollar and the correlative appreciation of the other currencies of the participating countries in the same proportion, in addition to the enlargement of the fluctuation margin of the official parities of those currencies against the Dollar to ±2.25 percent.[18]

It should be noted that the inconvertibility of the Dollar into gold in no way prejudiced the prevailing and absolutely decisive rule of convertibility between all the currencies in the System – which was maintained. Just as there remained a general duty for IMF member States to notify the value of their currency either on entry into the System or whenever parities were changed, in accordance with the provisions of Article IV, sections 5 and 7 of the Articles of Association – although in fact many members no longer respected this commitment.[19]

Without imposing fixed exchange rates, the original Bretton Woods regime thus imposed strict stability in the value of the national currency in relation to the other currencies participating in the System, with the consequent prohibition of floating exchange rates.

Due to the extreme rigidity of this exchange rate regime, and the enormous difficulties of the States in complying with it, it was abandoned, first *de facto*, generally from March 1973, and then *de jure*, with the second amendment of the Fund's Articles of Agreement, concluded in Kingston, Jamaica, in 1974–1976, and in force since 1978, in obedience to the principle according to which "the essential purpose of the international monetary system is to provide a framework that facilitates the exchange of goods, services and capital between countries", with a view to "sustain sound economic growth", by permanently guaranteeing the "orderly underlying conditions that are necessary for financial and economic stability", in accordance with the provisions of Article IV, section 1.

With the revision of the IMF's Articles of Agreement, States were given complete freedom to choose their exchange rate regime (fixed, floating or other), although subject to a general set of general obligations to act, concerning domestic economic policy and external monetary policy, as well as the obligation to collaborate with the Fund, in addition to the specific obligation to notify the Fund, which was maintained.

With specific regard to the obligation regarding the unity of the exchange rates applied, this is provided for in Article VIII, section 3 of the Articles of Association. The justification for this, as mentioned above, is very clear: it aims to rule out any discrimination between countries and economic operators, irrespective of their place of residence, nationality or place of establishment.

Other obligations of members of the International Monetary System include the progressive elimination of exchange restrictions, provided for in Articles I-iv and VIII, mutual respect for national exchange regulations in conformity with the Articles of Association, namely Article VIII, section 2 - *(b)*, and the demonetization of gold (the previous regime of which, in force between 1945 and 1978, was changed on this date by virtue of the second amendment to the Articles of Association), in addition to the obligations of members to notify the Fund, on time and in full, of various national economic, financial and monetary information, pursuant to article VIII, section 5 - *(a)*, as well as to generally cooperate with the Fund, in accordance with the provisions of Articles I-i, and IV, section 4 - *(a)*, the grounds for which have already been briefly alluded to.

5 The right to IMF assistance and its accomplishment

Let us now look at what the right to assistance from the IMF in cases of need by its members consists of and how this is financially operationalised through the various instruments in force and the monetary resources made available to the Fund for this purpose – aspects which, like the others that are sometimes barely listed, warrant further development and also reflection, in addition to the corresponding considerations and decisions.

The original IMF Articles of Agreement provided for rigid and restricted financial assistance, based on own resources and mechanisms that subsequently had to be specified and adapted in the light of the crises and challenges that arose and had to be met over the years, as well as broadened and reformulated in order to be able to contribute effectively to the resolution of increasingly serious economic and financial problems requiring ampler resources.

Faced with the scarcity of the IMF's financial resources and the growing needs of members hit by severe economic and financial crises, other means of international liquidity were added to the traditional assistance instruments with the first amendment to its Articles of Agreement in 1969, through the creation of "Special Drawing Rights" (SDRs), issued *ex nihilo* as is usually the case with the issuance of currency by national authorities and credit institutions, in order to enhance the ability to help those that needed this. The SDRs then became the Fund's unit of account.[20]

From the outset, the IMF has had at its disposal a large pool of resources that members can draw on in the event of temporary difficulties in their balance of payments, whether internal or external in origin. These resources are partly the Fund's own – derived essentially from contributions or membership fees subscribed and payable by the members since their accession, the total amount of which corresponds to the international organisation's capital, which has been increased on several occasions – and partly from loans – either on a bilateral basis, dependent on the will of each of its members, or on a multilateral basis, reinforced especially from 1997–1998 onwards, with the "New Loan Agreements", which complement the older "General

Loan Agreements", renewed consecutively since their creation in 1961.[21]

Despite the greater openness and flexibility regarding the use of SDR (Special Drawing Rights) as a unit of account – with exchange rates that are obviously more stable than those of any other currency, including those of greater weight in international trade, given their composition – when the IMF Executive Board approved a new mechanism for issuing SDRs in July 2009 (the most far-reaching one to date), extraordinarily expanding international liquidity,[22] allocations and subscriptions remained reserved solely for Fund member States or their central banks, thus excluding private operators and markets.

The use of IMF financial resources by members may follow the general regime provided for in the Articles of Agreement, or else a specific, non-statutory regime, since the creation in the 1960s of the "New Lending Facilities", to seek a more flexible and effective response to the diversified problems of members, taking into account their economic and financial situations, when they need to resort to assistance from the Fund – that is, in general, when they really have no other viable alternative.[23]

The provision of IMF liquidity is essentially carried out through *(i)* withdrawals or drawings in the strict sense, the only instruments foreseen from the outset in the Articles of Agreement, or *(ii)* certificates of withdrawals or drawings, also known as "stand-by arrangements". The first type involves the spot purchase of foreign currency by the member concerned and beneficiary of the assistance in exchange for the immediate delivery of its own currency and the forward sale of that currency. Therefore, legally, we are not dealing with real mutual fund or loan agreements. Given the inflexibility of this mechanism, and because of the seriousness and urgency of the needs and problems of the members in need of assistance, since 1952 there has been a greater reliance on drawing certificates or "stand-by agreements".

Withdrawal or drawing certificates or stand-by arrangements provide for the opening of a credit line, the details of which are negotiated between the IMF and the member concerned, enabling the latter to drawdown an amount of liquidity over a given period of time against fixed interest rates and other obligations, in accordance with the principle of conditionality currently laid down in Article V-section 3 - *(a)* and in article XXX - *(b)* of the Statutes.

About 2/3 of the loans granted by the IMF since 1952 have taken the form of "stand-by arrangements" and have come to prominence among instruments for international monetary cooperation. They typically consist of two documents: *(i)* the first contains a set of standard clauses indicating the purpose, duration and amount to be financed, as well as the obligations of the beneficiary member; *(ii)* the second consists of a "letter of intent" or "memorandum" signed by the governor of the central bank and/or the minister of Finance, with a detailed, quantified and scheduled explanation of the financial, monetary and exchange rate policies to be adopted. As a rule, the IMF makes the conclusion of a stand-by agreement conditional on the strict implementation of an internal economic and financial adjustment or economic stabilisation plan, with economic and social effects that are often very deep and painful.[24]

Withdrawals from the Fund are only unconditional and automatic if they do not exceed the member's so-called "reserve tranche" (corresponding to the former "gold tranche"), precisely because they are covered and backed by the corresponding official reserves (of the member). On the other hand, withdrawals are subject to conditions (they become "non-automatic" or "conditional") when they cover "credit tranches", which may not, in principle, exceed 200 percent of the quota of the member concerned (taking into account actual deliveries and the member's existing national currency holdings in the Fund).

The rigid and strict limits on these conditions and the resources available made it difficult to resolve the most serious financial and monetary crises that affected several IMF members in a timely manner. This led to the creation of "New Lending Facilities" in 1963 for specific purposes, including cyclical assistance and, from 1986, also assistance of a structural nature (such as the "Systemic Transformation Facility", for the adjustment and transition of centrally directed socialist economies to market economies, of central and eastern European countries, and, since 1997, assistance to developing countries, especially the Heavily Indebted Poor Countries, in close coordination with the World Bank group).

In the face of worsening difficulties resulting from the 2007–8 economic and financial crisis, the IMF's financial assistance programmes were further relaxed and expanded from July 2009 to include the "Extended Credit Facility" to address members' medium-term balance of payments needs in connection with the poverty reduction objective, and the "Rapid Credit Facility" to address urgent financing needs caused by exogenous shocks, including natural disasters and armed conflict, which allowed for an increase in the Fund's overall lending capacity in this regard from SDR 8 billion to SDR 17 billion by 2014.

Since 2008, the various IMF assistance mechanisms have included the "Short Term Credit Facility" for countries hit hard by the financial crisis, which can reach up to 500 percent of the member's quota and is not subject to the usual conditionality criteria, with a commitment to implement a "sound macroeconomic policy". Furthermore, in order to better face the international financial crisis that began in 2007, the "Flexible Credit Line" was created in 2009, for members with "solid fundamentals" and "good track records", of a preventive nature, unconditional and, which was unprecedented, without a maximum limit on financing (for which Mexico, Poland and Colombia immediately applied).

This diversification and strengthening of the IMF's financial instruments could lead us to the conclusion that the greatest weaknesses of the International Monetary and Financial System mainly concern the scarcity of resources available to meet the scale of the problems and needs of its members, aggravated by the cadence of financial crises, which are increasingly serious and costly. Had this been the case, the problem would already have been largely resolved, with the successive reforms and expansion of the assistance mechanisms and the reinforcement of the resources allocated to them, in order to quickly and effectively contain and curb the spread of very serious financial crises. This is why recourse to the financial markets – with wider liquidity, especially until the general issue of SDRs in 2009, but always dependent on a high assessment regarding confidence and credibility, and risk for debtors, even sovereign ones – is neither sufficient nor viable.

The availability of resources and the flexibility of the IMF instruments are essential for the smooth functioning of the International Monetary and Financial System, for preventing financial and monetary crises and, should they occur, for addressing and resolving them effectively, with appropriate instruments, not only of a financial nature, but also of an economic and social, and even political nature – including ensuring respect for the economic, social and also political rights of all. Of course, sufficient financial resources are not enough for this. No less essential will be the review and fine-tuning of the Fund's set of instruments for monitoring and advising members, within the necessarily interdependent but complex and asymmetric current and future framework of the international economic, financial and monetary order, which is constantly being reformulated.

Notes

1   At least from a conceptual point of view, the option pointed out is immediately criticisable for its ostensible lack of terminological rigour, as it "assumes" or at the least "tolerates" a (relative) indistinction between the monetary and financial strands, which clearly do not mix, despite

their close interconnection. In addition to the obvious distinction between the two components, with profound implications both from an institutional and a material point of view, we should, pedagogically, add the clear distinction and separation between these major areas of economic organisation, one essentially private in nature *(financial)*, regardless of whether it is subject to public regulation and supervision, and the other relating to the field of public economy, normally studied in the subject of Public Finance *(fiscal, public finance)*, congenitally interconnected with the monetary and financial system. In another very frequent and useful structural subdivision, it is usual and understandable to consider that the (non-public) financial sector in the broad sense consists of various subsectors: the monetary and banking subsector, which are very closely related, the financial subsector in the strict sense, which includes the different markets or stock exchanges, and the insurance subsector. However, for the purposes set out below, the composite term "international monetary and financial system" is justified, given the unity that characterises it, despite the diversity of the elements covered.

2   A distinct, though related, domain is that of the global economic reality of public entities, which constitutes the object of study of, respectively, public economics, financial law or public finances, all of which pertain to public entities in general, with the inclusion (in the first and third fields – in public economics and also in public finances, with a broader and interdisciplinary (legal and economic) scope or, possibly, not (in the case of Financial Law, the inclusion in its object of financing governed by general rules, not exclusive to public entities, is controversial), as commented upon in the preceding note.

3   The membership of almost all the States of the world in the IMF (currently 190 members) contrasts, until recently, with the smaller number of countries that agreed to abide by the General Agreement on Tariffs and Trade (GATT) of 1947 and which later became members of the World Trade Organisation (WTO), created in 1995 (with 164 members as of the end of July 2016), despite the fact that they now represent almost all international trade. See the websites of the international economic organisations mentioned, where their statutes and other applicable sources of law are available:
    www.imf.org (IMF), www.worldbank.org (World Bank) and
    www.wto.org (WTO).

4   The European monetary authorities have taken a different view: the European Central Bank has always stressed the need to conclude an international agreement with the European Union, thus rejecting the possibility of any third country deciding unilaterally to make the Euro its "own" currency.

5   For a general and detailed introduction to this topic, see, among various other works, Eichengreen B. 2007: *Global Imbalances and the Lessons of Bretton Woods*, Cambridge, Massachusetts: The MIT Press; Krugman, P. and Obstfeld, M. 2012: *International Economics*, 8th ed., Boston:

Pearson, pp. 215 et seq.; Qureshi, A. and Ziegler, A. 2011: *International Economic Law*, 3rd ed., London: Sweet & Maxwell, pp. 133 et seq.; Carreau, D. and Juillard, P. 2017: *Droit International Économique*, 6th ed., Paris: Dalloz, esp. pp. 727 et seq.

6 The reduction of national sovereign powers may be as significant or more intense, in terms of their economic and social implications and the direct repercussions on people's lives, in terms of obligations to be met and perhaps sacrifices to be made, than membership of a defence organisation such as NATO, as noted by P. Schweitzer, former Managing Director of the IMF.

7 A kind of general reciprocal relationship can thus be identified between the IMF (as with other international economic organisations) and its member States, along the lines of that which usually happens between clubs and their members, which involves a set of rights and a set of obligations for both parties: the general benefits of cooperation through membership of the organisation and its operation, including the right to assistance in the case of need (risks and losses arising from the occurrence of financial crises), and all the instruments of monitoring and technical advice, which are matched by the acceptance of and compliance with a set of rules of good conduct and other requirements (obligations), including financial contributions. In other words, States only agreed (and agree) to lose part (or all) of their monetary sovereignty in exchange for, or in return for, and to some extent in proportion to the advantages offered (or expected to be offered) as members of the IMF (as in principle for other international organisations). This does not mean, however, that many members or even all of them cannot join and remain members in a spirit of strict cooperation and solidarity with others. And even less that expectations of possible future assistance from one or more Member States will be maintained over time and may or may not materialise. Who would have thought, until the sovereign debt crisis within the Eurozone from 2010 onwards, that two European countries would be the recipients of the largest volumes of IMF funding, rather than less developed countries? The aforementioned reciprocal correlation does not occur, for example, in the case of international financial organisations based primarily on the principle of solidarity, as is the case with the World Bank, the priority function of which is supporting development which means that its main donors, the more prosperous member States, do not normally expect to benefit from the financial support of the organisation, which is often non-refundable, unlike the less developed member States.

8 Despite their misleading name, the "euro-markets" (like the "eurocurrencies" and "eurobanks") which emerged in the 1960s and 1970s, have nothing to do with the Euro – which would only be created as a currency some three decades later, on 1 January 1999 – or even with the European continent. Instead, they have as a necessary reference the use of the United States Dollar (US $) or, in a broad sense, another currency, by financial institutions subject to foreign jurisdiction.

9　The availability of funding and the conditions required for access to each of the systems, including the fact that the public system is intended exclusively for its members, i. e. the States, as well as the actual costs of funding, were clearly distinct, although they have changed, both mainly due to market developments in one case, or due to statutory changes and political decisions in the other case.

10　International financing through private international financial markets or "Euromarkets" in the broad sense (encompassing different currencies and not only credits in US Dollars) surpassed the barrier of one trillion Dollars of financing available before the end of the 20th century, in 1997; it would have reached a level of 5 trillion Dollars in 2006 and, according to estimates, 13.8 trillion Dollars in 2016, and it should be much higher today. However, the difficulties of calculating "Euromarkets" are evident, given their specific aspects. They are by far the largest source of international finance (perhaps as much as 90% by some estimates), being created, ironically, by the Soviet Union in the 1950s and their main centre has always remained London, the world's financial capital for centuries, although several other locations with offshore status have emerged in the meantime. The evolution of these markets has fluctuated significantly according to various factors, both monetary and real, while noticeably declining in periods of crisis, as in 2008. Cf. Mishkin, F. 2013: *The Economics of Money, Banking and Financial Markets*, 10th ed., Boston: Pearson, pp. 346 et seq.; Heyneke, N. and Daya, M. 2016: "The rise and fall of the Eurodollar System", Nedbank, available online at
　https://www.nedbank.co.za/content/dam/nedbank-crp/reports/Strategy/NeelsAndMehul/2016/September/TheRiseAndFallOfTheEurodollar System_160907.pdf.

11　In this context, it has been argued that the contemporary international monetary and financial system, as a set of rules, agreements and practices that govern the conduct of monetary relations between States regarding the financing of international exchanges, has become effectively transnational, crossing the classic and often artificial boundaries between domestic law and international law and also between private and public law. Cf. Carreau, D. and Juillard, P. 2017: *Droit International Économique*, cit., pp. 715 et seq.

12　On these international economic organisations in general, see, for example, the already cited works of Eichengreen, B. 2007: *Global Imbalances and the Lessons of Bretton Woods*; Krugman, P. and Obstfeld, M. 2012: *International Economics*; Qureshi, A. and Ziegler, A. 2011: *International Economic Law*; Carreau, D. and Juillard, P. 2017: Droit *International Économique*, esp. pp. 727 et seq.; as well as the IMF, the World Bank and the WTO websites – www.imf.org, www.world-bank.org and www.wto.org (WTO) – where their statutes are also available. In addition to the international economic organisations mentioned, the Bank for International Settlements should be added – www.bis.org – created by the central banks of the various countries of the world, a kind of "central bank for central banks", with the aim of guaranteeing financial and monetary stability on a global scale.

13 At present, the IMF has 190 member States (as of 16 October 2020, with the entry of the Principality of Andorra, following the entry of Nauru in 2016, www.imf.org/external/np/sec/memdir/memdate.htm), while the WTO has 164 members (following the entries of Liberia and Afghanistan in July 2016). See the IMF and the WTO websites.

14 As is well known, the whole of International Economics is based on the economic advantages of opening countries to the outside world, in general in alignment with David Ricardo's theory of comparative advantages and costs, inspired by earlier constructions and, in particular, Adam Smith's theory of absolute costs, with significant subsequent in-depth additions and other equally relevant complementary contributions. For a synthesis on this theme, see, for example, the works cited above.

15 As monetary history of recent decades has amply demonstrated, it is not easy to determine whether or not a particular currency depreciation movement, or a specific set of currency devaluation movements, is solely or essentially aimed at achieving competitive gains on the international markets, or whether, on the contrary, it is simply the result of regular market developments, regardless of the criteria formulated for this judgement, which is in any case decisive to know whether or not there has been a breach of the obligations in force in this area. The assessment of the nature of the devaluation situations of a member State's currency unit against the currencies of other members during a given period of time will always be relative and must take into account particular circumstances, both from a temporal and territorial point of view, namely the structure and development of the balance of payments or the "international investment position" of the country or countries concerned.

16 The International Monetary System therefore defaulted to the US dollar. The parities of the currencies of the acceding States were administratively linked to the US dollar, and the respective market exchange rates could fluctuate within a range of ±1 percent of these parities. On the European continent, the member States of the European Communities that had signed the European Monetary Agreement decided to narrow the band of exchange rate fluctuations against the dollar to ±0.75 percent, implying that the maximum possible variation in exchange rates between two currencies would be 3 percent (which would only happen, in an extreme and unlikely scenario, if one of them first reached the maximum limit of appreciation and the other the minimum admissible limit and if, thereafter, there were a complete reversal of these limit positions in relation to the North American currency). The new international monetary regime obliged the monetary authorities of the United States of America to maintain the pegging of the Dollar to a fixed weight in fine gold (35 Dollars per ounce), as well as converting into gold the Dollars presented for this purpose by the other participating States, which did not raise any doubts in 1944, when the country held about 75 percent of the world

reserves of that precious metal, but did not require them to have to defend those parities whatever the circumstances.

17 In 1960 the short-term foreign debt of the United States of America exceeded the amount of its gold reserves, calling into question the principle of full convertibility, an imbalance which was aggravated by the country's gold rush following the request to exchange dollars for gold which had been made by France since 1962. In 1968 the United States stopped converting Dollars held by private operators into gold, giving rise to the distinction between the official gold price, which remained legally fixed at $35, and the private gold price, available on the market according to supply and demand conditions.

18 Through the Smithsonian Agreement, signed in Washington on 18 December 1971, the general margins for the fluctuation of the currencies participating in the International Monetary System were extended to ±2.25 percent (so that the disparity between two currencies could successively reach a maximum of 9 percent) and the (official) price of gold rose to USD 38 per ounce, confirming the inconvertibility of the US currency, unilaterally declared by the US President on 15 August of that year.

19 The members of the IMF were statutorily bound to notify the parity of their currency in relation to the reference currency of the System and to carry this out in the international economic relations undertaken, i.e., to ensure all exchange operations of their currency were carried out at this parity, using the appropriate means for this purpose. While the US pursued a policy of free convertibility of its currency into gold between 1945 and 1971, all other members of the Fund intervened in the foreign exchange markets on various occasions, through the central bank in order to readjust or "regularise" the exchange rates of their currencies. Precisely for operational reasons and frequent exchange rate adjustments, the Fund's Articles of Agreement enabled (narrow) fluctuation margins. Spot foreign exchange transactions could initially vary up to plus or minus 1 percent of each currency's official parity.

20 Special Drawing Rights (SDR – XDR) were created on 6 August 1969, on the occasion of the entry into force of the first amendment to the IMF's Articles of Agreement, following lengthy negotiations within the "Group of 10" (Belgium, Canada, France, Italy, Japan, the Netherlands, the United Kingdom, the United States and the central banks of the Federal Republic of Germany and Sweden) as a new supplementary international reserve asset for use by intending IMF members. The first tranche of SDRs was allocated on 1 January 1970, followed by two others in 1971 and 1972, totalling 9.3 billion. In December 1978, the IMF's Board of Governors approved a further SDR issue in the following two years (1979–1981) for an amount of 12.1 billion. A lack of consensus among the Fund's core members prevented further issuances in the following decades, until a new special allocation was approved in 2009 for those who became members after 1981. In the same year (2009), a new general issue was approved for all participating members in the SDR department

for an amount of SDR 161.2 billion, forming a total of SDR 204 billion. As of the first quarter of 2016, SDR 204 billion has been allocated by participating members of the department, who can freely purchase or encumber them in the market. The value of SDRs was first linked to a fixed weight in gold (0.888 g) and, from 1974 onwards, was based on a set of 16 currencies, chosen and weighted on the basis of their representativeness. As the values of all these fluctuate, SDRs have also fluctuated, with all the resulting consequences. Having the power to modify the definition of the SDRs, the IMF exercised this power in 1978 and 1980 by reference to members' positions in international trade and foreign exchange reserves. Currently making up the basket of (new) SDRs, which is reviewed every five years and is considered an international reserve currency, are the US Dollar (worth 41.73 percent of that currency unit), the Euro (30.93 percent), the Japanese Yen (8.33 percent), the UK Pound (8.09% percent) and, since 1 October 2016, the Chinese Renminbi (10.92 percent). This composition of the SDRs ("new SDRs") was decided by the Executive Board of the Fund on 30 November 2015, with effect from 1 October of the following year. This was the first change to the SDR basket since the creation of the Euro on 1 January 1999, which involved the replacement of the Deutsche Mark and the French Franc by the new common European Union currency in that basket. SDR exchange rates (XDR) are updated on a dedicated page on the IMF website: https://www.imf.org/external/np/fin/data/sdr_ir.aspx.

21   The IMF's "General Lending Agreements", the global amount of which exceeds 17 billion Special Drawing Rights (SDR), have been in existence since 1962, involving the "Group of Ten", to be joined shortly afterwards in 1964 by Switzerland (which was not an IMF member at the time), and which were significantly revised in 1983. As for the "New Lending Arrangements", involving 25 members or their central banks and supplementing the liquidity of the General Lending Agreements, they provided SDR 34 billion. (see press release of 19.11.1998, https://www.imf.org/en/News/Articles/2015/09/14/01/49/pr9857). Both agreements were aimed at expanding the IMF's capacity for financial assistance.

22   To the 21.4 billion SDRs created in the early 1970s and early 1980s, the IMF Executive Board decided in July 2009 to add 21.5 billion SDRs from a special issue and a further 161.2 billion SDRs created in a new general issue approved on the same date, making an impressive total of 204 billion SDRs available to the Fund since then – a size that is difficult to compare with the very limited initial amounts.

23   It should be noted that IMF assistance to its members is not essentially financial in nature. Admittedly, this (financial) component is a necessary condition for the success of the Fund in pursuing its objectives: the resources available must be sufficient in relation to the absolute and relative size and severity of the crises affecting individual members. If resources are insufficient to help resolve crises fully, their effects will be

prolonged and may even worsen in various aspects. In any case, IMF assistance to its members typically transcends the strictly financial dimension of opening up credit in the amounts lent. In addition to the advisory and technical components monitoring the evolution of the economic and financial situation of the countries, it is necessary to add in particular the indirect and cross effects in terms of the credibility of each individual member in relation to the economic and financial policies resulting from the conclusion of negotiations and the entering into of adjustment agreements with the IMF, which cannot but be taken into consideration in the assessment of national economic and financial capacities and potential, as well as the corresponding risks, especially in the markets, involved in the usual effect of a (greater) openness of the creditors of these markets to grant (more) financing, with less demanding conditions and lower costs (interest), depending on the quality and adequacy of the agreed and approved assistance programme(s), which transcends the temporary provision of a certain amount of liquidity by the Fund.

24 The "letter of intent" signed by the IMF member justifies the opening of the credit line for its benefit. Despite the form followed, we are not simply dealing here with merely internal decisions of the Fund, but with real international agreements, the terms of which are binding on both the Fund and the beneficiary member, even though the new wording of the Articles of Agreement refers to "internal decision", in line with the position always maintained by the IMF's management bodies, in order to avoid possible contentious disputes. These agreements are generally not published, and when they are, they are only published by the member, not by the Fund.

References

Carreau, D. and Juillard, P. 2017: *Droit International Économique*, 6th ed., Paris: Dalloz

Eichengreen. B. 2007: *Global Imbalances and the Lessons of Bretton Woods*, Cambridge, Massachusetts: The MIT Press.

Heyneke, N. and Daya, M. 2016:"The rise and fall of the Eurodollar System", Nedbank, available online at https://www.nedbank.co.za/content/dam/nedbank-crp/reports/Strategy/NeelsAndMehul/2016/September/TheRiseAndFallOfTheEurodollarSystem_160907.pdf.

International Monetary Fund (IMF) website: www.imf.org.

Krugman, P. and Obstfeld, M. 2012: *International Economics*, 8th ed., Boston: Pearson.

Qureshi, A. and Ziegler, A. 2011: *International Economic Law*, 3rd ed., London: Sweet & Maxwell.

Mishkin, F. 2013: *The Economics of Money, Banking and Financial Markets*, 10th ed., Boston: Pearson.

World Trade Organization (WTO) website: www.wto.org.

Conclusion
External Funding and Portugal's Unstable Development

RICARDO PAES MAMEDE

Financing by international institutions has been a recurrent feature of modern Portugal. The arrival of funds was often related to macro-economic imbalances and led to significant changes in economic policy and institutions. Understanding the causes and consequences of external funding in Portugal is therefore an illuminating entry point to the study of the country's economic and institutional evolution over the past century.

The contributions to this volume provide much evidence regarding the conditions that led to each external financing event and the impacts these had on the Portuguese economy and society. In this final chapter, I discuss what we can learn from the joint reading of these events. The chapter is divided into three sections. The first deals with the constraints imposed by external accounts on economic growth, which is a recurrent cause of external funding by less advanced national economies. The second section focuses on the economic and institutional consequences of external funding for the recipient countries. The last section discusses how the literature on the causes and consequences of external financing sheds light on the experience and future challenges faced by Portugal.

The balance of payments as a constraint to economic growth

Instability in the course of economic growth is a common phenomenon, especially in the case of nations that fall short of the development frontier. For what matters in this context, less advanced economies have two main and interrelated characteristics: they generate relatively low levels of per capita income in each period of time, when compared to richer national economies; and their ability to grow is dependent on external sources. In such economies, growth always implies obtaining external means to acquire capital goods and intermediate products. In this sense, growth is limited by the ability to obtain such resources.

External dependence, in itself, is a common source of instability in the development process. This is a central point of the structuralist (e.g. Ocampo et al., 2009) and post-Keynesian (e.g. Thirlwall, 1979, 2019) traditions in economics. The constraints imposed on economic growth by external dependence can be briefly portrayed as follows.

Less advanced economies obtain the financial resources they need to finance growth either through exports (net of imports), capital inflows (including foreign investment and credit) or net transfers (especially, remittances). As far as net exports are concerned, these countries face several challenges. First, the terms of trade may tend to deteriorate, as the export prices of countries with less technologically advanced economies typically grow more slowly than import prices (namely because less sophisticated products face a higher degree of competition from other less advanced economies). This means that these countries must export a larger quantity of the goods they produce to cover the cost of imports. A second problem arises from the relationship between rising incomes and consumption patterns (i.e. the income elasticity of demand): as the country's purchasing power increases, domestic consumers tend to devote a greater share of their income to import products, worsening its external accounts. Third, less advanced economies often specialise in export products that face stagnant (or slow-growing) international demand, in contrast to the dynamism of high-tech goods and services, meaning that export growth does not keep pace with import growth.

As a result of the fragility of their export and import structures, less advanced economies tend to incur trade deficits whenever their growth rate is above a certain threshold. Fast growing domestic demand – whether through consumption or investment – leads to an increase in imports that can hardly be offset by export growth. Thus, in the absence of alternative sources of financing, continued high growth will soon become unsustainable: external indebtedness will reach a point where international investors will no longer be willing to provide funds to the country. When that point is reached, the national economy may experience a financial/currency crisis and/or a prolonged period of stagnation.

Some less advanced economies can finance long-lasting trade

deficits through migrants' remittances. Their less developed status means that a significant proportion of the domestic workforce is drawn to more advanced economies where they expect to earn higher wages. Part of their income is sent home, helping to finance trade deficits – put differently, allowing domestic demand to be higher without incurring unsustainable external imbalances. Note, however, that a stable amount of remittances does not allow a permanently higher growth rate compatible with external balance: the level of wealth increases, but the sustainable growth rate remains unchanged.

A similar reasoning can be applied to capital flows, which can relate either to foreign aid or to foreign investment/credit. If, for some reason, capital flows increase permanently, this leads to an increase in overall wealth, but not necessarily to a higher growth rate compatible with the external balance.

All this leads to the conclusion that the average income of less advanced economies is unlikely to converge with that of richer nations in the long run unless these economies manage to improve their export and import structures. Otherwise, periods of rapid growth and convergence will typically be followed by financial crises and economic stagnation.

Periods of unsustainable growth in less advanced economies may result from several factors. National governments may decide to pursue growth-friendly fiscal and/or income policies for different reasons, leading to a rapid increase in domestic demand, which ultimately translates into higher imports and often trade deficits. Periods of rapid growth can also result from external factors, including increases in external demand for specific goods or services (e.g. commodities, tourism) and in capital flows (including development assistance, foreign direct investment, portfolio investment and credit). Small open economies are especially prone to such externally-induced growth spurts.

Despite their positive and immediate impact on economic growth, the strong inflow of external funds in a country can lead to unfavourable developments in its production structure, ultimately having detrimental effects on financial sustainability and jeopardising long-term growth. These problems have been the focus of the "Dutch Disease" or "resource curse" literature (e.g. Magud & Sosa, 2010). In simple terms, a significant inflow of external funds leads to higher prices, making domestic exports less competitive and/or the tradable sector less profitable. As a result, a greater proportion of domestic resources will be allocated to economic activities less exposed to international competition. As incomes grow, imports will follow suit, while export growth is constrained by the appreciation of the real exchange rate, leading to a deterioration in the trade balance. Unless the inflow of external funds is permanent, the country will soon find it difficult to meet its financing needs, making macroeconomic adjustment inevitable.

Even in the case of permanent inflows of external funds (for example, due to persistently high international demand for a specific product or permanent transfers from official sources), such Dutch disease effects may have long-term impacts on economic growth and convergence. The decline in tradable activities, especially in manufacturing, may reduce growth prospects, as this sector has a higher potential for productivity improvement.

On the other hand, non-permanent flows of external funds can be another source of instability in a country's development path. Reversals in demand growth for crucial exports, for example, can lead to a deterioration of the trade balance, forcing the country to adjust in order to comply with its external financing constraints. The impact of sudden stops in capital flows can be even worse.

Periods of strong capital inflows followed by sudden stops in external financing have been a recurring phenomenon in less advanced economies in recent decades (e.g. Calvo et al., 1996; Eichengreen & Gupta, 2016). Initially, private capital flows are self-reinforcing as they lead to higher capital earnings, thereby attracting more investment from abroad and deepening the trend towards real exchange rate appreciation. Moreover, capital flows are often associated with credit reallocation to non-tradable activities (e.g. construction and real estate; Samarina and Bezemer, 2016), reinforcing the relative contraction of the export sector. Capital flows to less advanced economies are thus associated with aggregate demand growth, higher inflation, real exchange rate appreciation, and widening current account deficits. At some point, growing macroeconomic imbalances can become – or be perceived as – unsustainable, leading to sudden stops in external financing and capital inflows, and giving rise to financial crises and economic stagnation. Countries with high external indebtedness become particularly vulnerable to interest rate increases and, in general, to periods of high international financial instability.

Balance of payments constraints on growth – and the related instability in the development of less advanced economies – can be alleviated by various means. At the structural level, countries can improve their production profile by diversifying into more dynamic export products and/or becoming less dependent on imports to meet their development needs. To reduce financial instability, governments can impose restrictions on capital flows or the allocation of these funds throughout the national economy. Governments can also restrict the impact of economic expansion on imports by imposing strict limits on wage growth and/or forcing savings by domestic agents (including the government itself). Success stories of laggards – that is, previously less developed economies that were able to converge rapidly with those on the development frontier – typically involve the use of a combination of these strategies to support sustained growth while reducing insta-bility (e.g. Wade, 1990; Reinert, 2007).

Such development strategies require policy instruments that may not be available, however. During their development process, today's most advanced economies and the most successful laggards have made extensive use of export subsidies, import tariffs and quantitative restrictions, local content and trade balance requirements on foreign investment, state-owned enterprises and banks, capital controls and exchange rates, among other policy instruments. However, the use of these instruments is currently restricted by international rules and institutions, such as the World Trade Organization or the European Union (e.g. Chang, 2002, 2007; Rodrik, 2008). Moreover, wage repression and forced savings during periods of high growth are hardly compatible with democratic societies in which redistributive pressures are expected to constrain government choices (e.g. Przeworski & Limongi, 1993).

The reduction of the policy space available to manage the develop-ment process does not imply that convergence with richer nations becomes an impossibility for less advanced economies. It does mean, however, that the pace of growth is likely to be slower in the long run and occasionally disrupted by financial crises. The frequency of crises will depend on the country's structural conditions (both economic and institutional), the policy choices of national authorities, the evolution of the external environment, among other factors.

While national politics and policies can be crucial determinants of financial crises, this is not necessarily the case and is probably becoming less relevant as an explanatory cause. For example, Eichengreen & Gupta (2016) show that improvements in macro-economic management since the turn of the millennium have not insulated emerging markets from financial crises. As the authors put it, "with the continued growth of international financial markets and transactions, countries are now exposed to greater reversals of capital flows, and these greater reversals have more disruptive production effects" (p. 11).

The discussion above leads us to reject simplistic and unique explanations for different crisis events in less advanced economies. The productive structure of these countries, together with their institutional weaknesses (which are both cause and consequence of the former), make them particularly prone to crises, as we have seen. In this sense, episodes of external financing by international institutions are largely caused by these structural characteristics. Beyond this common cause, however, each episode is determined by distinct factors, of which only a part depends on the choices and behaviour of national agents.

I will deal later with the implications of the above discussion for the Portuguese case. I now turn to the consequences of external financing for the economy and institutions of the recipient country.

The economic and institutional consequences of external financing

External financing programmes generally encompass two distinct dimensions: financial support and institutional reform. In either of these, the consequences of external financing are largely indeterminate.

When external financing results from external imbalances in the recipient country, external assistance can help restore financial stability, thereby creating the conditions for economic recovery. However, external aid can also have less favourable structural implications. As discussed in the previous section, external financing flows are one possible source of "Dutch disease" effects. In a nutshell, increased domestic liquidity may lead to price increases in the non-tradable sector, leading to a real appreciation of the exchange rate and deterioration of external accounts. Such effects can be offset by adjustments in macroeconomic policies (e.g. nominal exchange rate devaluations, credit controls or fiscal constraints – when these are available), as well as by allocating foreign resources to cost-reducing investments (e.g. transport and energy infrastructure) (Rajan and Subramanian, 2011). In sum, the economic consequences of external financing depend on the cyclical and structural conditions of the recipient country, the allocation of funds and accompanying policy measures.

With regard to institutional structure, external funding can affect the recipient country's evolution through different channels (Bourguignon and Gunning, 2020). Institutional change may be a mere by-product of the planning and use of external funds (e.g. resulting from close interaction between technical staff from donor institutions and the recipient country), but may also be part of the conditions imposed by donors for the release of funds. Conditionality can go as far as imposing changes in political systems (for example, when donors require multi-party elections for autocratic regimes) or focus on governance issues (such as the autonomy of regulatory and audit bodies, independent policy evaluation, expenditure reviews, transparency practices, among others).

Improved governance is often necessary to minimise the risks associated with foreign aid, as the availability of funds leads to increased corruption and rent-seeking, diverting resources from more productive uses. However, the effectiveness of governance reforms depends largely on the commitment of the recipient country's authorities to such reforms and the capacity of donors to monitor their adoption (and to punish non-compliance).

The institutional consequences of external funding are also related to changes in the relative power of different groups in the recipient country. For example, funds may prioritise investments in non-traditional sectors (e.g. manufacturing in mainly rural countries, or technology-intensive activities in less advanced industrial economies); funding agencies may favour contacts with specific institutions (e.g. the central bank or the Ministry of Finance) or individuals (e.g. technical experts, academics); funding rules may require the empowerment of regulatory and auditing bodies (e.g. the Court of Auditors). In any case, external funding tends to alter the relative power of groups and individuals, as well as the prevailing coalitions. This may be necessary to unlock development, but it is also a common source of political instability, adding an extra layer of uncertainty about the consequences of external financing on the economy and society of recipient countries.

Finally, external financing can also have an impact on the geopolitical position of recipient countries by fostering economic and diplomatic ties between the latter and donors. This is often reflected in international trade and investment patterns, national power coalitions, as well as the institutional setup (when external financing is related to participation in international organisations or agreements).

The economic and institutional consequences of external financing will often depend on the duration of the intervention. In principle, programmes that last longer, involve greater volumes of funding, and comprise a greater diversity of policy areas are likely to transform the recipient country more profoundly.

A special case worth mentioning in this context is the EU's Cohesion Policy. Although it is often perceived as having an essentially redistributive objective, EU Cohesion Policy goes far beyond this objective (e.g. Mairate, 2006). Like other development-oriented international interventions, it aims to improve the growth potential of less favoured regional and national economies by concentrating investment in physical and human capital.[1] However, it goes much further than most external funding programmes as regards its governance framework.

EU Cohesion Policy is based on multi-annual strategic planning, focusing on medium-term investments to foster long-term development. Its rules and practices imply the adoption by all member countries of specific management and accountability systems, with detailed guidelines concerning monitoring, evaluation, control and audit procedures, as well as the involvement of stakeholders. The information and feedback mechanisms in place promote the exchange of experiences and the dissemination of good practices across the EU. Since Cohesion Policy is a major source of funds for various policy areas at national level (especially in less advantaged countries), it helps shape the institutional configuration of policy-making in most areas of government.

In sum, the institutional consequences of external funding related to EU cohesion funding tend to be broader, deeper and more lasting than those associated with non-permanent external funding mechanisms.

Portugal's experience and future challenges

The previous discussion on the causes and consequences of external financing helps to understand the evolution of the Portuguese economy in the last century.

Like many less advanced economies, Portugal had to face the challenge of reconciling economic growth, domestic expectations and external macroeconomic balance on several occasions. Although domestic developments played a relevant role in some episodes of external imbalances, outside factors were decisive in all of them.

Table 9.1 summarises the relationship between four episodes of temporary external financing in Portugal and their main determinants, both internal and external. As the contributions to this volume show, all these external financing episodes were associated with external macroeconomic imbalances. However, the main determinants of these imbalances vary across episodes.

Prior to Portugal's participation in the Marshall Plan (see Fernanda Rollo, chapter 1), gold and currency reserves declined significantly, as a result of both an increase in imports (in conditions of international shortages of essential consumer goods and a domestic context marked by social upheaval) and a decrease in export earnings (reflecting a sharp fall in external demand for several goods that were abnormally

Four external financing episodes in Portugal and their main determinants

		Marshall plan 1948	IMF 1977	IMF 1983	Troika 2011
External imbalances...		x	x	x	x
... due to internal factors	Pro-cyclical fiscal policy		x	x	x
	Overgenerous income policy		x		
... due to mixed factors	Reversals in net remittances or capital inflows		x		x
	Reversals in the external demand of exports	x	x		
... due to external factors	Increased foreign competition				x
	International interest rate increases		x	x	x
	Steep rise in the price crucial imports (especially oil)	x	x	x	x

valued during the war). The first IMF intervention in 1977 (see Luciano Amaral, chapter 2), instead, was preceded by a sharp rise in oil prices, an international recession that reduced external demand for exports, disruptions in domestic production associated with the revolutionary period, lower net remittances related to both the international crisis and political instability in the country, and high inflation resulting from both an expansionary fiscal stance and over-generous incomes policies. The second IMF intervention in 1983 (see João Zorrinho, chapter 3) followed the second oil shock, a sharp increase in international interest rates and pro-cyclical fiscal policies. Finally, the Troika intervention in 2011 (see Joaquim Ramos Silva, chapter 4) followed a decade of accumulation of exceptionally high external debt[2] as a result of (Mamede et al., 2016; Barradas et al., 2018; Mamede, 2020): a credit boom associated with international capital flows from the mid-1990s, pro-cyclical fiscal policies in the late 1990s, a succession of competitiveness shocks since the turn of the century (China's entry into the WTO, the EU's eastward enlargement and the strong appreciation of the euro), a sharp increase in oil prices,[3] a rise in interest rates[4] and, as a final trigger, a sudden halt in international capital flows to the eurozone periphery in 2010 following the 2007/2008 international financial crisis.

These four external financing episodes show both the vulnerability of the Portuguese economy to external imbalances and the diversity of factors that may lead to such imbalances. In some cases, they were associated with periods of rapid growth, driven by fiscal policy, income policy, capital flows or increases in demand and/or export prices. In other cases, external imbalances resulted from international interest rate increases, oil price hikes and/or external competitiveness shocks. In the most severe crises, several of these factors occurred in the same period.

The main factors behind external imbalances, or their absence, have changed over time. Like in many underdeveloped economies, for several decades Portugal's trade deficits were financed by a high level of net emigrant remittances, avoiding the accumulation of external debt.[5] In addition, wage repression through authoritarian means and underinvestment in social expenditures (health, education, housing and social protection) allowed the dictatorship to control the increase in consumer imports, while the rapid industrialisation of the country after Portugal's accession to EFTA in 1960 led to a strong increase in exports (Lopes, 1999). During the 1970s, rising oil prices and the instability of the revolutionary period were responsible for a large part of the external deficits. In the 1980s and 1990s, the financing of the Portuguese economy was facilitated by lower interest rates, strong private capital inflows, large amounts of EU subsidies and low oil prices. From the mid-1990s onwards, high external deficits persisted as a result of a credit-fuelled demand boom, competitiveness shocks and rising oil prices. After the euro periphery crisis of 2010–2013, external balance was restored due to low investment, stagnating real wages and a boom in tourism revenues.

The policy instruments available at the national level to address external imbalances have changed significantly over the period under analysis. Most notably, since the 1990s, as a result of Portugal's participation in the EU and the euro, the national authorities have no control over the exchange rate, the interest rate, capital flows and international trade, and have little influence on banking supervision and credit allocation.

In addition, the country's exposure to capital flows has increased dramatically, due to the EU internal capital markets and the euro. Typically, capital flows are conditioned by different risks, including political risks (e.g. expropriation), credit risks, and exchange rate risks. In the case of the eurozone, exchange rate risks do not exist, and political risks are minimal. In this context, credit risks are the most relevant. While the latter partly reflect the financial position of the national economy (proxied, for example, by external debt and its recent evolution), credit risks are also determined by the country's ability to secure access to capital in the event of a financial crisis. It is therefore not surprising that capital flows to Portugal since the late 1990s have largely followed international investors' perception of the willingness of the EU authorities to intervene in case of need. Until the euro crisis, international investors behaved as if credit risks were minimal across the EU, possibly assuming that eurozone members would benefit from a bailout by EU institutions in case of problems (Baldwin and Giavazzi, 2015). Ultimately, they were right. However, in 2009/2010, uncertainty surrounding the EU's strategy for dealing with the crisis led to a sudden halt in international capital movements to the eurozone periphery. Capital flows were restored, and interest rates fell sharply after the ECB's determination to ensure financial stability in the euro zone became clear, from 2012 onwards. These developments show how financial crisis risks related to external imbalances in Portugal (and elsewhere) are now strictly related to ECB monetary policy.

The interdependence between eurozone monetary policy and the external balance of member countries helps to explain the growing concern of EU authorities about national developments that may affect international trade and capital flows. Many of the policy reforms included in the adjustment programme agreed with the troika in 2011 (see Nuno Cunha Rodrigues, in this volume) were guided by such concerns – namely, labour market liberalization, energy price deregulation, judicial system reform, and fiscal surveillance. Pressure from the EU authorities on these areas became especially visible during the 2011–2014 troika intervention, and has become a permanent feature of the country-specific recommendations made annually to Portugal by the European Commission in the context of the so-called European Semester.[6] Such pressure is also evident in the design of the Recovery and Resilience Mechanism, created to address the impact of the COVID-19 pandemic (see the chapter by Guilherme Waldemar d'Oliveira Martins and Joana Graça Moura).

Although institutional reforms were highly visible – and quite controversial – during the troika intervention, earlier external financing events also involved some degree of change in institutional practices. For example, the Marshall Plan aid (again, see Fernanda Rollo in this volume) boosted the effort and practice of economic planning, forcing the Portuguese government to formally structure a four-year economic development programme. IMF interventions in 1977 and 1983 (see the chapters by Luciano Amaral and João Zorrinho) were associated with medium-term reforms, such as changes in the tax system, control of public finances (including public enterprises), the evolution of financial markets, and labour market flexibility. The use of EU funds, both before (see Paulo Alves Pardal in this volume) and after accession to the EEC, implied changes in the planning, monitoring and evaluation of public policies, state aid rules, territorial and multi-level governance, among others.

In short, external financing to Portugal is both a consequence and a cause of some of the most relevant developments in Portuguese economy and politics in the last century. Although domestic and external conditions have changed over the period, the country's export and import structures and its exposure to international capital and trade flows continue to be a potential source of instability. In other words, the need to resort to external financing in the future cannot be ruled out. It is therefore wise to look to the past for useful insights, as the chapters in this volume do.

Notes

1   The EU structural funds are also instrumental in the pursuit of many supranational objectives. In particular, they play a crucial role in promoting the Union's internal market – not only through their support for cross-border transport, energy and communication networks, but also by providing the European Commission with additional instruments to enforce competition rules at national level (for example, by preventing

discriminatory practices in public procurement or in government support for businesses). Cohesion Policy is also crucial in making the EU more visible to citizens, business and local authorities, thus playing an important legitimising role (Mairate, 2006).

2   The international investment position of Portugal went from −11,5% in 1996 to −43% of GDP in 2000 and −107,2% in 2010.

3   The price of the Brent crude went from nearly 10 USD/Bbl in 1999 to 140 USD/Bbl in 2008.

4   The ECB rate for the main refinancing operations increased from 2% in 2003 to 4.25% in 2008, coinciding with a period when Portugal's external debt was already at historically high levels.

5   According to Bank of Portugal historical data, net remittances were equivalent to 2% of GDP in 1953, peaked in 1979 at more than 10% and declined steadily thereafter, reaching 1% in 2010.

6   Each year, the European Commission undertakes a detailed analysis of each Member States' budgetary plan and macroeconomic challenges, producing country-specific recommendations for the next 12–18 months (see https://ec.europa.eu/info/business-economy-euro/economic-and-fiscal-policy-coordination/eu-economic-governance-monitoring-prevention-correction/european-semester_en).

References

Barradas, R. *et al.* 2018: Financialisation in The European Periphery and The Sovereign Debt Crisis: The Portuguese Case. *Journal of Economic Issues*, 52 (4), 1056–1083.

Bourguignon, F. and Gunning, J. W. 2020: Foreign aid and governance: A survey. In J.-M. Baland *et al.* (eds.), *The Handbook of Economic Development and Institutions*, Princeton: Princeton University Press, Ch. 9.

Calvo, G. A., Leiderman, L., and Reinhart, C. M. 1996: Inflows of Capital to Developing Countries in the 1990s. *Journal of Economic Perspectives*, 10 (2), 123–139.

Chang, H. J. 2002: *Kicking Away the Ladder: Development strategy in historical perspective*. London: Anthem Press.

Chang, H. J. 2007: *Bad Samaritans: Rich nations, poor policies, and the threat to the developing world*. New York: Random House Business.

Eichengreen, B. and Gupta, P. 2016: Managing sudden stops. World Bank Policy Research Working Paper N.7639. Washington: The World Bank Group.

Lopes, J. S. 1999: *A Economia Portuguesa desde 1960*. Lisboa: Gradiva.

Magud, N. and Sosa, S. 2010: When and Why Worry about Real Exchange Rate Appreciation? The Missing Link between Dutch Disease and Growth. IMF Working Paper, WP/10/271. International Monetary Fund: Washington, DC.

Mairate, A. 2006: The 'added value' of European Union Cohesion policy. *Regional Studies*, 40 (02), 167–177.

Mamede, R. P. 2020: Financialisation and structural change in Portugal: A Euro-resource-curse?. In A. C. Santos and N. Teles (eds.), *Financialisation in the European Periphery: Work and Social Reproduction in Portugal.* London: Routledge. Ch. 4.

Mamede, R. *et. al.* 2016: The Long Boom and the Early Bust: The Portuguese Economy in the Era of Financialisation. In E. Hein, D. Detzer and N. Dodig (Eds.), *Financialisation and the Financial and Economic Crises: Country Studies.* Cheltenham, UK: Edward Elgar.

Ocampo, J. A., Rada, C. and Taylor, L. 2009: *Growth and policy in developing countries: A structuralist approach.* New York: Columbia University Press.

Przeworski, A. and Limongi, F. 1993: Political regimes and economic growth. *Journal of Economic Perspectives*, 7(3), 51–69.

Rajan, R. G., and Subramanian, A. 2011: Aid, Dutch disease, and manufacturing growth. *Journal of Development Economics*, 94(1), 106–118.

Reinert, E.S. 2007: *How Rich Countries Got Rich and Why Poor Countries Stay Poor.* New York: Carroll & Graf Publishers.

Rodrik, D. 2008: *One Economics, Many Recipes.* Princeton: Princeton University Press.

Samarina, A. and Bezemer, D. 2016: Do capital flows change domestic credit allocation?. *Journal of International Money and Finance*, 62, 98–121.

Thirlwall, A. P. 1979: The balance of payments constraint as an explanation of international growth rate differences. BNL Quarterly Review, 32(128), 45–53.

Thirlwall, A. P. 2019: Thoughts on balance-of-payments-constrained growth after 40 years. *Review of Keynesian Economics*, 7(4), 554–567.

Wade, R. 1990: *Governing the Market: Economic Theory and the Role of Government in Taiwan's Industrialization.* Princeton: Princeton University Press.

The Editors and Contributors

Dr. Alice Cunha is Research Fellow at the Portuguese Institute of International Relations (IPRI-NOVA University Lisbon), where she works on European Integration, an area in which she has published extensively. Her main research interests are related to the history of European integration, enlargement studies, Europeanization and European funds. She is a member of the European Union Liaison Committee of Historians.

Guilherme Waldemar d'Oliveira Martins is Auxiliary Professor of Lisbon Law School (FDL) and Lisbon Accounting School (ISCAL). PhD in Public Finance, MD on Tax Law and Law Degree. Former Secretary of State for Infrastructures and Telecommunications for Portuguese Government (2015-2019). Chaired the Legislative Commission of Budgetary Framework Law (2014-2015). Lawyer and Former Partner of Portuguese Audit Firm. Author of several books and articles in Public Finance, Tax Law and Audit.

Joana Graça Moura has a Degree in Law. Lawyer in Portuguese Law Firm. He is a tax law Specialist in Portuguese and Francophone countries and the author of articles on tax law.

João Zorrinho was born in Évora in 1991. He graduated in Political Science and International Relations at Universidade Nova de Lisboa – FCSH. In 2014 he completed the master's in international economics at the University of Lisbon – ISEG and in 2019 the master's in political science and International Relations at the Universidade Nova de Lisboa – FCSH. Practices his professional activity, since 2015, at Portugal Global – Trade & Investment Agency (AICEP), where he performs functions as Senior Technician in the commercial direction of the Agency. Currently, he is attending an interdisciplinary doctorate in Political Economy at ISCTE; FEUC, ISEG-UL.

Joaquim Ramos Silva is Full Professor ("Jubilado") of Lisbon School of Economics and Management, University of Lisbon, and a member of SOCIUS/CSG, a FCT research center. PhD in Economic Policy and

Analysis at the École des Hautes Études en Sciences Sociales, Paris. Head of the Department of Economics at ISEG/UL, 2014–2018. He is the author of several books, and participated in the edition of eight other books. He published around one hundred articles and chapters, including in outstanding journals such as *Tourism Management, Technological Forecasting & Social Change, Journal of Economic Studies, Business Process Management Journal*. His research interests are focused on international and European economics: analysis, policies, and strategies of trade and foreign direct investment; the internationalization of firms and economies; sustainable development and entrepreneurship; the globalization process, emergent markets and international organizations. Empirical research has been mainly centered on the cases of Portugal and Brazil.

Luciano Amaral obtained his PhD from the European University Institute in Florence, Italy, and is Associate Professor at Nova School of Business and Economics, where he has taught different courses on modern economic history as well as modern general history. His research has been mostly dedicated to economic growth in the twentieth century, but also to banking history and the history of business groups in the same period, with particular attention to Portugal. He has published in various international publishing houses and economic history journals.

Maria Fernanda Rollo is Historian, PhD and Aggregate in Contemporary History. Full Professor at the History Department of the Faculty of Social Sciences and Humanities NOVA University of Lisbon. Coordinator of the Ph.D. program in History. Coordinator of the post-graduation course Management and Policy in Science and Technology. Member of Research Council of Europen University Institut. Researcher at History, Territories and Communities - CFE. State Secretary for Science, Technology and Higher Education (2015-2018). Researcher of the UNESCO Biodiversity and Conservation Chair for Sustainable Development and the of TERRA Associated Laboratory. Administrator of the Mário Soares and Maria Barroso Foundation. Research areas include the history of Portugal in the 20th century, the participation of Portugal in the European economic cooperation movements, the history of economy, industry, engineering and contemporary innovation, history of the organization of science in Portugal.

Nuno Cunha Rodrigues is Associate Professor at the Faculty of Law of the University of Lisbon. Jean Monnet Chair. Lawyer. Author of several books and papers in the field of EU Law; Competition Law; Public Procurement and Public Finance.

Paulo Alves Pardal has a PhD in Law and Economics and is an Assistant Professor of Law and Economics at the Faculty of Law of the University of Lisbon (Faculdade de Direito da Universidade de Lisboa).

Renato Gonçalves has a PhD in Law and Economics (European Economic and Monetary Union) and is an Associate Professor of law and economics at Lisbon University School of Law (Faculdade de Direito da Universidade de Lisboa).

Ricardo Paes Mamede holds a Ph.D. in Economics by Bocconi University, Italy. He is Associate Professor at the Department of Political Economy of ISCTE – University Institute of Lisbon and Integrated Researcher at Dinâmia'CET – Centre for Socioeconomic and Territorial Studies.

Index